American Politics and Society Today

American Politics
and Society Today

Edited by Robert Singh

polity

First published in 2002 by Polity Press in association with Blackwell Publishers Ltd

Editorial office:
Polity Press
65 Bridge Street
Cambridge CB2 1UR, UK

Marketing and production:
Blackwell Publishers Ltd
108 Cowley Road
Oxford OX4 1JF, UK

Published in the USA by
Blackwell Publishers Inc.
350 Main Street
Malden, MA 02148, USA

ISBN 0-7456-2526-6
ISBN 0-7456-2527-4 (pb)

A catalogue record for this book is available from the British Library.

Library of Congress Cataloging-in-Publication Data

American politics and society today/edited by Robert Singh.
    p.   cm. — (Politics today)
Includes bibliographical references and index.
    ISBN 0-7456-2526-6 (acid-free paper)—ISBN 0-7456-2527-4 (pbk. : acid-free paper)
    1. United States—Politics and government—1989– 2. United States—Social conditions—1980– 3. Political culture—United States—History—20th century. 4. Popular culture—United States—History—20th century. I. Singh, Robert. II. Politics today (Polity Press)
E839.5 .A667 2002
973.929—dc21

                                                                                    2002001453

Typeset in 10 on 12 pt Sabon
by SNP Best-set Typesetter Ltd., Hong Kong
Printed in Great Britain by TJ International, Padstow, Cornwall

This book is printed on acid-free paper.

Contents

Tables

Contributors

Nigel Bowles teaches in the Department of Politics and International Relations, University of Oxford, and at St Anne's College, Oxford. His main research interest is the US Presidency.

Paul Frymer is Assistant Professor of Sociology at the University of California, San Diego. He has a doctorate in political science from Yale University and is the author of *Uneasy Alliances: Race and Party Competition in America* (1999) as well as numerous articles on party politics and divided government.

Abigail Halcli is a Senior Lecturer in Sociology at Oxford Brookes University. She holds a Ph.D. from Ohio State University. She has published research on women in politics, the AIDS activist movement, and the funding of American social movement organizations. She is the co-editor of *Understanding Contemporary Society: Theories of the Present* (2000).

Desmond King is Professor of Politics and Fellow of St John's College, University of Oxford. His most recent book is *Making Americans: Immigration, Race and the Origins of the Diverse Democracy* (2000).

Paul Martin is Fellow and Tutor in Politics at Wadham College, University of Oxford. He recently completed a doctorate on US Supreme Court decision making, and the effects on judicial institutions of the so-called 'digital economy'. He is the author, with Patrick Schmidt, of 'To the Internet and Beyond: The Entry of State Supreme Courts to the World Wide Web', *Judicature*, 84, no. 6 (May 2001).

Robert Mason is Lecturer in History at the University of Edinburgh. He is currently working on a book about Richard Nixon and the Republican Party.

Julian Murphet has been a Research Fellow at St John's College, University of Oxford since 1998 and was Visiting Professor in the Department of African American Studies at the University of California, Berkeley in autumn 2000. His publications include *Literature and Race in Los Angeles* (2001).

Fiona Ross is a Lecturer in the Department of Politics at the University of Bristol. Her current research examines the politics of welfare restructuring in affluent societies, with a special emphasis on the United States. She is the author of recent articles in *Governance*, the *Journal of Public Policy*, and *West European Politics*.

Robert Singh is Lecturer in Politics at Birkbeck College, University of London and Director of the M.Sc./M.Res. programme in American Politics. He is the author of *The Farrakhan Phenomenon: Race, Reaction and the Paranoid Style in American Politics* (1997) and *The Congressional Black Caucus: Racial Politics in the US Congress* (1998).

Marc Stears is Official Fellow in Politics at Emmanuel College, Cambridge and teaches politics in the Faculty of Social and Political Sciences, University of Cambridge. His research concentrates on the relationship between political ideas and political institutions. He is currently completing a book comparing the American progressive movement of the early twentieth century with British socialism of the same period.

Editor's Preface

In the aftermath of the terrorist attacks on New York City and Washington DC of 11 September 2001, many commentators rushed to pronounce America and the world as having entered a new era. Certainly the strikes opened another chapter in the 'American experiment'. Without warning, on American soil, against landmark targets and causing thousands of innocent deaths, the atrocities represented the most 'clear and present danger' to America's national security and democratic values since Japanese forces struck at Pearl Harbor on 7 December 1941.

But the attention rightly accorded the changes wrought by the terrorist threat should not obscure the fundamental continuities that exist in America's governing arrangements, social foundations and contemporary domestic politics – and these form the central focus of the essays in *American Politics and Society Today*. Indeed, it is precisely these elements that contributed to the relative neglect of foreign policy in general – and counterterrorism in particular – under the Clinton administration and that now, in an entirely new context, shape America's response to terrorism under President George W. Bush.

In regard to the former, the post-Cold War era and the defeat of an avowed 'foreign policy' president, George H. W. Bush, in 1992, contributed powerfully to a renewed emphasis on domestic politics by Bill Clinton and Al Gore. Accusations that Clinton's foreign policy followed a *Wag the Dog* pattern remain unproven and, perhaps, unfair. But the articulation of a 'Third Way', the emphasis accorded to deficit reduction, welfare reform and the appropriate spending of an unanticipated budget surplus, and the succession of political scandals that dominated American politics from 1992 to 2000 helped to shape an approach to international politics that was tentative, inconsistent, and only intermittently preoccupied by foreign and defence policy.

Despite the attempts of the Bush–Cheney ticket to place national security matters on the election agenda of 2000 (particularly with regard to ballistic missile defence), the issues that dominated the presidential and congressional campaigns remained resolutely domestic in character: tax cuts versus increased social spending; education; and health care. During an era of unprecedented peace and prosperity and despite terrorist attacks on US targets from the World Trade Center in 1993 to the *USS Cole* in the Yemen on 12 October 2000, the public and media attention accorded the threats facing America – notwithstanding the efforts of many politicians within both main parties – remained strictly limited.

In terms of America's response to the terrorist threats, the central themes that this volume addresses as cornerstones of contemporary American politics remain fundamental: the intense competition between and within the institutions of the federal government and the two main political parties; fragmented and mostly parochial mass media; the centrality of issues of race and ethnicity – at home and abroad – to American political development; the constant struggle to make the promise of American ideals a reality; and the crucial role that popular culture plays in shaping perceptions of America's values, people and policies, both within and outside the United States.

How these features of American government, politics and society evolve and interact will shape some of the most crucial challenges now facing the United States: in reconciling civil liberties with the imperatives of domestic security; in a citizenry famously suspicious of centralized authority acceding to an enhanced role for the federal government; in identifying and eliminating terrorist threats while extending tolerance and equality of respect to Arab Americans and Muslims; and, most critically, in re-establishing America's national security on an enduring basis.

The United States remains a divided democracy, for the many reasons that this volume highlights. But America also possesses a resolute and capacious ability to overcome its divisions, especially in times of crisis. However profound the problems still are that confront a remarkably fragmented governmental system and fractious polity, the imperatives to overcome them are at least as powerful. More than ever, American faith in the traditional tenet of *e pluribus unum* ('from many, one') has been reinvigorated by the evils that befell the nation on September 11. In this respect, the ten essays in this volume demonstrate not only the complexity of America's democracy but also the courage, tenacity and resilience of its people in overcoming the immense challenges – old and new – currently confronting the American experiment.

R.S.

Acknowledgements

Three thanks and a fond farewell:

First, I would like to thank my fellow contributors for participating in the project when all of them faced many other burdens, both research related and otherwise, and for producing such accomplished essays.

Secondly, thanks are due to David Held and Lynn Dunlop of Polity Press for approaching me with the idea of a volume of critical essays on the current state of American politics, approving its design and helping the project on its way. Louise Knight took over from Lynn midway through and shepherded the collection to completion, for which I'm very grateful. Ann Bone was a wonderful copy-editor.

Thirdly, the production of the book has benefited greatly from the highly supportive environment of the School of Politics and Sociology at Birkbeck College and I would like to express my gratitude to my colleagues there – in particular, Samantha Ashenden, Anthony Butler, Paul Hirst and Bill Tompson – and the many hard-working mature students at Birkbeck who have suffered my undergraduate and graduate American politics courses with patience and good humour.

A fond farewell is owed Professor Byron E. Shafer, who will have departed these shores by the time this volume is published. In his distinguished tenure as the Andrew W. Mellon Professor of American Government at Oxford University and a Professorial Fellow at Nuffield College, Byron contributed tremendously to the building of the American politics discipline not only at Oxford but also in the United Kingdom as a whole. Several of the contributors to this volume – including myself – had the good fortune to encounter Byron as colleagues, undergraduate and graduate students, research assistants and co-authors.

This volume is therefore, in a sense, an indirect product of his labours and – although he had no part in it and will almost certainly disagree with much herein – we hope that it expresses the same combination of seriousness and good humour that he brought to the Americanist community in the UK, and will no doubt offer a new set of colleagues and students at the University of Wisconsin.

One final word, sadly, is merited here. If those of us outside America can continue, however modestly and inadequately, to honour the memory of the victims of the barbaric attacks of September 11, 2001 on New York, Virginia and Pennsylvania, this may at least partly consist in committing ourselves ever more carefully and consistently to the dispassionate, informed and reasoned study of the United States. Hopefully, this edited collection may help a little towards that end.

Robert Singh

Introduction:
Dubya's Divided Democracy

Robert Singh

The eventual triumph of Governor George W. Bush over Vice-President Al Gore in the 2000 presidential election occasioned a predictable outburst of anti-American sentiment outside the United States. The narrow, contested and politicized manner of Bush's eventual victory, the mix of 'compassionate' and not-so-compassionate conservative policies advocated by Bush, and the particular personal traits of the former Texas governor together provided ample opportunities for many non-Americans to indulge a familiar pastime: deriding the world's sole remaining superpower, its public life and people. In office, Bush's appointment of former senator John Ashcroft as US Attorney General, the initiation of rapid policy changes on abortion, the environment and national missile defence, and a sharp shift in diplomatic relations with Russia and China offered confirmation to his many critics within and outside America of a neophyte and parochial president seeking to reassert Reaganite conservatism and small-town isolationism under the guises of pragmatism, bipartisan civility and a foreign policy based on 'humility'.

For students of American politics, such developments have proved at once exasperating and exhilarating. On the one hand, the eminently newsworthy character of recent American politics has allowed anti-American prejudices and stereotypes – sometimes latent, often explicit – to surface with alarming regularity. The varied and seemingly unceasing travails of the Clintons offered evidence to America's critics of a burlesque public life dominated by money, legal niceties ('it all depends what the meaning of "is" is') and a shallow lack of principle masquerading as post-Cold War and post-budget deficit political pragmatism. Clinton's failed impeachment in 1998–9 and the thirty-six days of bitter controversy following the disputed November 2000 election elicited a mixture of bafflement and amusement at American foibles. By the spring of 2001, a book of 'Bushisms' had already been published and emails circulated listing the supposed verbal gaffes of America's President (that many of these were in fact coined by former vice-president Dan Quayle did little to alter public perceptions of Bush's lack of fitness for the highest office). Not since Ronald Reagan's first term has an American president occasioned such disrespect, derision and apprehension outside the United States.

On the other hand, behind the commonplace popular stereotypes, such events have offered rich and compelling opportunities to re-examine the distinctive features of the world's leading industrialized liberal democracy. For all their mix of partisanship, tragedy and farce, Clinton's impeachment and the deadlock in Florida at least were boons to the study of American government. Only rarely have questions about the constitutional meaning of 'high crimes and misdemeanours', the pros and cons of the Electoral College or the nature of 'pregnant chads' excited student awareness, much less enthusiasm. In addition, of course, international attention to matters American is rarely so great as when far-reaching changes to the prevailing international economic and security order appear imminent – not least when such attention is animated by a mixture of fear and fascination as to what the United States under a 'new' administration (given its composition, the qualification seems in order) may do next. This combination makes for a particularly opportune moment to analyse the state of American politics and society today.

That is especially so given that America is once more at a transitional point in its relatively brief but remarkable history. The pronounced continuity in its constitutional framework and governing institutions now confronts profound changes as an industrial era economy increasingly gives way to the information age; as 'wired workers' emerge as a new, distinctive and consequential social group; as the New Deal generation finally draws to a close; as the steady demographic shift to the suburbs gains further pace; as dramatic changes to the New Deal's constitutional, legal and social order – from federal–state relations to welfare policy – rapidly advance; and as the increasing ethnic, racial and religious diversity of America's social base brings renewed opportunities and challenges to the politics of cultural values and national identity in the United States. American political life currently offers a compelling and complex spectacle that marries far-reaching social, economic and political changes to an underlying continuity in governing arrangements.

These themes form the background to this volume of essays. The basic aim of this collection was to bring together a range of academics to tackle, in a thematic and critical fashion, a selection of important contemporary issues that have generated both academic disagreement and popular attention in America. In several instances, the controversies of 2000 and the shift in party control of the Senate in June 2001 have lent these essays an added dimension, sometimes confirming but occasionally questioning long-held conventional wisdoms on American politics.

Three observations should also be made at the outset. First, the essays that follow are not intended as an exhaustive survey of all aspects of contemporary American politics. Such an enterprise is barely feasible given the vast scope of political conflict and the rapid pace of social, economic and political change in the United States. Rather, the chapters that follow offer a series of critical interpretations of American politics and society at the end of the Clinton years and the early stages of the Bush presidency. Some key issues and controversies were selected to illustrate what is most distinctive and important (if by no means new or unique) about the current nature of politics in the United States. Moreover, as will become clearly apparent, the contributors have not shied away from stating clearly their own arguments on the subjects they address. The result is a set of essays that are doubly critical – providing a dispassionate analysis of their subject-matter but also offering a clear interpretation that cannot be accused of 'cheerleading' for America. The objective here has been not merely to inform but also to provoke critical reflection on contemporary politics and society in the United States.

Second, the contributors to the collection have assumed a reasonable amount of existing knowledge among our readers of the basic structure and dynamics of American politics (the US Constitution, the structure of the federal government, the relative weakness of political parties and so on). The essays here are therefore intended to supplement and extend the reader's knowledge while providing some distinctive reflections that may generate new ideas, interpretations and opinions – whether in agreement or opposition.

Third, as the title of the book suggests, the volume expressly deals with American society. Some material has been included that might not otherwise be anticipated in a specifically 'politics' book. This was a deliberate editorial decision reflecting practical and critical considerations of pedagogy and, it has to be confessed, personal prejudice. In terms of the former, many students come to study American politics – especially outside the States – because of an abiding fascination with aspects of America gleaned from popular culture: films about Pearl Harbor or Vietnam, popular music, television dramas such as *The West Wing*, and even cartoons. (This basic fact is one that perhaps has not been addressed adequately as yet by academic analysts of American politics.) In terms of the latter, the unapologetic abuse of editorial privilege that has been indulged here is one that reflects a personal interest in American popular culture and a conviction that it can, and should, be taken seriously (not to mention, of course, an abiding fascination with the activities of the residents of Springfield and South Park). This volume is one that therefore seeks to take certain aspects of American popular culture seriously, precisely because they both reflect and contribute to an understanding of American politics in its current state of flux.

Partly to this end, then, rather than drawing exclusively on political scientists, the team assembled for this volume brings together leading academics from the disciplines of politics (both empirical and theoretical), sociology, history and cultural studies. The contributors range far and wide in their treatments but rarely accept the prevailing orthodoxies of textbooks that sometimes accept too uncritically the essentially benign or 'neutral' nature of American government institutions and intermediary organizations.

In a volume that seeks to emphasize the continuing distinctiveness and complexity of the United States, chapter 1 does so through an explicitly comparative focus. Marc Stears offers an interpretation – perhaps better, a post-mortem – of the rise and fall of the so-called 'Third Way' in the United States and United Kingdom. By placing the debate over the Third Way in both a historical and comparative context, Stears illustrates how marked has been the gulf not simply between American and British political cultures and institutions but also between practising politicians in search of new ideas and the intellectuals keen to supply them. Stears concludes by noting that, however advanced the transatlantic exchange of both personnel and policies, the prospects for progressive politics to succeed on either side of the Atlantic – and, one could add, for conservative politics also – rest powerfully on forging public policies tailored to the distinct political conditions and government institutions of the two nations.

Chapter 2 then deals with the federal elections of 2000. Therein, I argue that the presidential election was more lost by Al Gore than won by George W. Bush – notwithstanding the problems associated with the notion of a Bush 'victory'. But whatever the rights and wrongs of the 'Florida moment' in particular and the Electoral College more generally, the presidential and congressional elections illustrated more continuity in America's underlying 'electoral order' than they did change. The Clinton years accelerated a long-standing partisan and ideological polarization that has steadily transformed the character of American party politics. That few (if any) observers discussed the possibility of a Republican realignment in the face of the first undivided Republican government in forty-five years spoke volumes about the frailty of the victories of the 'grand old party' (GOP) and the party's hold on the House and Senate – even prior to the defection of a moderate Republican in May 2001 that gave control of the Senate to the Democrats. In confirming the volatility of contemporary electoral politics, the near evenly matched Republican and Democratic party coalitions, and the sharp regional, cultural and ideological fissures in America's electoral geography, the stalemate of 2000 reflected and reinforced the fundamental fault-lines within a deeply divided American polity.

One of the most notable results of the election was the decisive refusal of African Americans to support Governor Bush, despite his high profile efforts to make the Republican Party more inclusive. But the Democratic Party's most loyal constituency has often found that its votes have been only poorly rewarded by policy changes under Democratic administrations and majorities in Congress, much less Republican ones. The dilemmas confronting black voters are examined in chapter 3, where Paul Frymer assesses the important consequences that the particular design of American institutions has for the representation and political influence of African Americans. Frymer makes a powerful case – strongly echoed in other chapters – that the supposedly 'neutral' institutional architecture of American government has profoundly negative effects on particular social groups, most importantly blacks. Examining both the sources of, and constraints on, black influence in American politics, Frymer concludes that the most propitious source of potential leverage for African Americans in the American system (short of its own radical overhaul) is for a credible black candidacy within the Democratic Party's presidential primaries to force the post-1964 home of racial liberalism to address the urgent concerns of its most loyal source of electoral support.

If the institutional features of American government continue to exert a profound influence on the character of current politics, however, so too do the mass media. Indeed, rarely has the nexus between politics and the media been so vividly apparent as during the elections of 2000. In chapter 4, Robert Mason focuses on the key medium in politics: television. Ranging widely across the several criticisms regularly levelled at American television since the end of the 1960s, Mason argues that the balance sheet is, overall, decidedly uncongenial to television journalists. While some traditional criticisms – such as purposive political bias – prove more or less unfounded, the failure of a relentlessly commercially driven American television to perform its key functions in the West's premier liberal democracy casts a broad and serious shadow on America's democratic pretensions. In this respect, the particularly graphic failings of the evening of 7 November 2000 merely proved pellucidly illustrative of more fundamental and persistent deficiencies in the quality of American democracy – failings that Mason persuasively argues are unlikely to be corrected in the foreseeable future.

The theme of America's divided democracy is also strongly present in the next three chapters that provide concise but vivid portraits of the fragmented and fractious nature of the institutional architecture of American government. In chapter 5, Paul Martin analyses the 'partial revolution' wrought by the Rehnquist Court since 1986. Frequently characterized as a 'conservative' body – not least in the aftermath of the *Bush v. Gore* decision in December 2000 that halted the Florida recount and thereby handed Bush the election – Martin demonstrates the strongly conflicting political tendencies that the Court exhibits. Examining abortion rights and the rights of criminal defendants, he shows how the expectations of a conservative reversal of established policies have mostly failed to be realized. In this respect, like its predecessor, the Burger Court, the Rehnquist Court remains for conservatives the 'counterrevolution that wasn't'. Examining nine recent federalism cases, however, Martin goes on to show how a radical reshaping of federal–state relations has nonetheless been pioneered by a narrow Court majority seemingly intent on reversing the New Deal settlement in favour of an enhanced respect for 'states' rights'. In illustrating the marked divisions between the nine Justices, Martin also shows precisely why the composition of the federal judiciary has become such an important part of the intense competition between Republicans and Democrats for control of the White House and Congress.

Prior to the shift in partisan control of the Senate in June 2001, the composition of the Supreme Court was widely expected to alter with new appointments under President Bush. The appointment issue was merely one element, however, in the turbulent politics of the period from 2001 to 2003 that offers new opportunities to assess the nature of the post-Cold War presidency. In chapter 6, in a challenge to the three dominant approaches to understanding the relationship between the presidency and Congress, Nigel Bowles sets out a 'trifocal' approach to analysing presidential power. Using two illustrative case studies of Clinton and trade policy, he demonstrates how political relationships between the two ends of Pennsylvania Avenue are invariably conditioned by three sets of distinct, but related, factors: the authority granted the President and Congress by the US Constitution; the configuration of parties, electoral cycles and coalitional dynamics; and what Bowles terms 'power politics'. In elaborating this threefold framework, Bowles reminds students of American politics that understanding particular presidential successes or failures is highly case specific and that, consequently, making generalizations about presidential–congressional dynamics remains a tremendously difficult (if unavoidable) academic enterprise.

The complex and multifaceted nature of political bargaining and the vital importance of coalitional politics within the American system is documented further in chapter 7. Fiona Ross, an expert in the politics of 'unpopular policies', sets the landmark welfare reforms of 1996 in the broader context of America's separated system of government. Challenging some of the established scholarly wisdom about the consequences of divided party control, she demonstrates how competitive electoral dynamics between the two main political parties can yield policy innovation rather than the governmental stasis or 'gridlock' conventionally said to characterize the American system. By emphasizing the extent to which both political authority and power are widely scattered and shared in the United States, Ross echoes Bowles in offering a forceful corrective to presidency-centred views of American government and a powerful reminder that coalitional politics – the 'politics of power-sharing' – is as much the province of the United States as continental Europe.

As chapter 3 noted, the particular design of American government has posed powerful constraints on the influence of African Americans. Chapter 8 revisits this theme by examining the fate of another important 'minority' group: American women. In addressing the topic of 'Women in American Politics', Abigail Halcli illustrates the remarkable progress of, but also the continued limits to, female participation and political influence in the United States. Reinforcing the themes of prior chapters, she demonstrates how the institutional design of American government has profound consequences for the fate of women not only in terms of participation and representation but also in regard to the policy outcomes that flow from these. Ironically, 2000 was much more the 'year of the woman' than 1992, yielding the greatest number of female senators in office in American history. At the same time, however, Halcli shows how divided American women remain among themselves – a source both of their centrality to two-party competition and election outcomes and their limited (though increasing) impact in government institutions.

The two final essays in the volume offer thematically complementary but politically contrasting interpretations on an increasingly prominent theme in American political life: the politics of identity and (popular) culture. In chapter 9, in a provocative and wide-ranging essay, Desmond King and Julian Murphet address the vexed issue of the relationship between American identity and multiculturalism (or 'the politics of difference') through the prism of two distinctively 'American' forms of music: jazz and rap/hip-hop. King and Murphet contend that, in its 'bebop' phase, jazz was a genuinely distinctive cultural moment in American history. Rap and hip-hop, by contrast, while originating in a particular time and place, have become subject to the Americanizing forces that condemn distinctive expressions of ethnic or racial identity to a standardized American outcome. Ironically, then, while white America consumes 'blackness' to an unparalleled degree in terms of its popular culture, King and Murphet argue that 'multiculturalism' ultimately represents 'just one more excuse for not redressing the extreme political grievances against urban conditions for African Americans which rap music continues to pronounce'.

By contrast with the prior chapter's argument that an originally subversive music is 'Americanized' and thereby shorn of its radical edge, the final chapter challenges the widely accepted notions that the satirical image of America presented in the two cartoons *The Simpsons* and *South Park* is subversive rather than traditionalist. To the extent that the 2000 elections and their aftermath confirmed an American polity riven by division, the two animated shows not only reflect the nature and scope of these divisions but are also subject to the politicization of popular culture. In particular, that 'moral panics' about American culture should encompass the cartoons – ranging from presidential criticism and evangelical condemnation to public school prohibitions – illustrates precisely how central, rather than peripheral, political conflicts over American culture and identity remain to the evolution of the 'first new nation'. Ironically, however, the cartoons do more to affirm long-standing American values than subvert them.

For many outside America, the United States remains as much a foreign country in terms not only of its governing arrangements but also its values as the rest of the world is to many Americans. While the abolition of capital punishment is now a precondition for membership of the European Union, for example, eighty-five judicial executions occurred in America in 2000. While the United Kingdom banned all private ownership of handguns in 1997, most American states enacted laws allowing the concealed carrying of firearms by their citizens. Yet in many European nations (including the UK, France and Italy), polls suggest most citizens wish to see the death penalty re-established. In the UK the number of handguns in circulation increased after 1997 despite their prohibition, and rates of violent crime – other than homicide – now exceed those in America. When assessing American democracy, then, it is invariably worth heeding Judge Learned Hand's cautionary dictum that 'The spirit of liberty is the spirit that is not too sure it is right.'

A divided democracy by constitutional design, historical evolution and social composition, the United States remains the most militarily powerful, diplomatically influential and economically dominant power in the world. Despite the current intensity of political competition, the sharpness of partisan conflict, and the extent of its social divisions, the United States has shown a tenacious capacity to absorb and transcend its social, economic and political problems. The ten essays that follow should assist readers to arrive at their own critical interpretations of the state of the American experiment at the beginning of the twenty-first century and the nation's prospects for resolving the problems and conflicts that remain.

1

Reaching across the Atlantic: Ideological Aspiration and Institutional Constraints in the United States and Britain

Marc Stears

On hearing that George W. Bush had won, or at least almost won, the American presidential election of November 2000, the British Foreign Secretary Robin Cook welcomed his victory warmly. There was nothing unusual in that itself; foreign secretaries always welcome incoming foreign leaders with whom they will have to work. But the content of the welcome was far more surprising. For Cook argued that although there had been differences between the British Labour Party and the Republican Party of George W. Bush in the past, the causes of such disagreements were now largely at an end. President Bush's 'compassionate conservatism', Cook continued, entailed that Bush's Republicans were closer to British New Labour than they were to the British Conservative Party. There had been a pattern of ideological convergence over recent years, the Foreign Secretary implied. As British Labour had learnt the electoral lessons of Bill Clinton's 'New Democrats' and moved from the left to the centre, so Mr Bush, in turn, had moved his Republican Party from the right to the centre in the pursuit of a response to the Clinton team's continued success.[1]

This was probably one of the more surprising, not to say ludicrous, of the welcomes that Bush enjoyed. It was presumably motivated far more by a sense of realpolitik than by ideological conviction for, as any reader of this book should know, the policy differences between the British Labour Party and the American Republicans are, and will in all likelihood remain, widely divergent. Yet, nonetheless, there remains something instructive in this welcome. It clearly illustrates the ways in which politicians in Britain and the United States continue to interact with each other, commenting not only on international affairs and the economic interests of their states but seeking also to compare their respective domestic programmes and to find potential connections. Such a pattern in itself is far from new or unimportant. Throughout the twentieth century, British and American politicians, activists and intellectuals have continuously exchanged ideas and opinions. Many, indeed, have believed that they were constructing transatlantic programmes of reform, arguing in a number of cases that early developments in one society act as predictor to later developments in the other. Despite the frequency and occasional intensity of these exchanges, however, they have generally not played any significant role in the scholarly accounts of the politics and history of the United States. Indeed, at least until fairly recently, most academic commentators have sought to explain America's political development with almost no reference to the role of outside interlocutors. For many such scholars looking at outsiders would automatically invite mistake, for the United States is said to follow an 'exceptional' path primarily shaped by its distinctive political and social structures. Its historic codified constitution, opportunities for social mobility, constantly growing ethnic diversity, unsurpassed economic strength, and culture of individualism all marking out its development as distinctive in comparison to European states in general and to Britain in particular.[2]

There is, then, a conflict between the perspectives of active participants and distanced scholars. On the one hand, those who have been involved in the transatlantic exchange have often claimed that their dialogue holds the secret of future political development. On the other hand, most academics generally conclude that these exchanges of ideas have appeared more important to the participants than they really have been, for few, if any, have had any significant impact on the politics of the United States. This chapter examines both of these claims by closely analysing two key moments of exchange. To make comparison easier, the chapter looks at two events in the history of the relationship between the political parties and ideologues of the 'progressive' centre and left in Britain and the United States, one at the beginning of the twentieth century and one at its end. In examining the strengths and weaknesses of these exchanges, it shows how this mismatch of attitudes between political actors – who believe that their exchanges can have an important effect – and academic commentators – who believe those exchanges are inevitably limited in their impact – has actually been of some important consequence itself. It has, that is, been the cause not only of substantial analytic confusion but also of some real and concrete political mistakes. Across the last hundred years, it will be shown, politicians have tended to overlook the sorts of arguments that academics make about the distinctive social and political environment of the US, but in so doing, the mistakes they have made have not been without important political consequences. If this analysis is correct, then we can conclude that a closer comparative study of the causes of political change in the United States should be helpful for both political actors and for those seeking better scholarly explanations.

From Britain to the United States:
Building an American Labour Party

In February 1918, the British Labour Party published a draft of its first real manifesto, entitled *Labour and the New Social Order*. It has long been noted that the document marked a turning point in British politics, marking as it did the end of one two-party system and the beginning of another. It is far less frequently recalled, however, that its significant impact was not confined to Britain alone. The draft manifesto caused comment and discussion throughout the developed world and the most striking of these international responses was the welcome accorded to it by those on the left of mainstream American politics, the progressives. Their response was clearly symbolized by the weekly magazine, the *New Republic*, which reprinted the draft manifesto in its entirety within days of its British publication, along with these words:

> Many American readers who are accustomed to the timidities and tepid-ity of American progressivism will shrink from the drastic character of much of the proposed social and financial legislation. But they must harden themselves ... The British Labor party has lifted quantitative socialism of the kind long advocated by the Fabian Society up to the level of imme-diate political discussion ... It will go ill with us unless a party is formed in America which will formulate and fight for a program of American reconstruction which, however different from ... [this] document, will at least not fall below it in courageous, scientific and thorough-going radicalism.[3]

The *New Republic* was far from alone in the United States in embrac-ing *Labour and the New Social Order* in this way. The other leading American progressive journals – *Survey*, *The Public* and the *Independent* – all enthusiastically endorsed the British Labour Party's new statement of purpose.[4] The building of a political party out of the massed forces of organized labour, with a programme apparently penned by the Fabian Society, these organs of progressive opinion uniformly concluded, was 'quite the most promising political and social enterprise taking place in the world of today'.[5] The *New Republic*'s positive welcome of the manifesto was not isolated nor was it short-lived. For several years following the end of the First World War, a large number of leading progressive intellectuals, especially those who had previously shaped the 'New Nationalism' of Theodore Roosevelt's Progressive Party, demanded the creation in the United States of an independent political party based on the model of the British Labour Party. 'The time has come', these American progressive intellectuals insisted, for the American trade unions 'to go into politics'.[6] This demand may have found its apotheosis in the response accorded to *Labour and the New Social Order* but it was reiterated well into the 1920s.

This commitment, although appearing surprising to many latter-day commentators, was rooted in almost a decade of close interconnection. Throughout the first decade of the twentieth century there had been a continuous exchange of ideas between the British Fabian socialists, including Sidney Webb, the author of Labour's constitution, and a group of American reformers called the 'nationalist progressives', who included the *New Republic*'s editors Herbert Croly, Walter Lippmann and Walter Weyl. Through a continual dialogue conducted in person, in academic journals and in shared political weeklies, both groups came to the view that their societies were blighted with the same essential problem: the arrival of serious class conflict. During the last years of the nineteenth century and the beginning of the twentieth, both groups argued, the overwhelming characteristic of Britain and the United States had become the 'clamour, bewilderment' and 'almost tremulous unrest' of class tension.[7] Such a challenge found its clearest expression in the exponential growth of a trade union movement that appeared to be challenging the very foundations of the predominant political and social order. British trade union membership increased by more than 250 per cent from 1890 to the outbreak of the First World War, and it doubled again during the conflict itself. In the United States, the growth was more dramatic still. There was a fivefold expansion of American union membership during the first decade and a half of the twentieth century alone.[8] And with the increase in size came an increase in militancy. All the major industries of the new economy – coal-mining, iron and steel production, railroad transport – were almost continually racked with discord and, in the United States at least, that discord was often violent. No politically engaged thinker could ignore it; the strength and discontent of organized labour was, it seemed, daily 'forced upon the attention of the public at large'.[9] 'The sword of class consciousness is being whetted,' Walter Weyl argued, and unless reform was quickly undertaken 'its sharp edge will cut clean through the body social, sundering us into two mutually antagonistic groups.'[10]

These British Fabians and American nationalist progressives both desired positively to respond to this crisis without embracing its potentially revolutionary extreme. They also agreed on the general outline of a solution. The avoidance of dangerous class struggle, both argued, was dependent on the enhancement of genuine social union and national harmony which could itself only be attained through purposeful government action. 'Social progress', Walter Weyl contended, entailed that all should be 'ordered, not jumbled, not left to the clash of egoistic interests'.[11] Across the Atlantic, Sidney Webb outlined an identical philosophy. 'Where our forefathers' relied on 'a jostling crowd of individuals each fighting for his own hand', the new generation desired 'a highly organized, far-reaching, patiently pursued communal enterprise'.[12] These general commitments led to two particular demands: there was an urgent need for a concerted government involvement in economic decision-making and for the construction of a substantial welfare state. Both groups thus dedicated themselves 'to a drastic reorganization of the . . . political and economic system. To the substitution of a frank social policy for the individualism of the past and the realization of this policy . . . by the use of efficient governmental instruments.'[13] While involving the government in industry and moving material resources from the rich to the poor could 'superficially be called class legislation', the *New Republic* thus argued, its essential justification for the British Fabians and the American nationalist progressives lay elsewhere. Any effort to improve the standing of the least well off should be considered because it 'seeks to remove the obstacles to national unity'.[14]

It was out of this ideal that the ideological justification for building a Labour Party emerged. Constructing a political party out of the massed ranks of the organized workers would assist in two essential ways. First, it would encourage the workers themselves to abandon any potentially revolutionary tactics and also lead them to move from a simple concern with their own interest to a more rounded interest in the community as a whole. If workers were to form their own party, it was thus continually argued, they would be led by the realities of democratic coalition building to 'assume the responsibility for adapting their class program and needs to those of the other classes and to that of the community as a whole'.[15] Direct political involvement would thus move the workers from sectionalism to communalism. In this way, these ideal Labour parties would also possess the advantage of being directed not by class-conscious workers but by removed, impartial experts, by, in other words, Fabians or the nationalist progressives themselves. Second, the arrival of a party of labour would also make the state itself far more likely to pursue the necessary reforming agenda. For even if the Labour Party did not attain power outright, its presence in elections and in the legislature would exert a powerful influence on others. There was, of course, also a clear electoral motivation here. Both Fabians and nationalist progressives had previously been dependent on the good-will of alternative political parties: mainly the Liberals in Britain and the Republicans in the United States. Increasingly, however, they felt let down by their chosen partisan vehicles and longed for an alternative of their own. The arrival of a mass working-class electorate and a powerful organized trade union movement seemed to bring that within reach.

For all its ideological attractiveness to American progressives, however, this demand was destined to remain unfulfilled in the United States for one very simple reason. Whereas the ideal and aspiration were shared across the Atlantic, the actual political situation in the United States differed greatly from that in Britain. In Britain, politics in the early twentieth century was already characterized by the emergence of a union-dominated Labour Party, equipped with resources and supporters, whose policy-making processes could be easily permeated by dedicated intellectual activists; in the United States the situation could not have been more sharply divergent. There, however much progressive ideologists desired it, it quickly became clear that the American trade union movement felt little need or desire for a partisan reorganization. The American Federation of Labor (AFL), led by Samuel Gompers, had always been suspicious of political engagement, believing, among other things, that the vast divisions among the American working class – cleavages of ethnicity, region and skill – would always prevent the development of any sustained sense of common involvement necessary for successful political endeavour. Even those few unions who were interested in pursuing the Labour Party ideal found their path blocked by several peculiar features of American political life. The Chicago Federation of Labor attempted to establish a National Labor Party which 'frankly admit[ted] its kinship to the British Labour Party' in November 1918 in an explicit challenge to the AFL's formal apolitical stance.[16] But despite high-level progressive expectations that such an organization would have 'an excellent chance of capturing the White House', the party failed to make any significant headway.[17] Unsuccessful in its attempt to persuade the left-leaning Senator Robert La Follette to stand as its candidate for the presidency, it ran in 1920 as a Farmer-Labor party with the relatively unknown attorney Parley Parker Christensen at its head. It polled only 290,000 votes, less than half the amount that the imprisoned radical Eugene Debs won for an American Socialist Party which had itself been severely weakened by the First World War.[18]

There were so many reasons for this failure – institutional, cultural, economic – that latter-day scholars have often described the failure of the Labour Party ideal in the United States as almost 'overdetermined'. Sifting through the various explanations for the lack of a political party of organized labour in America – explanations that range from the peculiarly exclusive nature of American trade unionism to the role of the Supreme Court in restricting the scope of legislative action in the United States – has thus become a staple of recent scholarship.[19] What united them, however, was that they were all distinctive and characteristic features of American politics and society. Whatever the precise causes, then, it is clear that all efforts at building a party of organized labour were always destined to come to nothing in the United States whereas such a party was perfectly well suited to conditions in Great Britain. The essential problem facing this effort, then, was that the transatlantic dialogue had – for reasons we shall return to shortly – taken almost no notice of ingrained local peculiarities. Fabians and nationalist progressives had collectively built up an ideal theory in glorious isolation from the political realities of their two very distinctive polities. The result, unsurprisingly, was intellectual success and, in the United States at least, political failure.

From the United States to Britain: The Third Way and the 'New' Approach to Progressive Politics

In the aftermath of the failure of the American Labor Party experiment, there were to be few serious attempts to forge a transatlantic agreement on progressive political strategy, even though there were continual discussions of individual policies, for eighty years. In April 1999, though, the *New Democrat* published an account of transatlantic political exchange that was just as dramatic in its own way as the *New Republic*'s coverage of eighty years earlier. In the White House earlier that month, Democratic President Bill Clinton and British Prime Minister Tony Blair had met together with other Western European leaders publicly to celebrate the construction of a 'new international public philosophy'. In a meeting dubbed 'the Third Way Homecoming', the President contended that 'Third Way thinking' was 'reshaping progressive politics' in both the United States and Britain.[20] The British centre-left itself was in no doubt that this view was right. 'A unifying thread of ideology runs throughout the changes we are making,' Tony Blair argued in a speech at the State Department in Washington DC. 'There is a new radical-centre being born' in Britain and 'when I spell out the key themes' there will clearly 'be familiar echoes to what you are doing here'.[21] Among those academics adding a scholarly gloss to this political enthusiasm were the American communitarian philosopher Amitai Etzioni and Anthony Giddens, ironically head of the most impressive monument to the British Fabianism of old, the London School of Economics.[22]

In its most ambitious form, the Third Way was intended to be a new approach to politics itself. The *New Democrat* argued that it was best characterized by three essential principles: 'the idea that government should promote equal opportunity for all while granting special privilege for none; an ethic of mutual responsibility that equally rejects the politics of entitlement and the politics of social abandonment; and a new approach to governing that empowers citizens to act for themselves.'[23] The essence of these principles themselves becomes clearer when it is appreciated that they were premised on one further idea; all the Third Way advocates believed that the old reformist techniques no longer provided effective means to the attainment of progressives' desired goals. Simple observation, it was thus argued, demonstrated that poverty and inequality had failed to be eliminated either by the initial welfare efforts of Franklin Roosevelt or Clement Attlee or by the later fine-tunings of Lyndon Johnson and Harold Wilson.[24] The economic difficulties of the late 1970s and early 1980s further put paid to the interventionist basis of earlier progressive macroeconomic policy, and the effective collapse of the trade union movement in both nations had further added to the need to find a new direction for economic policy. It was necessary, Third Way advocates thus claimed, to stand midway between the espousal of market mechanisms that characterized much of the politics of the 1980s and the faith in large-scale state intervention that had been characteristic of left-leaning politics at least since the First World War. The essence of that alternative strategy lay in resisting the call for the straightforward expansion of government intervention, and crafting instead a closer working relationship between the public and the private sectors. Voluntary agencies, community activists and private firms should thus be brought into the heart of many areas of public provision, while the large bureaucracies of old would be dramatically pared down. These techniques, it was argued, would guarantee that 'fundamental progressive principles' are 'furthered by modern means and innovative ideas'.[25]

In addition to this intellectual reasoning, the emergence of the Third Way was also driven by an explicit political calculation. The early twentieth-century efforts at intellectual and political exchange had also had an electoral dimension, of course, but whereas those earlier ambitions were born of optimism about the direction of social change, late twentieth-century views were shaped by pessimism. For most of the 1980s, both the United States and Britain had been subject to continuous and relatively radical right-wing governments. Throughout that time, political commentators on both sides of the Atlantic had also begun to worry that the old coalition of electoral support that both parties had relied on was breaking down. The very working class who had provided the backbone of electoral support for progressive endeavours was both shrinking and losing its homogeneous pattern of partisan allegiance. Increasing opportunities for social mobility apparently characterized both societies and, especially as these opportunities were attended by further demographic shifts, this made it increasingly unlikely that either the Democrats or Labour could happily rely on the simple majorities of old.[26] These trends had been notable for far longer in the United States than in Britain, accompanying the election of Richard Nixon there and not really emerging in Britain until almost a decade later. They were, on the other hand, felt more fiercely in Britain than the United States, as class had always played a more significant role in shaping British political allegiances. The Third Way offered a way out for both the Democrats and British Labour, intellectually and politically. Parties of the left, Third Way advocates argued, should continue to appeal to the remaining sections of the working class and to the economically disadvantaged, while at the same time incorporating the needs and values of the newly affluent and the traditional middle class. The question that remained was how to combine the two groups.

Rhetorically this was to be achieved by continually emphasizing the essential 'commonality of values' between these two groups, in a manner not dissimilar to earlier patterns.[27] In concrete terms, though, it entailed developing policy instruments that were capable of responding to the economic and social interests of both sections, and avoiding the use of those that might cause more difficulty.[28] This entailed, in particular, that Democrats and Labour abandon the bold objectives of the past that might alienate many potential voters. Third Way advocates urged the parties to move strongly away from any explicit efforts to redistribute wealth from rich to poor, via a traditional tax-and-benefits system, or to direct economic affairs from the centre. At the same time, it led both parties to seek improvements (and usually gradual ones) in the sorts of public services that might benefit old and new electoral constituencies alike; it was for this reason that health and education were both granted a central role. It still further entailed abandoning the active social agenda suggested by the cultural liberalism that was popular largely among committed activists, and embracing instead a firm style of cultural conservatism – tough on crime, demanding on welfare recipients, tentative on race – whose appeal was believed to cross class boundaries.[29] Combining these two themes, representatives of both Democratic and Labour parties even used the same language in continually committing themselves to serve the interests of those 'ordinary people who worked hard, played by the rules, and took responsibility for their own actions'.[30]

This looked on the surface like a spectacular international change of direction, beginning in 1992 with the election of Bill Clinton in the United States. After successfully capturing the White House and even managing to hold on to both Houses of Congress in that year, Clinton initially pursued what he described as the 'New Democratic agenda', later to be dubbed the Third Way, almost to the letter. Two years later, Tony Blair was elected leader of the Labour Party in Britain and, in clear emulation of Clinton, rebranded it 'New Labour'. In addition to adopting the broad policy agenda outlined by Third Way advocates on both sides of the Atlantic, Blair's Labour Party also employed the polling and presentational techniques that had characterized the New Democrat approach. Blair 'modernizers' adopted the Machiavellian internal politicking of the Clinton Democratic Leadership Council, ousting opponents and relying on broad appeals to public opinion rather than building up party activist support to forward his agenda, and relied heavily on the increasingly professional experts of political communications for advice. In office, indeed, Blair readily embraced the Clinton role, preferring to style himself in the manner of President rather than Prime Minister.[31] The celebrations by the *New Democrat* of a Third Way hegemony in Britain and the United States did not appear to be out of place.

Yet, despite all of this, it is already clear by the outset of the twenty-first century that the Third Way has failed to build a genuine trans-atlantic political order. It has also failed, to varying degrees, in both the United States and Britain. And, just as eighty years ago, the essential cause lies in the failure of the two groups to appreciate and to respond to the entrenched institutional and social differences of the two societies in which they operate. The American Third Way vision was explicitly designed for an institutional order where policy success was extremely difficult. For most of his administration, Bill Clinton faced a divided government. His first two years of office were the only time when he could have expected a legislative agenda to succeed. Even then, however, his efforts to introduce a complex form of universal health care provision failed to overcome not public hostility – there was indeed wide public support – but entrenched institutional obstacles. Attempts also to reform education stumbled on the simple institutional reality that the American federal government has very little effective control over educational provision. In so far as the Third Way survived at all, therefore, it was because it was peculiarly well suited to an institutional environment which made policy innovation extremely difficult. As a public philosophy that committed its advocates to relatively little in the form of concrete reform, it could just about sustain itself in such an environment but it could not hope to be able to promise solutions to remaining social problems in the long run.[32]

The situation in Britain was equally difficult, but for dramatically different reasons. Faced with a uniform system of government and far less regular elections, British voters were left with a stark choice in 1997: they had effectively to choose one-party government for another four years. In making that choice, there was little surprise that they turned their back entirely on a Conservative Party increasingly characterized by sleaze and managerial incompetence. The result was an overwhelming parliamentary majority for Blair. But Blair's majority presented problems to the 'do-nothing' mentality of the Third Way, a mentality which had been peculiarly well suited to the institutional conditions of the United States. For, in reality, Blair was presented with significant opportunities for reform, his parliamentary majority far outstripping that of all three of twentieth-century Britain's most reform-minded prime ministers, Herbert Asquith, Margaret Thatcher and Clement Attlee. His attempted answer partly lay in an attempt to avoid commitment. As Hugo Young has argued, 'Tony Blair had two objectives during the election. The first was to win, the second was to minimize every expectation of what would happen then. He wanted to over-perform, but under-promise.'[33] This was, however, an unsustainable scenario in the long run. There was a limit to how persuasive a British government would ever seem in claiming that it was incapable of responding to remaining social, and especially infrastructural, problems. It was as such that the last years of the first New Labour administration witnessed continual demands from many diverse groups for a return to at least some of the policies of old. Gordon Brown as Chancellor of the Exchequer was thus widely held to be courting the abandonment of the Third Way and a return to a more identifiably British form of social democracy.[34] Whatever the electoral appeal of 'New Labour', the politics of the transatlantic Third Way provided no straightforward answer to the peculiar difficulties with which Britain was faced.

Convergence and the Limits of Adaptability

To many outside the immediate circle of both of these movements, the failure of both efforts to craft a genuinely transatlantic political agenda did not come as much of a surprise. A large number of politicians and an even larger number of intellectuals have consistently warned of the potential problems and difficulties involved in attempting to borrow ideas and political strategies directly from one society to another. In the early twentieth century, for example, the leaders of the American Federation of Labor itself insisted that radical politicians in the United States should stay away from attempting to politicize its activities even if such approaches had appeared successful elsewhere. In the last months of the First World War, Matthew Woll, deputy leader of the AFL, specifically enjoined progressives not to try to follow the British model. 'We must not be unmindful', Woll argued, 'of the fact that our domestic problems are quite different from those found to exist in Great Britain.'[35] Although Woll's and the AFL's arguments could be attributed to the organization's innate opposition to the idea of party political engagement, friendly and informed critics also raised objections. Worried by signs of an unstable ideological export, Edward Pease of the British Fabian Society argued long before the end of the war that 'America must not borrow . . . Fabianism from England, but must create its own Socialism to suit its own political and social and industrial conditions.'[36] The same voices of concern were heard during the Third Way project, although they were rather more muted. *Tribune* the voice of the left wing of the Labour Party continually warned against the 'Americanization' of British Labour, suggesting that it was an inappropriate model to follow in the current circumstances.

   The failure of both groups to heed these warnings and their desire to jump right into potentially dangerous transatlantic alliances requires careful explanation. The answer is surprisingly similar in both historical cases. For both the progressives of the early twentieth century and the Third Way advocates of the century's end constructed a narrative of *convergence* to account for their decision to overlook protestations of differences. Both groups, that is, argued that the United States and Britain were inevitably beginning to resemble one another in fundamental social and political ways, and it was that resemblance that excused the decision to ignore apparently entrenched differences.

   In the early years of the twentieth century, the American nationalist progressives argued that it was Britain that was more advanced along a single trajectory for Western civilization, a trajectory provided most clearly by the growth and radicalism of the industrial working class.[37] All industrial societies, it was argued, were faced with essentially the same dilemma – how to maintain social harmony and stability in the face of ever-increasing class tension – and would thus have to seek essentially similar solutions. As Britain had industrialized earlier, as the popular industrial correspondent Ordway Tead put it in 1918, the 'peculiar advantage of drawing on the English experience' was thus that 'we see England a little ahead of us on the road that the capitalistic system is travelling.'[38] Even the leading political scientist of the day, Harold Laski, generally so astute an observer of irrevocable differences between Britain and the United States, occasionally fell into the trap of perceiving social progress according to a linear chronology. The underlying problem for progressives trying to politicize American unions, he once insisted, was simply that the American Federation of Labor 'is in social ideas . . . a generation behind the English labor movement.'[39]

In the late twentieth century, this narrative of convergence was maintained, but the pattern was reversed. Now it was the United States which was further ahead and Britain which was inevitably forced to catch up. Moreover, where convergence theory in the past was used to justify the inevitable growth of government intervention, in the late twentieth century it was employed to justify the inevitable withdrawal of the government from key sectors of economic and social life. As such, British Third Way advocates have thus been found arguing that a series of structural changes in British politics have called into question the very possibility of a more interventionist politics. These changes are most frequently described in the language of 'globalization'. The increasing mobility of global capital, it is thus argued, entails that only nations with relatively low tax burdens and non-interventionist governments will be able to maintain reasonable levels of investment and thus of economic growth. Capital, it is argued, will only locate to those societies governed by those committed to 'fiscal responsibility, prudence and a rules-bounded economic policy'.[40] The United States, then, which holders of capital apparently believe already largely fits this bill, must almost inevitably become the model, and not only for Britain but for the rest of the world. All countries, Blair and his allies thus argue, should be led to 'ratchet down' once ambitious progressive programmes of government action.[41] The Third Way, with its minimal ambitions and its reliance on non-governmental forms of intervention, is not simply one option among others, it is the *only* means of maintaining any form of workable progressive commitment.[42]

Both these narratives of inevitable convergence no doubt have some truth in them. It would be mistaken to argue that class was not a central issue in early twentieth-century politics, and equally misleading simply to claim that globalization posed no difficulties to interventionist administrations at the century's close. These are not, however, the only reasons for the adoption of such a narrative. Their first advantage is that they provide those engaged in transatlantic exchange with an excuse for overlooking the peculiarities of their own society. For if nations are converging, it seems to be claimed, there is no need to attend to the very real differences that currently exist. Moreover, the *inevitability* involved in both these narratives is designed to ensure that ideologues remain immune from any of the problems their own theories throw up. For if their ideas are the unavoidable consequence of immutable social change then there is little way in which they can be held accountable for the shortcomings. The ease of their own personal transatlantic academic engagement undoubtedly also contributed to the apparent inability of these groups to notice how deeply entrenched were the social and institutional differences that obtained between their two countries. Working together intellectually with their British allies, the editors of *New Republic* reported in 1918, had revealed to them that 'the problems confronting Britain are essentially the same as the problems confronting America.' As the wartime crisis gathered steam, that same intellectual exchange convinced them that the problems of the new world could thus be resolved 'only as [they are] being worked out in Great Britain'.[43] The same could no doubt be said of reformers in the later period. As *they* had become closer as the years went by, these British and American political theorists seemed to suggest, so inevitably their *societies* would follow suit.

   Whatever its root cause, this faith in convergence has crowded out any careful analysis of actual institutional and social differences between the two countries in both cases. As the First World War reached its conclusion, the progressive theorists of the *New Republic* often argued that there were no 'political . . . barriers to cooperation' across the Atlantic, and no barriers therefore to the easy adaptation of measures originating in one country to the circumstances of another.[44] Instead, of course, they simply failed to recognize how firmly entrenched these obstacles actually were. As the AFL's deputy leader Matthew Woll argued, to many of 'those who have come to be styled as advanced thinkers . . . the complete reformation of the world's social order may be readily secured simply by the formation of a labor party directed and led, of course, by the self-same intellectuals and advanced thinkers.' These thinkers, he continued, apparently believe that the long list of institutional, social and economic obstacles that in fact prevent that development 'may be easily swept aside as if by the waving of a magic wand'.[45] Although Woll's self-satisfied rhetoric jars even these eighty years later, his basic conclusion remains justified nonetheless. To put all that has gone before another way, where Daniel Rodgers argues that in 'talking about Britain' these progressive intellectuals were 'thinking about America', he would be advised rather to suggest that while talking about Britain, these progressives *ought* to have been thinking about America.[46]

Conclusion

It is not always thus. The mistake of the early twentieth century did not fail to be instructive. A generation later the American theorists that helped to shape and legitimate the programmes of the New Deal learnt relatively quickly the necessity of being constantly aware of the opportunities and limitations posed by their own social, institutional and economic environment. After a few early difficulties, they shaped an ideological vision that was broadly compatible with those constraints but which was radical nonetheless. They pulled the system as far as it would go without ever really attempting to break it.[47] Such an approach is vital to the success of progressive politics and it is for that reason that we have much to learn from the study of comparative politics and the individual study of polities that are foreign to us. For such scholarly investigation should best be used to remind us not only what countries have in common – although that is important – but also what distinguishes them. Such an emphasis has long been a key element of the very best scholarly analysis and it has occasionally percolated into politics too. In observing international labour developments just before the First World War broke out, another participant in that same Anglo-American progressive exchange, G. D. H. Cole, sagely noted that 'the American movement is as characteristically American as ours is characteristically English.' From this observation, Cole drew the conclusion that many activists in his own time and hence have appeared to miss. 'It is a truth to be remembered', he argued, 'that institutions are born and not made.' And as such, the 'greatest service that can be done us by the intelligent study of foreign' politics 'is to save us at least from becoming cosmopolitans'.[48]

NOTES

The first version of this paper was delivered at a conference to celebrate the hundredth anniversary of the British Labour Party held at the University of Bristol in February 2000. I thank all the participants at that event, especially Rodney Lowe, Kenneth O. Morgan, and Mark Wickham-Jones, for their very helpful comments. I should also like to thank Nigel Bowles, Liz Irwin, Eugenia Low, Karma Nabulsi, and Paul Martin for insightful observations. All remaining problems and omissions are, of course, my fault alone.

1   As reported on
    http://news.bbc.co.uk/hi/english/uk_politics/newsid_1009000/1009633.stm
2   For excellent overviews of these trends see Byron E. Shafer (ed.), *Is America Different? A New Look at American Exceptionalism* (Oxford: Clarendon Press, 1991) and David Englander (ed.), *Britain and America: Studies in Comparative History 1760–1970* (New Haven: Yale University Press, 1997). For notable exceptions to the general trend see Peter Hall, *The Political Power of Economic Ideas: Keynesianism across Nations* (Princeton: Princeton University Press, 1989) and Desmond King, *In the Name of Liberalism: Illiberal Social Policy in Britain and the United States* (Oxford: Oxford University Press, 1998).
3   Editors, 'Labour and the New Social Order', Supplement to *New Republic*, 16 Feb. 1918, p. 1.
4   See Paul U. Kellogg, 'The British Labor Offensive', *Survey*, 2 Mar. 1918, pp. 585–8 and, for an overview, John A. Thompson, *Reformers and War: American Progressive Publicists and the First World War* (Cambridge: Cambridge University Press, 1987), esp. pp. 208–32.
5   Editors, 'The Rising Tide of British Labor', *New Republic*, 19 Dec. 1923, p. 82.
6   Editors, 'Labor in Politics', *New Republic*, 19 Nov. 1919, p. 336.
7   Walter Weyl, *The New Democracy* (New York: Macmillan, 1912), p. 1.
8   See Gary Marks, *Unions in Politics: Britain, Germany and the United States in the Nineteenth and Early Twentieth Centuries* (Princeton: Princeton University Press, 1989), esp. pp. 83–5 and Joseph A. McCartin, *Labor's Great War: The Struggle for Industrial Democracy and the Origins of Modern American Labor Relations, 1912–1921* (Chapel Hill: North Carolina University Press, 1997).
9   Arthur Gleason, *What the Workers Want: A Study of British Labor* (New York: Harcourt, Brace, and Howe, 1920), p. 5 and Charles Beard, 'Introduction', in Savel Zimmand (ed.), *Modern Social Movements: Descriptive Summaries and Bibliographies* (New York: H. W. Wilson, 1921). For an overview, see David Brody, *Workers in Industrial America: Essays on the Twentieth Century Struggle* (New York: Oxford University Press, 1980).
10 Walter Weyl, *Tired Radicals and Other Essays* (New York: Macmillan, 1921), pp. 24–5.

11   Walter Weyl, 'From Chaos to City', MS in the Walter Weyl Papers, Rutgers University Library, Special Collections, box 2, folder 7, p. 2.

12   Sidney Webb, *The Principles of the Labour Party* (London: Labour Party, 1918), p. 4.

13   Herbert Croly, *Progressive Democracy* (New York: Macmillan, 1915), p. 15.

14   Editors, 'The Nationalism of the British Labour Party', *New Republic*, 17 Apr. 1918, pp. 63–5.

15   Editors, 'Labour in Politics', *New Republic*, 15 Mar. 1922, p. 336. See too 'Why a Labor Party?', *New Republic*, 26 Apr. 1919, p. 399 and 'A New National Party', 24 Mar. 1920, pp. 108–11, and Ordway Tead, 'A National Labor Policy', *New Republic*, 17 Nov. 1917, pp. 67–9.

16   Editors, 'The Labor Party', *Survey*, 13 Dec. 1919, p. 229. See too, Editors, 'Independent Labor Party Launched', *Survey*, 30 Nov. 1918, pp. 264–5 and 'Growing Support for a Labor Party', *Survey*, 14 Dec. 1918, p. 354.

17   Frank P. Walsh cited in McCartin, *Labor's Great War*, p. 197.

18   See C. Merz, 'Enter: The Labor Party', *New Republic*, 10 Dec. 1919, pp. 53–5. On the Socialists, see James Weinstein, *The Decline of Socialism in America, 1912–1925* (New York: Monthly Review Press, 1967).

19   Marks, *Unions in Politics* convincingly argues that the combination of the closed nature of American unions and the ethnic heterogeneity of the work-force limited the possibilities of political action on the part of organized labour. An explanation centred on the contrasting institutional character of Britain and America – and especially the supremacy of the judicial branch in the latter – is provided in Victoria C. Hattam, *Labour Visions and State Power: The Origins of Business Unionism in the United States* (Princeton: Princeton University Press, 1993) and Theda Skocpol, *Protecting Soldiers and Mothers: The Political Origins of Social Policy in the United States* (Cambridge, Mass.: Belknap Press, 1992), pp. 205–43. Informed scepticism about this dominant form of explanation is present in Robin Archer, 'Unions, Courts, and Parties: Judicial Repression and Labor Politics in Late-Nineteenth-Century America', *Politics and Society*, 26, no. 3 (1998), pp. 391–442. An overview of all the various arguments can be found in Neville Kirk, *Labor and Society in Britain and the USA*, vol. 2 (Aldershot: Scholar Press, 1994), esp. pp. 246–62.

20   Editors, in *New Democrat*, 25 Apr. 1999, republished at www.ndol.org

21   Tony Blair, speech to State Department, 6 Feb. 1998, republished at www.ndol.org

22   See Amitai Etzioni, *The Spirit of Community* (New York: Crown, 1993) and Anthony Giddens, *The Third Way* (Cambridge: Polity, 1993).

23   'The Third Way: Progressive Governance for the 21st Century', *New Democrat*, 25 Apr. 1999, republished at www.ndol.org

24   For classic accounts of the early period, see among a voluminous literature, Arthur M. Schlesinger Jr, *The Coming of the New Deal* (Boston: Houghton-Mifflin, 1959) and Kenneth O. Morgan, *Labour in Power, 1945–1951* (Oxford: Oxford University Press, 1984). For the later efforts at refinement

see Gareth Davies, *From Opportunity to Entitlement: The Transformation and Decline of Great Society Liberalism* (Lawrence: Kansas University Press, 1996) and Michael Stewart, *The Jekyll and Hyde Years: Politics and Economic Policy since 1964* (London: Routledge, 1977).

25 Al From, 'The Third Way: Reshaping Politics throughout the World', *New Democrat*, 14 July 1999, republished at www.ndol.org

26 See Ivor Crewe, Neil Day and Anthony Fox, *The British Electorate, 1963–1987* (Cambridge: Cambridge University Press, 1991) and W. E. Miller and S. A. Traugott, compilers, *American National Election Studies Data Handbook 1952–1986* (Cambridge, Mass.: Harvard University Press, 1989).

27 See Tony Blair, *Social-ism* (London: Fabian Society, 1994) and *New Britain: My Vision of a Young Country* (London: Fourth Estate, 1996).

28 See Margaret Weir, 'The Collapse of Bill Clinton's Third Way', in Stuart White (ed.), *New Labour: The Progressive Future* (Basingstoke: Palgrave, 2001), p. 189.

29 For the classic account of this dimension, see chapter 4 of Seymour M. Lipset, *Political Man: The Social Bases of Politics* (London: Heinemann, 1960). A detailed recent account is Byron E. Shafer and William J. M. Claggett, *The Two Majorities: The Issue Context of Modern American Politics* (Baltimore: Johns Hopkins University Press, 1995). For a comparative account, see Byron E. Shafer and Marc D. Stears, 'From Social Welfare to Cultural Values', *Journal of Policy History*, 11, no. 4 (1999), pp. 331–66.

30 Bill J. Clinton, 'The New Covenant', speech to Georgetown University, 23 Oct. 1991, (republished at www.ndol.org). Compare with Peter Mandelson and Roger Liddle, *The Blair Revolution: Can New Labour Deliver?* (London: Faber, 1996), pp. 6–8.

31 For an authoritative statement of intent in this regard, see Mandelson and Liddle, *Blair Revolution*, pp. 232–55. See too C. Campbell and B. A. Rockman, 'Third Way Leadership, Old Way Government: Blair, Clinton, and the Power to Govern', *British Journal of Politics and International Relations*, 3, no. 1 (2001), p. 45.

32 For a detailed account see Weir, 'Collapse of Bill Clinton's Third Way', pp. 137–48.

33 Hugo Young cited in Colin Hay, *The Political Economy of New Labour: Labouring under False Pretences?* (Manchester: Manchester University Press, 1999), pp. 133–4.

34 See Hay, *Political Economy of New Labour, passim.*

35 Matthew Woll, 'American Labor Readjustment Proposals', *Proceedings of the Academy of Political Science*, 7 (1919), p. 181.

36 Edward Pease, 'The Legislative Programme of the Socialist Party', *Fabian News*, Jan. 1914, p. 76.

37 See Arthur Mann, 'British Social Thought and American Reformers of the Progressive Era', *Mississippi Valley Historical Review*, 42 (1956), p. 691.

38 Ordway Tead, 'The American Situation in War Time', *Century Magazine*, Jan. 1918, p. 355.

39   Harold Laski, 'Industrial Self-Government', *New Republic*, 27 Apr. 1918, p. 392. See too Harold Laski, 'British Labor and the War', *New Republic*, 23 July 1919, p. 400.

40   Colin Hay, 'The Invocation of External Economic Constraint', *European Legacy*, 6, no. 2 (2001), p. 238.

41   See Peter Seyd, 'Tony Blair and New Labour', in Anthony King (ed.), *Britain at the Polls: New Labour Triumphs* (Chatham: Chatham House, 1998).

42   For a full account of this vision see D. Coates, *Models of Capitalism: Growth and Stagnation in the Modern Era* (Cambridge: Polity, 2000), esp. pp. 258–9 and Adam Przeworski and Michael Wallerstein, 'Structural Dependence of the State on Capital', *American Political Science Review*, 82, no. 1 (1998), pp. 11–29.

43   Editors, 'Towards Industrial Democracy', *New Republic* (1918), p. 123.

44   Melvyn Stokes, 'American Progressives and the European Left', *Journal of American Studies*, 17 (1983), p. 28.

45   Woll, 'American Labor', p. 182.

46   Daniel T. Rodgers, *Atlantic Crossings: Social Politics in a Progressive Age* (Cambridge, Mass.: Harvard University Press, 1998), p. 311.

47   See Alan Brinkley, *Liberalism and its Discontents* (Cambridge: Harvard University Press, 1998), pp. 37–62. As Brinkley argues at p. 62: 'By 1945 American liberals, as the result of countless small adaptations to a broad range of experiences, had reached an accommodation with capitalism that served in effect to settle many of the most divisive conflicts of the first decades of the century.'

48   G. D. H. Cole, *The World of Labour* (London: Macmillan, 1928), p. 165.

2

A New Electoral Disorder?
The American Elections
of 2000

Robert Singh

For all the political and legal controversy surrounding their final resolution, there was something richly apposite in the stalemate results of the 2000 presidential and congressional elections. At the dawn of a new millennium, with the United States enjoying unprecedented prosperity and peace, the closest presidential election since 1960 precipitated a constitutional crisis of epic – albeit brief – proportions. Only two years after America's most powerful and polarizing political figure was engulfed in impeachment proceedings as a result of an episodic series of sexual encounters with a White House intern, the nation was once again convulsed by a political soap opera with a colourful cast of characters that included a dead man elected to the US Senate and the prospect that the then ninety-eight year old Senator Strom Thurmond (R-SC) might succeed to the White House. The presidential election was effectively decided by a one-vote margin in the US Supreme Court, whose members included some who had themselves been praised and censured by the main contestants in the campaign, as well as some whose prospects of retirement or promotion rested on the outcome. Yet again, the capacity of American public life simultaneously to inspire, baffle and bemuse the world appeared almost limitless.

Ironically, the American election results of 2000 signified more continuity than change in recent politics in the United States. But that continuity was itself a matter of maintaining a trend of polarized partisan and ideological competition, near parity in the main parties' electoral strengths, and a deeply divided electorate. The election results confirmed the turbulent pattern of politics since 1968 in which divided party control of the federal government has emerged as the norm, accompanying presidential as well as mid-term elections. More particularly, since 1988, all possible partisan outcomes had occurred at the federal level in just twelve years: a Republican president facing a Democratic Congress (1989–93); undivided Democratic Party control of the White House and Capitol Hill (1993–4); a Democratic president confronted by a Republican Congress (1995–2001); and, for the first four months of 2001, an outcome that had proven elusive for forty-six years – undivided Republican control of both the White House and Capitol Hill. Not since the years immediately following the Second World War have such rapid changes in government accompanied such close partisan competition.

Even prior to the Democrats regaining the Senate in June 2001 as a result of James Jeffords (I-VT) leaving the GOP, however, the description of the federal results as yielding 'undivided' Republican control obscured not only the precariousness of the party's majorities but also the profound social, economic and political divisions manifested in the 2000 elections. Not since 1948, when Harry Truman had defied the odds to win re-election in a four-way presidential race, had all possible partisan outcomes at the federal level been realistic possibilities. But the election was notable not only for the closeness of the presidential race, its competitiveness and the bitter partisan controversy that dogged its eventual results. The narrowness of the congressional elections also revealed a profoundly divided post-Clinton America, riven by conflicts based on ideology, geography and demographics. These predated the Arkansan's tenure in the White House but Clinton helped to sharpen and intensify them greatly. Consequently, the two national parties have emerged more evenly matched in terms of popular support than at any time since the nineteenth century, but with distinct regional, ideological and cultural divides between their respective electoral coalitions.

For students of American elections, the 2000 election outcomes reinforced rather than resolved long-standing academic disagreements about how best to characterize the post-1968 'sixth party system' in the United States.[1] The absence of a clear, decisive and enduring partisan victory lent credence to proponents of Everett Carl Ladd's 'no majority' realignment thesis – the notion that Republicans have mostly won the battle of ideas among Americans but not reaped commensurate electoral rewards.[2] But those scholars for whom the party system remains 'dealigned' could also discern support for their views in the absence of a national partisan tide and the importance of 'swing' voters and the key battleground states in 2000.[3] For still others, and notwithstanding the relative shallowness of the electorate's partisan moorings, American voters behaved – given the relative economic and security context – with some predictability. The 2000 elections confirmed what Byron Shafer terms an 'electoral order'[4] that rests upon 'two majorities': a majority preference for a tempered liberal economics on the one hand (one that rejects radical reforms of either a conservative or progressive cast), and broadly traditionalist cultural values and nationalist foreign policy on the other. The elections were, in this sense, the continuation of a long-standing battle for the 'new centre' of American politics that had commenced in 1968 and intensified dramatically after 1992. The key questions that this chapter seeks to answer are why the results narrowly favoured the Republicans in 2000 and what this signifies about the state of the contemporary American party system.

The Clinton Legacies

The 2000 contest was as much a retrospective verdict on Bill Clinton as it was a choice between George W. Bush and Al Gore. In concluding a volume on 'the Clinton legacy', Bert Rockman raised a simple but vexing question as to whether Clinton 'has been an unprincipled opportunist, quick to shed ideas, commitments, and associates when they become inconvenient, or a pragmatic idealist who played a bad hand skillfully'.[5] On this, the jury is still out, and seems likely to remain so for some years to come in the face of America's most Zelig-like, chameleon president of the modern era.

Clinton entered office with his fellow Democrats solidly in control of the House and Senate and became the first Democratic president to win re-election since FDR in 1936. But by the time he left office the Republicans had not only captured control of both Houses of Congress in 1994 after a forty-year hiatus, but also (briefly) achieved full control of the federal government in 2000 for the first time since 1954. Clinton failed to secure a majority of the popular vote in either presidential election that he contested, yet he left office with job approval ratings in the high-60 per cent range. Elected as a 'New Democrat', his initial two years saw him labelled as an old one (notable for the failed attempt at comprehensive health care reform, support for gays in the military, gun control, and a tax increase) before reverting to type – or 'triangulation' – in the face of the Newt Gingrich-led GOP from 1995. Clinton ulti-mately left office with America more prosperous and seemingly secure than when he entered. Yet how far this was attributable to the President, and how far opportunities for progress were squandered rather than seized, remained unclear.[6]

There can, however, be little doubt that Clinton's second term saw him consolidate the 'Reagan Revolution'. But Clinton was a centrist, not a revolutionary, and his actions were born more of political necessity (or opportunism) than principled enthusiasm. As Rockman notes, 'Like Eisenhower, Clinton may be known for having put a tepid but confirmatory seal of approval on popular policies of the other party.'[7] Clinton rarely instigated conservative policies but frequently found their language politically appealing and ventured further in conservative directions on policies such as welfare reform (see chapter 7), capital punishment and same-sex unions than Reagan ever dared. Admittedly, Clinton used his veto (and veto threats) to substantial effect, tempering Republican ambitions on issues as varied as capital gains tax reductions and the prohibition of partial-birth abortions. But few Democrats in 1992 could have anticipated that the resounding declaration that 'the era of big government is over' would be sounded a mere four years later not by Gingrich or Bob Dole but Bill Clinton.

That Clinton became such a polarizing figure and attracted such vilification on the right and steadfast support from progressives might then seem puzzling. But as Richard Posner noted in regard to the impeachment proceedings against the President:

> Clinton's opponents on the Right were so odious to the Left that many on the Left, including a number of prominent intellectuals, denied (or evaded the issue of) his guilt, while Clinton himself, though a centrist rather than a leftist ... became for many on the Right the preeminent symbol of all they hate ... exposure of Clinton's private life made him a symbol not merely of a political position (it is difficult to identify him with a political position) but of a way of life, and an attitude toward personal responsibility, revolting to much of the Right and congenial to, even defining of, much of the contemporary American Left.[8]

The origins of the partisan and ideological polarization manifest in the impeachment saga predated Clinton. But, from the 1992 primaries to his departure from the White House in January 2001, Clinton advanced this polarization to a new post-1968 high. Echoing Posner, Gary Jacobson notes that:

> Socially conservative Republicans associated with the Religious Right took a deep dislike to him from day one, viewing him as a pot-smoking, draft-dodging, womanizing liberal, who was fundamentally mendacious, conniving, and morally unfit to be president. They never saw fit to reconsider. Other Republicans have also generally taken a dim view of his morals, even while approving of his administration's performance on the

economy, budget deficit and other aspects of policy. Some Democratic constituencies, particularly African Americans, have been enthusiastic supporters; other Democrats have rallied to him because, whatever they think of Clinton, they loathe his many enemies on the Right even more.[9]

The 2000 elections therefore offered Americans the opportunity not merely to decide between two relatively uninspiring presidential candidates but, thereby, to repudiate or prolong the Clinton era. That era, however, had yielded two distinct and competing political legacies – of economic competence and ethical malaise – that were accordingly presented very differently in the two main parties' campaigns. While the Gore–Lieberman ticket consistently focused on 'eight years' of sustained and low-inflationary economic growth and mostly omitted any mention whatsoever of the incumbent President, the Bush campaign sought to make presidential character a centrepiece of its appeal alongside across-the-board tax reductions, education reform and national missile defence. While the Gore campaign consistently ventured 'experience' as the key to an effective presidency, the Bush campaign focused on the importance of personal 'integrity' and the restoration of 'dignity' to the White House. The coded messages were not difficult to decipher in the aftermath of the Whitewater investigation, dubious campaign fundraising, 'Monica-gate' and impeachment.

In terms of the structure of the campaign, however, the most obvious comparison was the presidential election of 1988, with the partisan identities of the main antagonists reversed: An incumbent vice-president of a two-term administration seeks the presidency during an era of economic prosperity where, despite a debilitating recent political scandal, the incumbent president enjoys widespread popular job approval ratings. Against him runs a governor of a state who possesses no experience in Washington DC and whose record of leadership was tinged by accusations of extremism. The vice-president's campaign emphasizes the experience of its nominee while portraying his rival as the governor of an 'out of the mainstream' state with unreliable personal qualities for the highest office. The governor's campaign seeks to downplay ideological divisions in favour of leadership qualities and the merits of a pragmatic approach, while also seeking to discredit the vice-president by associating him with some of the more 'ethically challenged' aspects of the preceding administration.

The parallels were indeed striking. Governor George W. Bush, like his father's opponent in 1988, Michael Dukakis, possessed a substantial lead over his rival in the opinion polls going into his party's summer convention in Philadelphia, Pennsylvania. He had earned a national reputation as a successful state governor of a populous state crucial to his party's national electoral coalition. That reputation was in turn consolidated by the 2000 primary campaign in which a range of opponents were summarily dispatched and in which the maverick threat posed by Senator John McCain (R-AZ) forced Bush to consolidate his ties to the party's right. Facing an incumbent vice-president with little support in the public opinion surveys and an as yet unclear identity of his own, the prospects for a successful campaign appeared strong. Yet that poll lead had evaporated after his rival's party convention and, by Labor Day, never threatened to reappear again. By contrast, Gore in 2000 imitated the role of Bush Sr twelve years previously in emphasizing the achievements of the previous eight years and the need to move forward with incremental change. In seizing control of the campaign without repudiating the incumbent, Gore stressed that 'I am my own man.' Even the language was uncannily familiar to observers of the 1988 campaign.

The 2000 election was, however, significantly different from 1988 in important respects. Most notably, the strong ideological features of the 1988 campaign that had helped to doom Dukakis were absent from the campaign (though not the election's aftermath) twelve years later. Partly as a result, the sharp and enduring lead that the Republican had opened up in 1988 was not repeated in 2000. Bush Sr had employed the themes of weakness on defence and permissive liberalism on social values to lacerating effect in 1988. But despite the attempts of the Bush–Cheney ticket to revive issues of Democratic weakness on defence in 2000, the post-Cold War era had essentially neutralized the salience of this issue in the public's mind. Similarly, where issues of cultural value conflict had worked powerfully for the Republicans in 1988 (capital punishment, the Pledge of Allegiance), in 2000 it was Bush who appeared to many Americans to be the more 'out of the mainstream' figure on issues such as gun control and the death penalty.

One final difference was the several scandals surrounding Clinton. For while it was true that both Reagan and Clinton left office with high approval ratings and a mixed legacy, Reagan had not suffered the ignominy of impeachment proceedings (though many held Iran–Contra a far more serious charge than Monicagate). Nor had Reagan's personal values been impugned with the regularity and intensity that had been directed at Clinton. In this sense, an appeal to restoring 'dignity' to the Oval Office might have been thought to have resonated more among the American electorate. Although the Democratic gains in the 1998 House elections helped to convince most Republicans by 2000 that the electorate's appetite for yet more direct Clinton-baiting was limited, the antipathy that cultural conservatives felt towards Clinton would inhibit and, ultimately, cost the Gore campaign dearly in an election in which non-economic issues played a critically influential role.

The 2000 Election Results: A 'Perfect Tie'

Like 'waiting for Godot', analysts of American elections have patiently anticipated a 'critical' election for the past thirty-four years, only to be regularly disappointed.[10] This is not to suggest that profound changes in the party system have been absent from post-1968 America. The substantial popular majority of party identifiers that the Democrats enjoyed from 1932 largely disappeared by the mid-1980s, eroded by the realignment of white southerners and social conservatives into the Republican base. Although the Democrats retained a marginal lead among party identifiers, the greater propensity to vote and more pronounced party loyalty of Republicans has made the balance between the parties in the electorate virtually even. However, the clear and decisive partisan realignments of prior eras have been conspicuously elusive. Watershed elections that reshaped the American political landscape for the decades that followed them remain, at least thus far, a phenomenon of the past: the 1860 election that ushered the Republicans into national power; that of 1896 that cemented the ascendancy of urban over rural America; and that of 1932 that launched the Democratic 'New Deal' coalition.

For all its historic qualities, the 2000 presidential election was not one of these. Despite its nominal outcome, the results provided neither a sweeping change in the identity of the party in government nor a sharp partisan redirection among the electorate. The election of 2000 was an important and memorable contest for precisely the opposite reason – the unusual closeness of the results, not only in the presidential race but also in the contests for the House of Representatives and the Senate. If these outcomes were, in several respects, the culmination of trends that had existed since at least 1980, they nonetheless heralded an era that has been unseen for more than a century in America – one in which neither of the two main political parties exerts more than a tenuous and temporary hold on either end of Pennsylvania Avenue. A remarkably close partisan balance now prevails in the United States and, in the absence of a strong partisan tide, the 2000 results reflected the broader and balanced partisan configuration among the electorate with rare clarity.

The unexpected closeness of the presidential election lent its character an exciting quality that the relative moderation of its main protagonists belied. The popular vote for President was the closest since 1960, when John F. Kennedy defeated Richard Nixon by a margin of fewer than 120,000 votes out of nearly 69 million cast. In 2000, Al Gore won a popular plurality by a margin of almost 540,000 votes, capturing 48.3 per cent of the popular vote to George W. Bush's 48.0 per cent, with Ralph Nader garnering 3.7 per cent. After more than five weeks of legal wrangling, with Florida's contested ballots ultimately going to the Republican, this translated into a Bush triumph in the Electoral College of just four votes: 271 to 267 (see table 2.1). This represented the closest electoral vote for President since the election of 1876, when Rutherford B. Hayes defeated Samuel Tilden by a margin of just one electoral vote. The 2000 election also marked the first time since 1888 that the identities of the popular and electoral vote winners differed in an American presidential election.

Bush's failure to win a majority of the popular vote was hardly unprecedented (Clinton had achieved only a plurality, not a majority, of the vote in 1992 and 1996, making 2000 the third consecutive presidential election in which the winner failed to secure a majority of the popular vote). But the fact that Gore ran ahead of Bush in the popular vote (and, in absolute numbers, attracted more votes than any presidential candidate since Reagan), combined with the controversy over ballots in Florida, assisted the perception among Democrats that Bush's victory was illegitimate. That victory in the popular vote is – as even Democratic partisans noted – constitutionally unnecessary in the American system did little to alter this (although, for all the criticism of the Electoral College at the end of 2000, few Americans outside academia seriously questioned its appropriateness once the result was settled).[11]

The remarkable closeness of the presidential result was mirrored at the other end of Pennsylvania Avenue. The Senate breakdown of 50–50 represented the first partisan tie in that chamber since the election of 1880. In the House, the partisan match of 221 Republicans to 212 Democrats (with two Independents) represented the most even balance between the parties since the election of 1952. Indeed, the GOP's successive majorities in the House since the historic 1994 victory have been the narrowest House majorities elected in any four consecutive elections in American history.

That the results proved so close was not widely anticipated by election analysts. We will return shortly to consider in detail the reasons for this, as well as the most convincing explanations for Bush's victory (or, more accurately, Gore's loss). But it is perhaps worth noting at this point that the virtual stalemate produced in Washington DC in 2000 reflected not merely the short-term dynamics of the campaign but longer-standing developments in American politics that have sustained remark-

Table 2.1   The Electoral College vote by candidate

BUSH		GORE	
State	*Electoral College votes*	*State*	*Electoral College votes*
Texas	32	California	54
Florida	25	New York	33
Ohio	21	Pennsylvania	23
North Carolina	14	Illinois	22
Georgia	13	Michigan	18
Virginia	13	New Jersey	15
Indiana	12	Massachusetts	12
Missouri	11	Wisconsin	11
Tennessee	11	Washington	11
Alabama	9	Minnesota	10
Louisiana	9	Maryland	10
Arizona	8	Connecticut	8
Colorado	8	Iowa	7
Kentucky	8	Oregon	7
Oklahoma	8	New Mexico	5
South Carolina	8	Hawaii	4
Mississippi	7	Maine	4
Arkansas	6	Rhode Island	4
Kansas	6	Delaware	3
Nebraska	5	District of Columbia	3
Utah	5	Vermont	3
West Virginia	5	**Total**	**267**
Idaho	4		
Nevada	4		
New Hampshire	4		
Alaska	3		
Montana	3		
North Dakota	3		
South Dakota	3		
Wyoming	3		
Total	**271**		

ably close party competition even as the electoral bases of the parties have shifted apart and their ideological profiles have polarized.

In retrospect, a close election was reasonably likely. At the presidential level, Gore benefited from the public's high job performance ratings for the Clinton administration (of which he had been a prominent and

Table 2.2   The House and Senate elections

	Republicans	Democrats	Independents	Vacant
House of Representatives				
Elected in 1998	223	211	1	–
At the 2000 election	222	209	2	2
Elected in 2000	221	212	2	–
Incumbents re-elected	193	199	2	–
Incumbents defeated	4	2	–	–
Open seats retained	20	4	–	–
Open seats lost	5	6	–	–
Senate				
Elected in 1998	55	45	–	–
At the 2000 election	54	46	–	–
Elected in 2000	50	50	–	–
Incumbents re-elected	13	10	–	–
Incumbents defeated	5	1	–	–
Open seats retained	0	3	–	–
Open seats lost	1	1	–	–

Source: Gary C. Jacobson, 'A House and Senate Divided: The Clinton Legacy and the Congressional Elections of 2000', *Political Science Quarterly*, 116, no. 1 (2001), p. 5.

influential part) and excellent economic conditions: modest inflation, low unemployment, rising family incomes, a growing federal budget surplus and declining rates of welfare dependency and crime. Economic models of the election were almost unanimous in predicting a Democratic presidential victory – mostly by some distance – simply in virtue of these indicators (in this regard it was not simply the television network journalists discussed in chapter 4 who called the election incorrectly on 7 November). Moreover, in their 'New Democrat' guise, Clinton and Gore had managed to recapture the White House twice already during the 1990s – albeit in three-way races against lack-lustre Republican nominees. Against this were Clinton's low personal ratings, especially among swing voters in the key battleground states of the Midwest, the structural dilemmas facing the incumbent party after eight years in office (the 'time for a change' factor), and a third party challenge in Ralph Nader that posed much more significant problems for Gore than did the conservative gadfly Patrick Buchanan for Bush. Given the Republicans' success in post-1968 presidential races – capturing five of the six elections preceding 1992 – and their evident hunger for the White House, a competitive race was a near certainty.

Ironically, good economic conditions also assisted the Republican efforts to recapture Congress. Like 1996 and 1998 (but unlike 1994) the electoral environment broadly favoured the congressional status quo, with the electorate apportioning credit for the robust economy not only to the White House (the Federal Reserve was not on the ballot, of course) but also to congressional incumbents generally. Although the congressional elections of the 1990s had been notably turbulent events that had witnessed substantial turnovers of membership in the House and, to a lesser extent, the Senate, incumbency remained the most powerful predictor of results. The 2000 elections were also especially important, not only in terms of the likely pattern of behaviour between the White House and Capitol Hill, but also because the state legislative outcomes would exert a profound impact on the redrawing of congressional boundaries for subsequent elections from 2002 to 2010. Moreover, congressional Democrats had been slowly but steadily regaining a position of near parity in the House after the disastrous 1994 elections. Finally, the playing field was not so much the 435 seats nominally up for grabs, but less than one-tenth that number. In the absence of a dramatic turn of events or an unusually extended set of presidential coattails, most districts were unlikely to see significant competition. (Indeed, ultimately, only eighteen House seats changed party hands – ten going to the Democrats, eight to the GOP – yielding a net Democratic gain of just two seats. Most of the switches came, as usual, in open seat races. Only six incumbents were defeated, producing an incumbent re-election rate of 97 per cent.) The closeness of the congressional results might therefore have been expected, given the narrowness of the GOP majorities.

A close call was also likely in the Senate, which has more potential for changes of party control than the House – a change that has occurred three times since Reagan's first election (1980, 1986, 1994). In 2000, Republicans had more seats to defend in the more competitive Senate races (nineteen, against the Democrats' fifteen), a vulnerability that was reflected in the results. Against most expectations, the Democrats made a net gain of four seats, mostly through the defeat of some of the more vulnerable of the large Republican class elected in the GOP tide of 1994: Rod Grams of Minnesota, Spencer Abraham of Michigan, and John Ashcroft of Missouri (who lost to the state's late governor, Mel Carnahan). Each party lost at least one veteran incumbent: the Democrats, Virginia's Chuck Robb; the Republicans, Delaware's William Roth and Washington's Slade Gorton. The parties also traded open seats, Democrats picking up one in Florida and the Republicans one in Nevada. Although the GOP did retain control, it was by the narrowest of margins, with Vice-President Dick Cheney acting to break tied votes. Even prior to James Jeffords (R-VT) abandoning the party in May 2001, the GOP Senate majority was vulnerable due to the ill-health of aging senators such as Strom Thurmond (ninety-eight) and Jesse Helms (seventy-nine), both of whose states had Democratic governors who would likely appoint a Democratic successor in the event of their deaths.

The Geographic and Social Bases of the 2000 Vote

If the election results were close, they were also graphically revealing in the patterns they showed of a politically divided nation. In most respects, the pattern of results strongly resembled those of the post-Lyndon Johnson, pre-Clinton era (1968–88) in which Republicans enjoyed an effective 'lock' on the White House. But the results also reflected a more sharply divided America than existed in that era, with the nation split into two distinct halves based on three dimensions of ideology, geography and demographics.

On the one hand, favouring the Republicans, there exists a Republican 'L-shaped' sector that comprises the South, the Plains and Mountain states, and Alaska; against this is a Democratic, bi-coastal and industrial heartland sector that now includes the Northeast and industrial Midwest, the Pacific Coast and Hawaii. The Republican-leaning 'L' comprises a total of 26 states with 223 electoral votes. The bi-coastal–industrial sector includes 24 states and the District of Columbia, with 315 electoral votes. The alignment is not new, inasmuch as GOP presidential candidates dominated the 'L' (then, but no longer, including California) so conclusively that they entered Democratic domains in campaigns from 1968 to 1988. In 1992 and 1996, Clinton reversed the pattern, cutting important swathes in the 'L' to assure his victories. What was crucial about 2000, however, was the extent to which Bush re-created decisive Republican majorities in the 'L' states, sufficient – just – to secure an electoral vote advantage over the decisive Democratic sector.

With the exception of New Mexico, for example, Bush made a clean sweep of the 'L' and won every state in the South. As Black and Black had argued in 1992, the South remains vital to the prospects of both main parties' presidential nominees.[12] Where Clinton had broken the Republican presidential 'lock' in 1992 and 1996 in part by winning states such as Arkansas, Georgia and Tennessee, Bush in 2000 denied Gore the effective southern key to the presidency. Beyond the South, the Rocky Mountain states and the Great Plains states were also virtually lock-solid for the GOP nominee. These areas – predominantly white, rural and culturally conservative – proved overwhelmingly Republican.

Gore, by contrast, had a near-complete lock on the Northeast, mid-Atlantic and the Pacific Coast, along with urban areas that included large contingents of ethnic and racial minorities. These proved as reliably and overwhelmingly Democratic as the 'L' group had been Republican. For example, of the 24 states outside the 'L' in the bi-coastal–industrial sector, Gore won 19 of them, securing a 262 to 53 electoral vote margin (against which Bush achieved a huge 218 to 5 lead in the GOP's 'L').

Key to the results, however, was a third group, at once geographically and demographically diverse but united by the common feature of living in the suburbs. These voters had proved reliably Republican in the elections of the 1980s, but 2000 marked the third consecutive presidential election in which they had shifted from those partisan moorings. In this instance, suburban voters split evenly between Gore and Bush, helping to ensure that the overall election result proved so close. It is this group, above all, that now holds the key to success in national elections, and that, consequently, both parties are targeting especially hard.

The reasons for this are straightforward when the sharply divergent nature of the two main parties' electoral coalitions is considered. Because as much as the electoral geography of 2000 provided a remarkable illustration of the fault-lines of American politics, it also illustrated the difficulties confronting both parties in forging a reliable majority on a narrowly partisan basis. Although Gore ran more than 500,000 votes ahead of Bush nationally, for example, Bush carried almost four times as many individual counties as his rival: 2,472 to 675 for Gore. The extent of Bush's sweep of relatively lightly populated, rural areas was remarkable and demonstrative of the success of the Texan's conservative appeal to his party's core electorate. Bush did not lose a single county, for example, in Nebraska, Utah and Wyoming. He lost only one county each in Idaho and Nevada, two each in Kansas and North Dakota, and five each in Montana and South Dakota. Pronounced rural support also enabled him to come close in Minnesota, Iowa and Wisconsin, states that had been anticipated to support Gore by large margins.

As table 2.3 indicates, the election demographics revealed a sharply divided social as well as geographic base to the presidential choice. Yet striking as such division appears, it is also a familiar post-1968 pattern. This election represented, in many respects, a peculiar case of 'back to the future'. With the exceptions of the presence of Nader and Buchanan, the pattern of partisan support would not have struck Nixon, Reagan or Bush Sr as especially unusual. Republicans could rely

Table 2.3 The presidential vote: electoral geography and issues (%)

	All	Gore	Bush	Buchanan	Nader
Sex and race/ethnicity					
Men	48	42	53	0	3
Women	52	54	43	0	2
White men	48	36	60	0	3
White women	52	48	49	0	2
White	81	42	54	0	3
Black	10	90	9	0	1
Latino	7	62	35	1	2
Asian	2	55	41	1	3
Age					
18–29	17	48	46	1	5
30–44	33	48	49	0	2
45–59	28	48	49	1	2
60+	22	51	47	0	2
Income ($)					
Under 15,000	7	57	37	1	4
15,000–29,999	16	54	41	1	3
30,000–49,999	24	49	48	0	2
50,000–74,999	25	46	51	0	2
75,000–100,000	13	45	52	0	2
100,000+	15	43	54	0	2
Region					
East	23	56	39	0	3
Midwest	26	48	49	1	2
South	31	43	55	0	1
West	21	48	46	0	4
Political ideology					
Liberal	20	80	13	1	6
Moderate	50	52	44	0	2
Conservative	29	17	81	0	1
Condition of the economy					
Excellent	28	53	46	0	1
Good	12	38	53	2	6
Not good	57	47	49	0	3
Most important issues and qualities					
World affairs	12	40	54	1	4
Medicare/PX drugs	7	60	39	0	1
Health care	8	64	33	0	3
Economy/jobs	18	59	37	0	2
Taxes	14	17	80	0	2
Education	15	52	44	0	3
Social security	14	58	40	1	1

For 'all', percentages read down; for individuals, percentages read across. A zero for Buchanan voters indicates less than 0.5 per cent.
Source: CNN exit poll data (www.cnn.com/ELECTION/2000).

disproportionately on the votes of whites in general, and white men in particular, actively religious and fundamentalist Christians in particular, abortion opponents and gun owners (48 per cent of voters in 2000 owned firearms, an increase from 37 per cent in 1996). Whites – and white men in particular – favoured the Republican candidate, making 2000 the ninth presidential election in succession in which the Democratic Party candidate has failed to win a majority of the white vote. Blacks voted overwhelmingly for Gore despite Bush's efforts to present an 'inclusive' party image. The Democrats also retained a substantial advantage among Jews, Latinos and, to a lesser but nonetheless significant extent, Asian Americans. (Surprisingly, Lieberman's candidacy appeared to make little difference to Jewish voting intentions, albeit that its effect may have been important in increasing Jewish turnout.)

But within the broad parameters of continuity, the results revealed some important changes. Potentially of greatest consequence was the shift in Latino votes to the Republican nominee. Admittedly, a majority of Latinos voted Democratic despite the best efforts of the Bush campaign to woo them. Nonetheless, the Latino GOP vote doubled from 1996. At a minimum, this has created nascent opportunities for the Republicans to make greater headway among what the census now confirms as America's largest ethnic/racial group, its fastest growing community, and one that is also located in some of the nation's key Electoral College states (California, Texas, Florida, New York, New Jersey). The problem here is the divisions within the Latino communities and the difficulties that these pose for a coherent partisan approach. Preserving conservative policies on immigration, multiculturalism and bilingual education poses strong barriers to expanding the Latino base of the party beyond its reliable Cuban base. The latter, moreover, is likely to become a more problematic constituency as pressures to normalize relations with Cuba increase from Midwestern elements within the GOP coalition.

Another important social development concerned the gender gap that first drew academic attention in 1980 and continues to help to define and polarize the two parties (see chapter 8 for a fuller analysis of this phenomenon). More than ever, the 2000 election yielded two competing landslides, one for Bush among men and another for Gore among women. But whereas this gap had worked to Clinton's advantage in 1992 and 1996, it assisted the Republicans in 2000. Men tended strongly to support Bush, in most exit polls by a margin of 53 to 42 per cent; women tended to endorse Gore, by 54 per cent to 43 per cent. But not only white men but white women also narrowly favoured Bush over Gore (49 to 48 per cent). Even Reagan, who was consistently more popular among men than women, nonetheless gained a plurality of the women's vote in both 1980 and 1984. In 2000, the gender gap was larger and more decisive than previously.

What is perhaps most intriguing about these results, however, is the complex picture presented by the issues rated as most significant by the respondents. On three of the most important – the economy/jobs, education, and social security – Gore achieved a decisive lead over his opponent. Similarly, Gore also notched up substantial leads on health care and one of the most prominent issues in the 2000 campaign, prescription drugs coverage. By contrast, Bush had decisive majorities on only two of the issues, world affairs (perhaps surprisingly, given that he had not travelled extensively outside America prior to becoming President) and taxes, where his 63 point advantage was the greatest of any of the important issues. This suggests strongly that – Florida notwithstanding – the election was more lost by Gore than won by Bush.

Why Did Gore Lose?

Popular attention to American elections invariably concentrates on the presidential contest. The close result and protracted controversy in the 2000 election merely compounded that tendency. In one sense, this is deeply misleading, since in a separated system of government where power-sharing is the norm the congressional results are at least as critical to the success of any administration. Against this, though, the relative lack of serious competition in most House districts and the comparatively small number of genuinely competitive Senate races frequently offer good reasons to concentrate on the presidential result. In 2000, especially, the main result that demanded analysis was Gore's crushing failure to translate strongly favourable economic conditions into a decisive electoral victory.

The 2000 results were hardly comparable to the stark repudiation of the Clinton administration that had been delivered in the 1994 mid-term elections (when not a single incumbent Republican senator, representative or governor lost their seat). Yet the 'scientific' election models so beloved of American psephologists had been almost unanimous during the run-up to the election. Even in the midst of Bush's strong and consistent lead over Gore during the first six months of 2000, these models had predicted Gore as the eventual victor. Moreover, some suggested not a narrow margin for the Vice-President but a landslide of between 53 and 56 per cent of the popular vote.[13]

The election of 2000 was one that was undoubtedly Gore's to lose. Such an approach is not to minimize Bush's appeal. In many respects, the Texas governor ran a shrewd campaign admirable for its lack of race-baiting (as Paul Frymer notes in chapter 3), its aversion to personal animus (albeit that this strategy facilitated capitalizing on the restoration of 'dignity' to the White House), and a general tone of moderation. In eschewing the more immoderate elements of his party's coalitional base, the Bush campaign resembled that of Clinton in 1992. Similarly, groups that might otherwise have sought to press their demands vocally on the party (from the Christian Coalition to pro-life groups and gun rights advocates) remained relatively quiescent in search of the Republican ally in the White House that had been denied them for the previous eight years. The single-minded prioritization of victory and pragmatism over political purity worked as well for Bush in 2000 as it had done for Clinton in 1992.

However, notwithstanding the generally well-organized campaigning of Bush, rarely had conditions so favoured his opponent. Internationally, the post-Cold War years had seen America secure, and its foray into Kosovo in 1999 saw not a single American casualty. The administration had presided over sustained non-inflationary economic growth and turned a substantial budget deficit into a surplus. Did Gore's loss therefore reveal evidence of underlying trends that would have proved fatal for any Democratic Party candidate or was it explicable simply at the level of the individual candidate's deficiencies? Had Clinton been eligible for a third term, for example, would the result have been different?

Explanations for the lack-lustre performance of the Gore candidacy conventionally fell broadly into three distinct (but not mutually exclusive) categories: the personal or character flaws of Gore; the Clinton 'shadow'; and the paradoxes of peace and prosperity for the Democratic ticket.

Gore's personal failings were a constant theme of media coverage throughout the campaign. Paradoxically, the Vice-President was criticized for being both a rigid bore and a quixotic chameleon. On the one hand, Gore's public manner was – to all but his immediate family and the most zealous Democratic partisans – stiff, uninspiring and wooden, not least by comparison with the incumbent President. The charisma that Clinton effortlessly exuded on the campaign trail and in office was simply absent from someone who appeared a cold, ruthless and uninspiring technocrat.[14] Yet, on the other hand, Gore resorted to every manner of personal reinvention to suggest a public figure of stature, an 'Alpha male'. Public impressions nonetheless seemed to confirm that each attempt to adopt a new approach reinforced the reality of a dull politician lacking in vision and oratorical skills, seeking office for the sake of power alone, and insulated from the real world of most Americans.

Certainly, at crucial moments of the campaign, the inability of Gore to carve out a clear, consistent and focused appeal appeared deeply problematic. As his biographers had noted prior to the general election, despite what could be described as a lack of intellectual curiosity, Bush has thrived both electorally and in office by being underestimated by his political opponents.[15] From the aftermath of defeat in February's New Hampshire Republican Party primary until 7 November, the governor's campaign was consistently shrewd in downplaying expectations of its candidate. Despite initial polls showing Gore the winner of the three presidential debates, for example, it became clear that Bush had ultimately proved the victor – in part through simply surviving, but also in causing Gore evident disquiet as to how best to project his own persona. Again, a sense that Gore was all things to all men pervaded his approach to electioneering.

Such personal flaws alternately compounded and highlighted the Banquo's ghost of the 2000 election, namely, Bill Clinton. Al was most definitely not Bill in terms of personal sexual rectitude, and the leaked press stories of their increasingly cool relationship helped make this clear as the campaign progressed. The famous 'kiss' with Tipper at the Democratic convention in August 2000 symbolically confirmed a solid marital life and an 'all-American' family. But in other important respects Al did resemble Bill in disturbing ways: a talent for prevarication and obfuscation, an apparently congenital inability to answer questions directly and fully, and a tendency to vastly exaggerate his claims of achievement. There was no Monica in Al's cupboard, but there were dubious tales of illegally raising campaign funds from the White House, hardball political tactics, serving as the inspiration for *Love Story* and the inventor of the internet, and policy U-turns of a greater or lesser magnitude that together suggested a continuation of the more unrelentingly ambitious, mendacious and thuggish aspects of Clinton.[16] Although some analysts had understandably predicted that 'the events that occur immediately before the 2000 elections will be important in voters' minds, whereas the Lewinsky scandal may be long forgotten',[17] the scandal did cast a lengthy shadow. The point about it – as Clinton's defenders tended to ignore during 1998–9 – was that the scandal was a symbol of more serious questions than simply adulterous sex.

The main thrust of critical commentary, however, focused on what has become a structural dilemma for vice-presidential candidates in the American system – how to craft a distinctive political appeal that at once claims legitimate (if partial) credit for the achievements of an incumbent president while setting out an agenda of one's own that does not repudiate the administration's accomplishments. Only two vice-presidents have been elected to office immediately following the presidential administration in which they served: Martin Van Buren and George Bush Sr. Ironically, Gore's problems were in this sense compounded by the structural dynamics of American primary and general elections. Having decided upon a populist-style approach that galvanized core Democratic constituencies (labour unions, abortion rights activists, environmentalists and minorities), some kind of demands for change were a functional necessity in the primaries. This was especially the case against a well-respected, well-financed and progressive opponent in former senator Bill Bradley. Yet for the general election, that approach ran up against a broader electorate for whom the watchword of 2000 was more continuity than change. By the time of the Democratic convention in Los Angeles in August 2000, Gore had therefore manoeuvred himself into the curious position of in effect claiming, 'We have unprecedented peace and prosperity – and I'm angry as hell about it.'

In Gore's defence – and recalling that he did win the popular vote – one might ask what else he could plausibly have done to advance his candidacy. The early relocation of his campaign to Nashville, Tennessee was a sensible move necessitated by the anti-Washington cast of recent American politics.[18] Gore's choice of Senator Joe Lieberman (D-CT) as his vice-presidential candidate was widely praised and strongly assisted the ticket, not only in the historic dimensions of selecting a practising Jew but also in thereby distancing the ticket from Clinton's many ethical failings.[19] Opinion surveys clearly demonstrated that among swing voters Clinton was not a personally popular figure, his administration's accomplishments notwithstanding. Arguably Gore could have made more of the substantive achievements of the Clinton administration without personally campaigning with the President. It also seems odd that more use was not made of Clinton to shore up and turn out the core Democratic base in swing states such as Arkansas, Tennessee and Georgia, though the cultural conservatism of these states probably placed them well into the GOP column anyway. That the most consummate campaigner of his generation was left largely to assist the First Lady's Senate campaign in New York was in this respect a limited, but not decisive, strategic blunder.

The fundamental problem remained, however, that Gore failed to capitalize effectively on the economic record of the Clinton administration while also failing to resolve how best to deal with the cultural conservatives alienated by Clinton's personal behaviour and, in many cases, policy positions. Gore eschewed tying his mast to Clinton in favour of a populist defence of 'the people against the powerful'. Yet he ran behind the expectations not so much of upper income voters but of those further down the scale (and, in particular, non-college educated whites among whom concerns about values were most pronounced). According to table 2.3 above, for example, 57 per cent of the electorate felt the economy to be in poor shape, yet a narrow plurality of these favoured Bush over Gore. Where Clinton had exploited the salience of economic bad times to substantial effect in 1992, Gore seemed curiously unable to take advantage either of good conditions or the perception that they were bad! Even among the 12 per cent who viewed economic conditions as good, for example, Bush achieved a substantial majority.

Although both campaigns focused on the states and districts where the partisan balance was sufficiently close to foster genuine competition, Gore's success amidst suburban voters was ultimately insufficient to outweigh Bush's success not only among the culturally conservative states in the Electoral College but also among key groups of culturally conservative voters in swing states. For example, Bush managed to win Missouri, Kentucky and Ohio and only narrowly lost Wisconsin and Iowa, all five of which had been carried by Clinton in both 1992 and 1996. Similarly, Gore lost Arkansas, Tennessee and West Virginia, states that Clinton had previously won.

The Aftermath of the Election

Cynics may answer the question of why Gore lost with a more straight-forward answer than that elaborated in the prior section: a Republican state legislature and Secretary of State in Florida, George Bush's brother Jeb Bush as governor and, ultimately, a narrow and partisan majority of the US Supreme Court. The controversies surrounding the contested ballots in Florida have already generated a voluminous literature and will no doubt continue to do so for many years to come.[20] Whatever the results of recounts in 2001, most of which suggested that Bush had indeed won the popular vote in Florida by the thinnest of margins, the perception that he lost will shape politics for years to come.

For analysts of the election, whatever the merits of the competing legal arguments, one of the greatest ironies of 2000 was that the profound partisan divisions that exist in America became most clearly manifest after the election rather than during the campaign. Both Bush and Gore had focused on the key districts and states and tempered partisan appeals accordingly. What was striking, however, was how rapidly the sharpness of partisan conflict returned once Gore had retracted his concession on the morning of 8 November.

In this respect, the post-election battle vividly recalled the acrimony of the impeachment proceedings of 1998, not merely among the elite protagonists but also in terms of the public response. The partisan reactions to post-election events in Florida illustrated how polarized national American politics has become. Among Bush voters, for example, 93 per cent expressed satisfaction with the election outcome, 92 per cent believed Bush had won legitimately, and 95 per cent approved of the Supreme Court's decision halting the manual recount of ballots in Florida. Among Gore voters, 89 per cent were dissatisfied with the result, 81 per cent thought Bush was not a legitimate victor, and 80 per cent disapproved of the *Bush v. Gore* ruling. Such figures echoed the division over Clinton's impeachment, where polls consistently revealed approximately 65 per cent of Republicans in favour and 85 per cent of Democrats opposed to impeachment.[21]

Making Sense of a Divided Democracy: A New Partisanship

The elections confirmed what has been the case for at least a decade: that the conventional textbook image of the Democrats and Republicans as two broad, centrist and non-ideological coalitions is now an outdated relic. Coalitions of diverse interests they certainly remain, but driven primarily by the activism of their core constituencies, the main parties have polarized dramatically since 1981. The consequence of increased intraparty homogeneity has been increased interparty conflict, broader in scope and more intense than at any period since the Depression. In the House elections of 2000, for example, there were only eighty-six members who were elected from districts carried by the opposing party's presidential candidate – the lowest incidence of split-ticket voting since 1952 (and a decrease from 110 in 1996 and 100 in 1992).[22] Twenty-four of the thirty-four states contested in 2000 cast a plurality for their votes for Senate and presidential candidates of the same party (the same figures as in 1992 and 1996). Senate and presidential voting has thus returned to the levels of consistency that existed in the 1950s and 1960s – unlike the 1968–88 period – when typically only about half the states were won by the same party's Senate and presidential candidates.

Such results attest to the degree to which interparty conflicts are now more consequential in American politics than intraparty ones. The

erosion of the southern presence in the Democratic Party and the conservative cast of the GOP's nominating base have together eliminated the
era in which the most liberal and conservative members of Congress were
both Democrats. Intraparty differences are still many, of course, and relative to European parties the health of the Democratic and Republican
parties in the electorate, as organizations and in government remains
poor. But whereas knowing the partisan affiliation of an American voter
or public official was a relatively poor predictor of where they stood on
specific issues in 1971, partisanship is now a fairly good indicator of
where Americans stand on issues such as tax cuts, education, defence,
gun control, abortion rights and many other national issues.

Unsurprisingly, then, the 2000 election was notable in the extent
to which the campaigns pressed sharply divergent programmes of
government even as they competed for marginal voters. Bush consistently
articulated conservative notions of market-based solutions for drug
prescription coverage, low taxation and an active role for religious and
civic organizations on issues such as welfare and drugs. Gore relied
heavily – much more so than any Democratic presidential candidate
since Walter Mondale in 1984 – on defending the nostrum that only
government-based solutions could adequately tackle problems of health,
education and environmental decay. To this extent there existed in 2000
a more genuine choice of distinct programmes of government than
had occurred since at least 1984 and, arguably, since 1972. The closeness of the results, moreover, signified the near even division of the
electorate between these competing programmes.

In Ladd's terminology, the 'no majority realignment' continues its
incremental but steady advance. The Republicans nominated a candidate
for President who managed, like Reagan in 1980, to paper over the substantial divisions within the fractious conservative base. A more-or-less
united front, combined with the formidable advantages of congressional
incumbency, briefly secured a prize that had eluded all Republicans since
Eisenhower: undivided GOP control of the White House and Congress.
At state level, too, and in terms of party identification, the Republicans
had made gains of genuine substance.

The problem remains, however, that the precarious nature of the GOP
victories belies any notion of a classical realignment. The Republican
victory did not occasion a massive shift in the loyalty of significant parts
of the electorate, whose support appears more uncertain than reliable.
The electorate did not endorse Bush's policy prescriptions on the issues
about which they cared most or on the issues for which Bush campaigned
most heavily. Moreover, the passage of a substantial tax cut by the

summer of 2001 owed at least as much to fears of an impending recession as to the persuasiveness of the Bush case. Depending on the surveys,
partisan identification among the electorate is either evenly divided or
accords the Republicans a narrow lead. This is certainly cause for GOP
optimism, but the fluctuations of recent years suggest that any such
advantages can evaporate as rapidly as they emerged.

Moreover, the dominance of white southerners and social conservatives in the party's base and congressional leadership poses problems for
the party's prospects of achieving a genuine majority status. In 1980, for
example, the South and border states sent 49 Republicans to the House,
the Northeast and Midwest seaboard states 46. By 1994, when the GOP
captured the House, the figures were 80 and 41, respectively. In the
Senate, the 13–10 balance in 1980 became 18–10 by 1994. After 2000,
Republicans held 63 per cent of House seats and 67 per cent of Senate
seats in the South, Plains and Mountain West states. The Democrats held
57 per cent of House and 69 per cent of Senate seats in the Northeast,
Midwest and West Coast. The danger for the GOP is that unless it can
recover its appeal in suburbs and the bi-coastal areas, it will consolidate
its position as a regional rather than a national party.

In this respect at least, Shafer's 'two majorities' analysis remains
of substantial value in understanding the dynamics of contemporary
American elections. For all the turbulence of recent years, the apparent
electoral disorder has nonetheless revealed underlying forces of substantial continuity. Prior to September 2001, the foreign policy issues that
assisted Republican presidential candidates from 1968 to 1988 receded
sharply in importance to the American public. But in the absence of
recession, economic issues have proved problematic for Democratic
candidates to use to re-create the 'New Deal' coalition in presidential
elections. In those circumstances, issues of cultural value conflict –
abortion, gun control, crime, but also presidential character – can
impinge substantially in determining who reaches the White House.
Bush's central success in 2000 was in limiting the GOP's extreme image
on social issues among swing voters while strongly mobilizing the
Republican base. However, as Shafer argued prior to the election, 'the
prospect of an extended era of unified Republican control of government
in the face of those crosscutting influences and in the absence of a shift
of partisan identification appears remote.'[23]

One reason for this is the current state of the two main parties. Since
its first publication, political analysts have quoted the 1950 report of the
American Political Science Association with regularity. The faults of the
American system were laid at the doors of the two main parties, whose

intraparty divisions were marked and whose influence had weakened among voters, in campaigns and in the halls of government. It was the inability of parties to bridge the divisions that the Constitution established that had rendered an inefficient system unworkable and a fragmented system impossible for voters to hold their leaders to account. Only a re-strengthening of parties could hold out reasonable hope for restoring some of those key properties either missing or weak in American politics: responsibility, accountability, and a genuine concern for public policy rather than electioneering.

In a remarkable turnabout, it is the parties that are now the authors of America's current democratic discontents. The types of problems once discussed have gone a substantial way to being corrected. Partisan coherence? The parties have not represented such clear choices rather than echoes for almost a century. Party responsibility? The parties have generated programmes for governing previously unheard of in American politics and few days of a congressional session now pass without party-orchestrated themes, sound-bites and issue-oriented appeals. (It was, after all, the pressures to maintain party unity, not to allow individualism to go unfettered, that prompted Jim Jeffords to leave the GOP and hand the Democrats control of the Senate in 2001.) Party accountability? The very volatility of American electoral politics in the 1990s suggested that the electorate can indeed 'read' national politics and render a clear partisan judgement – in rejecting Clinton's excessively liberal cast in 1994; in rebuking the Gingrich legions for overreaching their claimed 'mandate' for far-reaching conservative programmes in 1996 and their zealous pursuit of Clinton in 1998; and ultimately in denying either party a 'mandate' in 2000.

The irony here is profound. A politics of democratization and participation has yielded a partisan configuration in which compromise, concessions, conciliations – in short, the watchwords of effective legislating – have become much harder to achieve. The textbook image of American parties was one in which 'lowest common denominator' politics could dominate. From 1932 until 1992 the deep and broad intraparty divisions within both the Democratic and Republican parties meant that progress could be made because opportunities for exploiting cross-party dissent could be adroitly utilized. That environment has not disappeared, but it has diminished to a degree that would make the giants of congressional politics past – Sam Rayburn, Lyndon Johnson, Everett Dirksen – not only surprised but concerned. American politics has rarely lacked partisan conflict, but seldom has that conflict so neatly matched a set of issue divisions among the public over economic, social and foreign policy. Seldom have interparty divisions so strongly outweighed intraparty fissures. Nor, as the final element in the new era of American partisanship, has such partisan and ideological division so clearly and closely overlaid the divided institutional architecture of national government.

Conclusion

The 2000 elections were neither landmark nor 'critical' ones but they were important. In effect, the Republicans briefly gained undivided party control of the federal government by accident. Not only did the Electoral College and the Supreme Court's decision in *Bush v. Gore* hand the presidency to the Texas Governor, but the Constitution provided the GOP with its Senate majority – thanks to the Vice-President's casting vote. But the brief opportunity to advance a nascent Republican realignment – not least through appointing Supreme Court justices and, possibly, a new Chief Justice – was prematurely ended by Jeffords's departure just four months after Bush's inauguration. Whether President Bush manages relations with a Democratic Senate better than his father did will strongly condition the shape of national politics for the 2002 midterms and his own re-election prospects in 2004.

American electoral and party politics remain in a highly volatile state. Of the Senate seats up for election in 2002, Republicans must defend twenty-one against the Democrats' fourteen. Only five of the Republican seats, however, are in states won by Gore in 2000, while Democrats must defend three seats in states won by Bush. Republicans should also benefit from the reapportionment and redistricting that must occur before 2002 in accordance with the 2000 census. The states scheduled to gain seats are more Republican than those likely to lose them, and Republican governors and state legislatures will control the redistricting process in a slightly larger number of states where extensive changes are likely be needed. By mandating the creation of further 'majority-minority' House districts, voting rights laws against minority 'vote dilution' are also likely, again, to assist Republicans by expanding the number of 'lily-white' districts with few black and Latino voters. Against this, since the Civil War, only in 1934 and 1998 has the president's party not lost seats in midterm elections. Bush's performance in defeating terrorism, managing the economy and maintaining respectable approval ratings will be powerful influences on the outcomes, but only the bravest forecaster would bet against the prospect of continued divided party control of the White House and Capitol Hill.

NOTES

1   See Gerald M. Pomper (ed.), *The Election of 2000: Reports and Interpretations* (New York: Chatham House, 2001); James W. Ceaser and Andrew Busch, *The Perfect Tie: The True Story of the 2000 Presidential Election* (Boston: Rowman and Littlefield, 2001).

2   Everett Carl Ladd, 'The 1996 Vote: The "No Majority" Realignment Continues', *Political Science Quarterly*, 112, no. 1 (1997), pp. 1–28.

3   Martin Wattenberg, *The Decline of American Political Parties 1952–1996* (Cambridge: Harvard University Press, 1996).

4   The term was first coined by Byron Shafer in 'The Election of 1988 and the Structure of American Politics: Thought on Interpreting an Electoral Order', *Electoral Studies*, 8, no. 1 (1989), pp. 5–21. Shafer's approach was developed further, most notably in Byron E. Shafer (ed.), *The End of Realignment? Interpreting American Electoral Orders* (Madison: University of Wisconsin Press, 1991) and Byron E. Shafer and William J. M. Claggett, *The Two Majorities: The Issue Context of Modern American Politics* (Baltimore: Johns Hopkins University Press, 1995).

5   Bert A. Rockman, 'Cutting with the Grain: Is There a Clinton Leadership Legacy?', in Colin Campbell and Bert A. Rockman (eds), *The Clinton Legacy* (New York: Chatham House, 2000), p. 294.

6   See, for example, the mixed assessments of Clinton's foreign policy in 'Clinton's Foreign Policy', *Foreign Policy* (Nov./Dec. 2000), pp. 18–29.

7   Rockman, 'Cutting with the Grain', p. 293.

8   Richard Posner, *An Affair of State: The Investigation, Impeachment, and Trial of President Clinton* (Cambridge: Harvard University Press, 1999), pp. 12–13. See also Mark J. Rozell and Clyde Wilcox (eds), *The Clinton Scandal and the Future of American Government* (Washington DC: Georgetown University Press, 2000).

9   Gary C. Jacobson, 'A House and Senate Divided: The Clinton Legacy and the Congressional Elections of 2000', *Political Science Quarterly*, 116, no. 1 (2001), pp. 5–27.

10 Shafer, *The End of Realignment?*

11 A fairly typical response was Demetrios James Caraley, 'Editor's Opinion: Why Americans Need a Constitutional Right to Vote for Presidential Electors', *Political Science Quarterly*, 116, no. 1 (2001), pp. 1–3.

12 Earl Black and Merle Black, *The Vital South: How Presidents are Elected* (Cambridge: Harvard University Press, 1992).

13 An excellent summary is Jonathan Parker, 'Forecasting American Presidential Elections', *Talking Politics*, 13, no. 2 (2001), pp. 113–18.

14 See, for example, the accounts in Jake Tapper, *Down and Dirty: The Plot to Steal the Presidency* (Boston: Little, Brown, 2001) and Joel Aberbach, *It Looks Like a President Only Smaller: Trailing Campaign 2000* (New York: Simon and Schuster, 2001).

15 See, for example, Molly Ivins and Lou Dubose, *Shrub: The Short but Happy Political Life of George W. Bush* (New York: Random House, 2000).

16 See Christopher Hitchens, *No One Left to Lie To: The Triangulations of William Jefferson Clinton* (London: Verso, 1999). Although its polemical character undermines any pretensions to rigour or balance, Hitchens's discussion of Clinton's mendacity and single-minded pursuit of political office is as compelling as more scholarly treatments of the President's approach to government and politics.

17 Molly W. Andolina and Clyde Wilcox, 'Public Opinion: The Paradoxes of Clinton's Popularity', in Mark J. Rozell and Clyde Wilcox (eds), *The Clinton Scandal and the Future of American Government* (Washington DC: Georgetown University Press, 2000), p. 192.

18 See Michael Foley, *The Rise of the British Presidency* (Manchester: Manchester University Press, 1992). One of the most persuasive analyses of the mix of attitudes that Americans currently display towards government is Anthony King, 'Distrust of Government: Explaining American Exceptionalism', ch. 4 in Susan J. Pharr and Robert D. Putnam (eds), *Disaffected Democracies: What's Troubling the Trilateral Countries?* (Princeton: Princeton University Press, 2000).

19 On the importance of religiosity in 2000, see Gertrude Himmelfarb, 'Religion in the 2000 Election', *Public Interest*, 143 (2001), pp. 20–6.

20 See Vincent Bugliosi, *The Betrayal of America: How the Supreme Court Undermined the Constitution and Chose our President* (New York: Nation Books, 2001); Bill Sammon, *At Any Cost: How Al Gore Tried to Steal the Election* (Washington DC: Regnery, 2001); Roger Simon, *Divided We Stand: How Al Gore Beat George Bush and Lost the Presidency* (New York: Crown, 2001); and Tapper, *Down and Dirty*.

21 Jacobson, 'A House and Senate Divided', pp. 18–19.

22 Gregory L. Giroux, 'Split-Ticket Voting Lowest in 48 Years', *Congressional Quarterly Weekly*, 12 May 2001, p. 1052.

23 Byron E. Shafer, 'The Partisan Legacy', in Campbell and Rockman, *The Clinton Legacy*, p. 32.

3

Race, Representation and Elections: The Politics of Parties and Courts

Paul Frymer

Despite its dramatic conclusion, the 2000 presidential election was rather unremarkable on matters of race. No major candidate actively supported or opposed civil rights policy and no one engaged in the racial antagonisms that have marked recent presidential campaigns. There was no 2000 version of Willie Horton or Sister Souljah, infamous figures from past campaigns that emerged because presidential candidates wished to signal their sensitivity to white voters who feared black criminals. There was no Jesse Jackson running a campaign centred on civil rights and a 'Rainbow Coalition' agenda; but likewise, there was an only marginal Pat Buchanan spouting nineteenth-century notions of American community.

Even when race issues wove their way into the electoral debate, the candidates seemed sincerely reluctant to allow racial undertones to become a major feature of the campaign. George W. Bush, for example, quickly apologized when criticized for speaking at Bob Jones University, a school that prohibited interracial dating and has a history of hatred towards blacks, Jews and Catholics. The Republican presidential candidate maintained his commitment to civil rights during the campaign and in the nationally televised presidential debates, he made public efforts at mobilizing Latino voters, and he seemingly had no intention of attacking African Americans or the major tenets of the civil rights agenda. He avoided previous Republican efforts to subtly race bait on affirmative action, welfare or immigration rights. African Americans, Latinos and Asian Americans were prominent members of the Bush campaign and prominent faces at the National Republican Convention; he has since nominated people of colour such as General Colin Powell to prominent posts in his cabinet.

The other major presidential candidates, Al Gore, Ralph Nader and Pat Buchanan, were equally neutral in their actions and rhetoric. Buchanan promoted a hard-line conservative agenda but avoided the pointed attacks on racial minorities and gays that punctuated his previous campaigns. He even nominated an African-American woman as his vice-presidential candidate. Nader also nominated a person of colour as his vice-presidential candidate and campaigned on a radical environmental and labour agenda, but was criticized – fairly or unfairly – by many minority political figures for his lack of attention to race issues. Al Gore, meanwhile, played the role of the 1990s centrist Democrat initially carved out by Bill Clinton. He lacked firm views on anything controversial or related to the Democratic Party of the Civil Rights era. Gore stumped in African-American churches in the days just prior to the election, but his campaign was dominated by extreme prudence on potentially controversial matters involving the continuing inequities in civil rights.

Of course, this did not mean that racial undertones were absent from the election. It did mean, however, that such undertones were more or less neutralized by the unwillingness of any of the parties involved to provoke others over the issue. Consider two examples. Months before the election, Texas Governor George Bush approved the execution of a convicted murderer, Gary Graham. Graham's execution caused a great deal of outrage and controversy. Graham was convicted in a trial with little evidence and a single self-doubting witness, his lawyers were woefully unprepared for the case, and he had emphatically maintained his innocence until his death. Graham's execution symbolized the unfairness underlying the criminal legal system in which African-American men are sentenced to the death penalty in grossly disproportionate numbers.[1] Graham defiantly declared at his execution that 'this is what happens to black men in America', and the NAACP called the execution 'a gross travesty of justice'.[2] Even a majority of Texas citizens believed Graham was innocent, notable in a state that kills far more people than any other state in the nation. But the Governor heard no criticism from his chief rival, Al Gore. Gore remained silent throughout the controversy, maintaining his personal support for the death penalty, and stating on the day of the execution, 'I do not know the record in Texas. I have not examined the cases. I've always tried to stay away from issues in criminal courts.'[3]

The second example involves African-American voters in the state of Florida who may or may not have been denied their right to vote on the day of the election, or had their votes voided by confusing ballots and 'hanging chads'. Newspaper articles at the time reported widespread complaints by African Americans in the state. Some were stopped at roadblocks and prevented from voting. Some were told at polling booths that they were ineligible to vote because they were incorrectly labelled felons (and thus denied by law the right to vote in Florida) or because they were simply not on the relevant voter registers.[4] For whatever reason, African-American ballots in the state were also disproportionately voided for having holes punched incorrectly. Yet, while more than 90 per cent of African Americans voted for Al Gore nationally, and while the missing votes in Florida surely would have favoured Gore and probably would have provided the difference in the state and national election results, the Gore campaign did not precipitate these accusations or demand investigations into potential violations of the Voting Rights Act.[5] In fact, when African-American politicians such as Jesse Jackson and Al Sharpton attempted to rally public support around the potential voting rights violations, they were quietly asked by leaders of the Gore campaign to tone down their complaints.[6] Civility and silence on race matters dominated the 2000 campaign and election, and seemingly all of the candidates were willing to partake.

In some ways, we ought to be celebrating the absence of race from the campaign. An election that is unremarkable on race issues is indeed remarkable given the historical context. In recent decades, the Republican Party has too easily used race to drive a wedge into the Democratic Party's once reliable electoral coalition, a coalition unified on issues of economic liberalism but deeply fractured on issues pertaining to race. The absence of race in the 2000 campaign meant voters who agreed that they want better health care, more social services and improved labour conditions did not end up splitting their vote because of their differences on affirmative action, welfare, immigration, and crime. The lacunae of divisive race issues allowed Democrats to promote a modern-day twist on the New Deal economic liberalism that made the party so successful at the polls earlier in the twentieth century. Moreover, it's certainly a step in the right direction that the Ronald Reagan/Pete Wilson race-baiting strategies of the 1980s and early 1990s have been replaced by at least a skin-deep effort at inclusion. National leaders of all the political parties seem to recognize that racism is unappealing to the mainstream American voter. In a nation that fought a civil war over the issue of slavery, and followed this war with another century of legal racial apartheid, this newly found consensus is not to be minimized.

While this silence over race issues can be interpreted as an achievement in terms of national politicians maintaining civility, it is also a cause of concern for those interested in promoting a more vibrant and inclusive democracy. Racial harmony in our national election campaigns has come at a cost; it has meant avoiding discussion of causes and solutions to pressing policy issues concerning racial inequality, particularly with specific regard to African-American voters.[7] The major party candidates did not discuss issues of critical concern to African Americans such as racial segregation in housing and schools, the increasing racial divides in wealth and resources, and the continuing inequalities in criminal justice, health care, labour rights and equal access to a clean environment. African-American voices and interests were largely ignored during the campaign as the parties focused on various groups deemed by party strategists to be potentially determinative of the election campaign. The result is that African Americans have found their concerns marginalized in national campaigns and legislative policy-making, a problem exacerbated by a long history of racial oppression and continuing vestiges of inequality. White Americans are told little about race matters from political leaders and as a result remain largely ambivalent towards and unaware of critical inequalities. Even in the most civil of elections (such as 2000), national political discourse is merely racially generic – the parties focus on narrow sets of issues that are believed to be without any racial content. While this might seem good in theory, in practice it amounts to a discourse that is quite race specific, as it focuses on issues that can be discussed in white households without implicit connections to racial minorities.

This racialized discourse is a direct result of US electoral institutions. The ballot system, the rules governing the number of votes needed to win the election, and the number of parties favoured by such rules play a significant role in determining which issues are discussed during political campaigns. The Electoral College and the emphasis on 'first past the post' ballot counting are particularly repressive of minority concerns, racial issues foremost among them. To win elections, politicians must pander to swing voters. In recent US elections, it has seemed politically suicidal for national politicians to discuss racial inequality, racism or civil rights because Reagan Democrats, Perot supporters, and soccer moms have little interest in these issues. In a historically white majority nation with racially conservative swing voters, parties have little incentive – in fact, they often have great disincentive – to appeal to black voters. In the current context, this has resulted in a defensive politics: Democrats appeal to African-American issues at the base level calculated to keep blacks in the party, and Republicans address racial issues with only enough care not to frighten white voters with unattractive racism. Discussion of race by both parties is minimal and centres largely on the symbolic. The result is that race issues have been institutionalized outside the electoral arena, creating a large and problematic void in democratic politics in this country.

The next part of this essay explores the institutional dynamics that make discussion of racial equality unlikely in national party campaigns. The following part considers potential strategies to remedy this problem. The obstacles to reform are great and include not only the two major political parties but also the current Supreme Court's jurisprudence on voting rights and electoral law. In stark contrast to decades past when the Supreme Court was valiantly promoting Equal Protection in famous cases like *Brown v. Board of Education*, the current Court has favoured using the Fourteenth Amendment to deny race-specific efforts to enhance minority representation, has resisted applying Section 2 of the Voting Rights Act to respond to the problem of vote dilution, and has been a leading supporter in the hegemony of winner-takes-all electoral institutions that marginalize African-American representation. An alternative course of action is for African Americans to influence the political agenda through a concerted effort to run a candidate in the Democratic Party primaries. This would publicize the interests of African-American voters, mobilize these voters, and most importantly, keep keen political pressure on the Democratic Party to represent their concerns. This is a constant struggle, however, because Democratic Party leaders will work hard to keep such candidates out of the primaries since they will fear that it will lead to electoral defeat come November. The need to win national elections, seemingly at all costs given the stakes of the winner-takes-all electoral system, highlights the need for fundamental institutional reform. Such reform would change the tenor of long-term political discourse and increase the opportunities for a more inclusive representation by institutionalizing both a voice and a potential veto for minority interests that would no longer be silenced simply by politicians pursuing electoral incentives.[8] Although electoral reform efforts have rarely received much support in the past, the debated outcome of the 2000 election has energized discussions about such matters.[9] The Supreme Court has, perhaps inadvertently and with real irony given its current ideological composition, made Equal Protection in the voting booth a renewed national priority.[10] Given the power of our two-party system to maintain a racial discourse that is profoundly disadvantageous to racial equality, such reforms are vital in the promotion of a more inclusive democracy.

Race, Democracy and Institutions

How the two-party system denies discourse about race

Scholars who study US race politics tend to focus on the dramatic, and for good reason. Americans fought a civil war over slavery and, a century later, arguably fought a second civil war during the civil rights protest movements of the 1960s. Race issues have had huge consequences for national politics, precipitating two electoral realignments, the decline of urban political machines and the fall of the New Deal welfare state. The events in which race issues have dominated the political agenda, from Abraham Lincoln's Emancipation Proclamation to Martin Luther King's 'I Have a Dream' speech to the march on Selma to the Rodney King beating and subsequent riots in Los Angeles in 1992, are indelibly etched in our political memory.

In terms of understanding governance, however, it is problematic to consider racial politics solely in terms of a series of dramatic moments. Such a perspective minimizes the importance of race in broader under-standings of the institutional workings of American politics. Scholars have tended to create a dichotomy between moments when race is not a part of public debate – and institutions and politicians function in a 'normal' manner – and moments when race dominates the public sphere, and institutions and politicians behave irrationally because they are moti-vated by prejudice and anti-individualistic notions of society.[11] Dianne Pinderhughes reflects the views of many political scholars when she suggests, 'When political institutions handle racial issues, conventional rules go awry, individuals react irrationally, and constitutional rules are violated.'[12]

This view ignores, however, the ways in which US governing institu-tions were created and continue to function in response to racial con-siderations. Throughout most of US history, laws and institutions have been developed to avoid potentially divisive national conflicts over race. At the Constitutional Convention in 1787, to keep the nation from divid-ing over the issue, southern whites were given a veto power in the design of political institutions. As a result, many of the nation's institutions provided for compromises between a white racist South and anti-racist interests in the North. Although the compromise ultimately failed, as demonstrated by the American Civil War, the institutions it birthed have proven stalwart. Whether it is the protection of slave owner interests through the Senate, Electoral College, and Full Faith and Credit provi-sion of the Constitution, or the creation of racially separate spheres of welfare and labour politics during the New Deal, the implications of institutional design remain significant.[13] While designed to mitigate racial conflict, these institutions remain a powerful method of denying the salience of racial claims, resulting in a discourse and politics that gives primacy to white interests.

The development of the two-party system is a perfect example of an institution designed to alleviate the effects of racial conflict that continues to have subtle yet significant implications for modern-day race relations. While our electoral rules provide incentives for the development of a two-party system, its promulgation did not occur until the 1820s, when political leaders believed that such a system could effectively side-step divisiveness over slavery and concentrate national attention and party competition around moderate voters through appeals to patriotism and economic populism.[14] The two-party system would be able to successfully avoid the slave debate (until its breakdown in 1860 when a third party won the election with less than 40 per cent of the national vote) because both party coalitions necessarily needed to appeal to centrist voters in order to win the election. Andrew Jackson, the first president to be elected in a two-party system, was the perfect candidate for avoiding such a conflict. He was personally popular, unspecific in his ideas, and a war hero around whom moderate Americans could unite. But there was a severe cost to this development. Most other nations that have developed party systems around racial and ethnic division have created systems where each group is mandated some kind of voice and power-sharing.[15] In the United States, however, the party system denied voice to its racial minorities while creating a fiction of national unity around a self-imposed non-ideological political spectrum. It is a party system well equipped to handle a society that is generally unified around political goals. It is anti-democratic in a society that is deeply divided between a small minority and a large majority.[16]

The second problem with a scholarly focus on dramatic events is that scholars need to be wary about concluding that race ceases to matter in the actions and motivations of our political actors and institutions when it isn't being openly discussed. The construct of part-time race consciousness can misleadingly affirm a view of our governing institutions as fundamentally democratic and successful enhancers of racial equality. While silence may mean the absence of racist expressions, it can also mean the absence of opportunities for the promotion of racial equality. The successful denial of racial division does not enable the furthering of a healthier democracy in a society where the status quo is one of inequality. Instead, such denial simply deepens the level of racial inequity, and leads our political institutions to be complicit in this effort.

In contrast, one might well argue that this institutional dynamic has quite often silenced and marginalized the interests of other groups, including the very same white racists who would deny African Americans the right of political participation. In this sense, one could claim an important democratizing function of the two-party system – it keeps extremists of all stripes out of central political debate. Rabid pro-slave politicians were no more electable in a two-party system than passionate abolitionists. In the election of 1948 and again in the 1960s, supporters of southern segregation were effectively marginalized because they could not find direct expression within the two-party system and had to opt for third-party alternatives. George Wallace's 1968 third-party campaign endorsing racial segregation, for instance, captured a disturbing 15 per cent of the national vote and 46 of the 538 Electoral College votes, and yet he gained no political power from this because of our winner-takes-all electoral system. By 1972, he was only a marginal presence in national politics.

Still, there are many reasons why African Americans might find a political system that provides a greater voice to explicitly racist third parties in exchange for a greater voice to African Americans preferable to one that denies opportunities to both. One reason is that two-party politics already centres around white voters, enabling racist expression to remain viable in partisan politics. For much of America's history, this racism was quite explicit. But even since the civil rights era of the 1960s, a period in which racist hate speech is no longer an acceptable element in public discourse, code words with racial implications – such as 'crime', 'welfare' and 'affirmative action' – have taken their stead. Conservative political leaders utilized these code words during the 1970s and 1980s, engendering the support of large numbers of middle- and working-class white voters for the dismantling of many key New Deal social welfare programmes.[17] When Republicans in the 1970s and 1980s spoke of mothers on welfare driving expensive cars, or of the importance of states' rights during campaign speeches in the Deep South, they didn't mention race. They didn't have to; white Americans caught their reference. In the past decade, racial code words have been extended beyond African Americans to include new racial minority groups. For example, as influxes of Latino and Asian immigrants became a dominant concern in California, California governor and Republican presidential aspirant Pete Wilson successfully campaigned in his home state for an initiative denying all government welfare benefits to immigrants illegally residing in the state. Wilson's success, as well as the success of state propositions that end affirmative action, demonstrates the continuing relevance of race consciousness in political campaigns.

Given the historical context of racism in the US, African Americans need affirmative government measures to rectify a long history of past wrongs. Those who see race politics as an aberration ignore the ways in which race is subtly intertwined in almost all national campaigns and legislative battles. In most political contexts, the two parties are vying for a white moderate voter. This contest excludes competition for black voters, whether or not it is explicitly stated. In part this is because of the assumption by party leaders that black voters will vote Democrat regardless of any specific appeals. In every national election since 1964, African Americans have voted for the Democratic Party at rates of higher than 80 per cent.[18] Recognizing this, the Democratic Party tries to win elections by keeping race off the political agenda (in order not to startle conservative white voters) while delicately balancing subtle race-specific appeals at different moments to both black and white voters. Meanwhile, the Republican Party, a party almost totally disconnected from African-American voters, tries to win elections by making direct appeals to white voters without portraying the party as out of the mainstream on race matters. Both strategies leave African-American interests severely underrepresented. It is for this reason that many African-American scholars and politicians are among the most prominent opponents of two-party dominance.[19]

The capture of black interests in national politics is mirrored in the politics of the Democratic Party itself. Democratic representatives of black voters are faced with a quandary. While they push for civil rights goals as emphatically as they can, at the same time they have little choice but ultimately to unite behind party strategy designed to appeal to white swing voters. They oppose many of the specific actions of the Democratic Party leadership but endorse it because the party's stance is still better than the Republicans. For example, there has been a continuing battle in the Democratic Party between largely black politicians who favour the Voting Rights Act's creation of congressional districts specifically drawn to provide for African-American majorities, and largely white politicians who fear that such districts will decrease the overall number of Democrats elected to Congress. This same battle has extended to rules that govern how the Democratic Party operates in the House of Representatives: should the Democratic Party function as a majoritarian organization or should it support the fiefdoms of its individual members? Most white members of the party want a House organization that emphasizes the majority over the preferences of its individual members because it will help the party achieve more of its legislative goals. African-American members of Congress who perceive the party as unsympathetic to the interests of their own constituents have pushed for stronger opportunities for seniority and committee autonomy.[20] These rules would insulate more liberal African-American members of the House from the policy goals of the more moderate party majority. In the early 1990s, this conflict became most directly apparent when black members of Congress refused to vote for the Democratic Party's anti-crime legislation, budget plans and welfare proposals on grounds that they did too little to protect black voters.

The result of this is that vibrant two-party competition, particularly in the modern context, reflects the successful denial of racial salience by both of the major parties. In stark contrast to those who argue that two-party politics is essential for democratic progress, I argue that it instead serves as one of the most important ways in which the ideas and ideologies that are communicated in national political campaigns deny a multiracial political viewpoint. In fact, I argue that the reason we can have two-party competition in the US is exactly because racial matters are suppressed. Were African-American interests prominently advocated on a consistent basis in electoral politics, the two-party system would break down because one party would consistently win and the other would consistently lose. Thus an essential element of democratic freedom in US society exists precisely because race is kept out.

Race and party politics at the end of the twentieth century

The 2000 election was among the closest in American history and followed a series of similarly close elections in which no national party received a majority of the popular vote since 1988. The closeness of partisan electoral conflict in the last dozen years is a marked change from the prior two decades. Between 1968 and 1988, the Republicans dominated presidential contests, winning five of six elections. Many argue that the competitiveness of the past three elections is a direct result of the Democrats' re-emergence as a viable electoral organization. The Democratic Party had been widely criticized during the time of their electoral failure, not only for losing elections, but for being perceived as a decaying and irrelevant electoral institution. By any definition of the word 'party', the Democratic Party had trouble living up to it. Instead, it was fragmented between distinct interest groups and individual politicians who lacked a common goal, history or ideology. Nelson Polsby described the Democrats as a party of crazes, manias, and fads.[21] Byron

Shafer argued that 'at bottom, the result of all these reforms was *the diminution, the constriction, at times the elimination, of the regular party in politics of presidential selection*' (emphasis in original).[22]

Throughout this period, the party's decline was intrinsically linked to racial issues. Internally, party leadership was divided over how to incorporate and represent African-American interests. The Democrats changed the rules that governed the way in which its members would nominate a presidential candidate. These rule changes removed power from the hands of white city mayors and gave it to rank-and-file voters and party delegates, delegates that were racially diverse as a product of strict quotas. At the same time, these rules helped lead white delegates from the South and northern urban areas to flee to the Republican Party.

Externally, the party found itself under attack by the Republicans for policies that were perceived as simultaneously pro-black and anti-white. Party support for controversial issues such as government-enforced school busing to end racial segregation in schools, affirmative action, welfare rights, criminal procedure protections, and general government spending on national social programmes was blamed for the swing of white voters to the Republicans. Republicans further fuelled this exodus by white voters by subtly race baiting. Richard Nixon centred his 1968 campaign around two distinct groups whose identity was premised on racial politics: the 'silent majority', the group of voters who weren't protesting, who weren't breaking the law, who had jobs, families and home mortgages; and a southern strategy which targeted whites who opposed school integration policies and favoured states' rights.[23] Ronald Reagan courted the same groups, making specific appeals to southern whites on behalf of state rights, and appealing to northern working-class whites, then referred to as 'Reagan Democrats'. George Bush Sr followed in their footsteps, perhaps most dramatically with his references to Michael Dukakis as soft on crime, exemplified by the infamous Willie Horton television ad in which Horton's face was shown to American voters as representative of what happens when Democratic Party politicians are soft on black criminals.

The Democratic Party's initial response to its electoral defeats was uneven. Political parties in the United States are not unified organizations, nor are they clearly hierarchical. There is often ambiguity as to who the leader of the party is, particularly when the party hasn't elected the President, and even sometimes in the periods when it has. Certainly, each party's official leader – the elected chair of the Democratic National Committee and Republican National Committee – is rarely of much consequence in terms of party power and strategy. At different times, national party power has been centred in city mayors, congressional committee leaders, populist outsider candidates, and small interest groups.[24] More often, and particularly in the recent decades since the McGovern–Fraser reforms mandated the use of primaries in picking presidential nominees, no one individual or group has held command of the national parties. The result of this is that party strategy rarely has a great deal of coherence, as many different groups and individuals vie for leadership and have alternative goals and strategies for attaining those goals.

In recent years, the need to win national elections has encouraged the development of party unity among Democrats. Whether one believes that parties are simply instrumental in their desire to win elections or whether parties are composed of ideological individuals desiring policy agendas, winning elections is essential to the goal.[25] When parties lose elections, particularly when they have sustained losing streaks, the necessity to win becomes more and more dominant, and the party tends to unify more clearly around strategies directed at changing their losing ways. Ideologues who prefer to maintain policy agendas at the cost of winning are marginalized by those who can emphatically proclaim that winning through compromise is better than ending up with nothing at all.

The Democrats' strategy in the 1980s and 1990s reflects this process. With relatively consecutive losses to Nixon, Reagan and Bush, moderate Democrats slowly took control of the party away from the once passionate ideological agendas of the 1960s and the Great Society. After the party's loss in 1984, moderates in the party created the Democratic Leadership Council with the intent of changing the party's agenda and moving it away from the civil rights and social spending goals of previous decades. A study of traditionally white Democrats who were voting Republican in the suburbs of Detroit, Michigan, reported that the voters 'express[ed] a profound distaste for blacks, a sentiment that pervades almost everything they think about government and politics. . . . These sentiments have important implications for Democrats, as virtually all progressive symbols and themes have been redefined in racial and pejorative terms.'[26] With the subsequent loss in 1988 to George Bush Sr, a candidate perceived by the Democrats as very beatable, even progressive party leaders came to be persuaded by the importance of winning as opposed to ideological purity, and leading members of the party's left wing became critical in legitimating the promotion of centrist candidates such as Bill Clinton and Al Gore.

Clinton's election in 1992 and eventual success in office was seen as part of the triumph of 'third way' candidates throughout the United States, United Kingdom, and across the globe. He was tough on crime, making sure to participate in the execution of a mentally disabled

African-American man earlier on in his first presidential bid, and later making anti-crime legislation a major tenet of his legislative agenda. He was even tougher on welfare recipients, ending 'welfare as we know it' just prior to his 1996 re-election bid, effectively taking away one of the leading ways in which Republicans were able to race bait Democrats. Clinton's strategy was certainly a 'third way' as opposed to a straight-forward cooptation of conservative causes. He stood behind affirmative action programmes with a typically moderate but politically successful 'mend, don't end' solution, he promoted social spending and pro-grammes in a way far different from the Republicans, and he promoted an ambitious if merely symbolic and substantively empty dialogue on race. In the course of his impeachment hearings, he was even labelled by the famous African-American writer Toni Morrison as 'the first black president' and received overwhelming support from the black community.

Nonetheless, important concerns in the black community – racial seg-regation in housing and schools, unequal access to health care and other important social services, and dramatic disparities in arrests and sen-tencing for non-violent crimes – were entirely ignored by the President and other leaders of the Democratic Party. Leading African-American supporters of Clinton, promised opportunities for a race agenda after he was elected, would be hard pressed to argue that Clinton at any time turned to such an agenda. Members of the Congressional Black Caucus were continually at odds with the President in his early years regarding welfare, crime and social spending. The Caucus had some success – they pushed the President to invade Haiti and increased spending provisions in some of the budget debates.[27] But in a moment which in many ways symbolized the conflict between the Caucus and Clinton, when key members of the Caucus balked at a Clinton-sponsored Crime Bill in 1994 that they opposed because it failed to contain a provision about racial justice and the death penalty, Clinton simply moved further to the right in order to find additional votes to pass the legislation. He rarely went back in his subsequent years in office.

That Clinton made it safe for Democrats to be conservatives is un-deniable. He was exceptional at balancing acts that alienated African-American voters, such as the high-profile participation in the execution of an African-American criminal and the promise to end welfare, with acts that won wide approval, such as his simultaneous attendance at all-black events, his symbolic yet earnest appeals for dialogue on national race issues, and his endorsement of black politicians for high-ranking political posts – many of them his close friends, as he was arguably the first US president to have close African-American friends. At a certain level, he also made it safe for Republicans to make symbolic gestures at inclusion towards black and Latino voters. With the promise of a substantive discussion of racial issues no longer a primary point of division between the parties, candidates Bob Dole and Jack Kemp in 1996 and George Bush in 2000 found it safe to speak of African Americans as equal citizens with a place in the Republican Party. Bush, in fact, seemed fairly successful with a balancing act of his own: passionately opposing affirmative action, welfare and federally mandated school integration, but equally emphatic in his support of basic civil rights principles, his endorsement of black politicians for high-ranking political posts, and his campaign promise to leave no child behind.[28]

But if this is ideal, it is a strange ideal. Race, when present, is symbolic rather than substantive, a warm fuzzy gloss over a situation fraught with difficulty. In the only party even ambivalently committed to addressing minority concerns with substantive legislation, the consensus that the Democratic Party's strategy is necessary to win elections has further isolated African-American political leaders from the central party agenda. Al Gore, for instance, didn't even have to pay the usual lip-service to the notion that an African American ought to be considered as a vice-presidential nominee. Instead, he chose a candidate more conservative than he was – Joseph Lieberman – a candidate who has been outspoken in his opposition to affirmative action, welfare and other key elements of the civil rights agenda. African-American political leaders grumbled publicly about the Lieberman selection but within twenty-four hours were on television with the vice-presidential candidate offering their endorsement.

Alternatives to Party Marginalization

Court-based strategies

For much of the twentieth century, court litigation was an essential element of African-American political strategy. While African-American voters were finding their voices muted in national electoral politics, either because of systematic efforts to disenfranchise their votes or simply because national parties were ignoring their concerns, the US Supreme Court was providing a more sensitive ear. This jurisprudence was first laid out in an obscure footnote of an otherwise unmemorable case about dairy regulation, *United States v. Carolene Products*.[29] The Supreme Court began to justify increased scrutiny of laws and legislation that attempted to divide along racial lines, mandating additional protection for African Americans than that being offered by legislative and electoral politics. Employing the strict scrutiny standard, the Court struck down a series of laws that attempted to enforce different societies and opportunities for blacks and whites, and wrote a number of opinions that made meaningful the longstanding legal notions of Equal Protection. As a result, the Court was widely seen as a champion of African-American interests for much of the 1950s through the 1970s, passing landmark decisions regarding school segregation, criminal procedure and voting rights. These decisions, particularly when combined with mobilization by civil rights leaders and corresponding congressional activity, led to major civil rights gains during this period, particularly in areas of employment and voting rights, and ended the legal basis of Jim Crow laws in the South.[30] As the civil rights movement and Great Society started to fade into the background, courts remained a crucial battleground for African Americans in achieving political goals, as the Supreme Court made a number of quite radical rulings in the areas of affirmative action, employment discrimination, criminal procedure and civil procedure. As late as 1979, for example, the Court held that the Civil Rights Act endorsed workplace affirmative action programmes, despite strong evidence that Congress had no such intent when passing the law in 1964.[31] Leading legal scholars at the time argued, in fact, that the Court was uniquely suited to promoting the interests of disadvantaged groups, particularly when there was little opportunity in the electoral setting.[32]

But in the past two decades, the Supreme Court has seemingly turned the strict scrutiny standard on its head, using the doctrine to deny affirmative opportunities for African Americans to gain access to schools, jobs and politics. On the one hand, the Court has made it more difficult for African Americans and other racial minorities to prove that they were harmed by discriminatory action, as it has consistently denied the use of statistics and historical context, absent the finding of 'a discriminatory purpose' as a 'motivating factor' in the disputed action.[33] On the other hand, the Court has subjected legislation designed to curb the historical legacies of discrimination to strict scrutiny standards initially developed to promote civil rights; this has served to effectively overturn many race-specific programmes on the grounds that they specifically make reference to racial status.[34]

With regard to electoral politics, the Court has restricted opportunities for increased African-American representation in two critical ways. First of all, Supreme Court decisions in recent years have restricted the reach of the 1965 Voting Rights Act in enhancing minority representation. Prior to the Voting Rights Act and the Twenty-fourth Amendment, southern whites had used numerous methods to disenfranchise African Americans of their right to vote, from voting taxes, literacy tests, grandfather clauses, racial gerrymandering, and straightforward violence and discrimination.[35] As a result, the Voting Rights Act was designed to do more than give African Americans the right to vote, it was to ensure political representation in areas of the US that had been denying black voting privileges in spite of the Fifteenth Amendment right to vote, defining the right to vote as 'all action necessary to make a vote effective'.[36]

In the 1980s, the Voting Rights Act was extended to respond to problems in local and congressional elections where blacks and Latinos were finding their votes offset by white majorities that voted in blocs against minority candidates and at times changed the electoral rules to insulate themselves against black voting power.[37] Particularly problematic for voting rights supporters was that party loyalties were being trumped by racial considerations when white Democrats were faced with a ballot booth choice of a black Democratic candidate versus a white Republican candidate. As a result, in many areas of the South, black voters were faced with two choices – vote for a conservative white Democrat and win the election with the help of conservative white Democratic voters, or vote for a liberal black Democratic candidate and lose the election as white Democratic voters abandon the party for the Republican candidate.[38] In 1982, Congress amended the Voting Rights Act, and in particular Section 2 which deals specifically with government enforcement procedures, to allow for federal intervention in situations of vote dilution. The Court immediately followed Congress by mandating the drawing of legislative districts to respond to racial vote dilution.[39] These districts were designed to ensure that African-American populations were fairly represented in local and state politics, as well as in state-congressional delegations. If necessary, these districts were to be drawn in such a way that black voters from around the state would be artfully manoeuvred into a few districts where their majorities would enable the election of representative candidates.

In the 1990s, however, the Court had dramatically restricted this effort to respond to vote dilution. In 1993 the Court in *Shaw v. Reno* responded to the sometimes bizarre shape of these majority-minority districts. A congressional district that was an unusual shape because of the effort of party leaders to make black voters a majority of the district was 'so irrational on its face that it can only be understood as an effort to segregate voters into separate voting districts because of their race'.[40] The Court determined that any reapportionment scheme that was so clearly drawn along racial lines was subject to strict scrutiny, demanding that the legislation be narrowly tailored to further what the Court could deem a compelling governmental interest.[41] The Court has since expanded this holding to include districts that are not unusually shaped. As long as race is the 'predominant factor' in the drawing of congressional district lines, they are considered unconstitutional on Fourteenth Amendment Equal Protection grounds.[42]

The impact of these cases is potentially sizeable (redistricting occurs every ten years based on census counts – the next redistricting will be in place for the 2002 elections). The Congressional Black Caucus has never been more influential than in the years shortly after the creation of majority-minority districts with the 1990 redistricting that led to a 50 per cent increase in black members of Congress. While the CBC has been criticized for a variety of reasons regarding its strategy and successful exertion of political power, there is little question that between 1993 and 1994, when the Caucus was at its largest in a Democratic-controlled Congress, it was at its loudest and most successful.[43]

In addition to regulating (if usually opposing) congressional legislation designed to increase African-American representation within the existing political structure, the Court has also undercut African-American efforts at alternate approaches outside of the two-party system. Historically, African Americans have attempted to exert greater influence on electoral politics by participating in third party political movements, or at least making a threat of such participation, as Jesse Jackson, Harold Washington, Al Sharpton and many other black political leaders have done in recent years.[44] In the past decade, however, the Court has written a number of decisions that further entrench the hold that the Democratic and Republican parties have over the electoral process. Most notable was the Court's decision in *Timmons v. Twin Cities Area New Party*, which dealt with a third party nominating a candidate from one of the two major parties.[45] A Minnesota law prohibited 'fusion' or multiple party nomination of candidates. The New Party, a progressive multiracial party, argued that the fusion ban violated its rights under the First and Fourteenth Amendments. They had hoped to nominate a Democrat for state legislature (and the Democrats approved of this nomination). By nominating a major party candidate, the New Party and other third parties could attract candidates and voters with the assurance that no one is 'throwing away' their vote by affiliating with them. Instead, the Court endorsed the two-party system's positive role in democracy, holding that the 'States' interest permits them to enact reasonable election regulations that may, in practice, favour the traditional two-party system.'[46] More recently, the Court has allowed third parties to be excluded from televised political debates and denied efforts to open up party primaries to non-affiliated voters, both decisions that only further entrench the two-party system's hold over the electoral process.[47]

Opportunities existing in the two-party system

Despite the institutional disadvantages that exist for African Americans to have influence on national partisan politics, opportunities are not entirely absent within the two-party system. However, specific efforts need to be taken to make sure that such opportunities are manifested. Most important is to have a candidate that runs in the Democratic Party primaries. Since the McGovern–Fraser reforms of the late 1960s, both national parties pick their presidential candidates largely through state-by-state primaries in which voters of the respective parties choose their most liked candidate. This provides the opportunity for any individual who so chooses to run for office and influence the party's agenda by campaigning on issues of his or her choosing and potentially winning delegates by gaining the support of primary voters. In 1972, progressive candidate George McGovern first benefited from this strategy by winning the Democratic Party's nomination over a series of party insiders. Jimmy Carter and Ronald Reagan, candidates who ran opposed to the leaderships of their respective parties, had similar success in the following years. Jesse Jackson became the first prominent African-American candidate by running in the Democratic Party primaries in the 1980s and winning a number of primaries based overwhelmingly on the mobilized African-American vote. Pat Robertson ran a similar campaign in the Republican Party during this time, also achieving success through the mobilization of a single group – in his case, evangelical Christians.

Since the mid-1980s, party leadership has been active in changing the rules of the primary process to allow them to exert greater influence. These changes were most stark in the Democratic Party since they were the party losing presidential elections during this time, and as a result, their leadership was the most mobilized to make changes. The most important change in primary rules is the advent of Super Tuesday. Early on in the presidential nomination season, the Democrats hold several southern state primary elections on the same day: Super Tuesday. By grouping these southern primaries together early on, party leaders hope to attract candidates who will appeal to southern white voters, resulting in the nomination of a more moderate national candidate. If a conservative southern white candidate runs in Super Tuesday, he or she will most likely exit with a commanding lead over other Democratic Party contenders. Even if no southern candidate runs for President, the importance of Super Tuesday is that it forces all candidates to adopt policy stands consistent with the interests of southern voters.

While Super Tuesday represents a powerful constraint on outsider candidates, opportunities for influence remain. In 1988 for instance,

Jesse Jackson was able to win many of the state primaries on Super Tuesday because he mobilized large numbers of African Americans in those states to vote. Since Jackson was in a contest with two other Democrats – Al Gore and Michael Dukakis – black voters were able to provide enough votes to sway the election in his favour. In most Democratic primaries, registered Republicans cannot vote. Moreover, turnout in primaries is consistently much lower than general elections. The result is that groups that are too small to have influence in national elections can be a majority or near-majority in presidential primaries. This is a particularly powerful strategy when more than two candidates are running in the primary, thus further lowering the number of votes needed to win.

In the past few elections, neither Jackson nor any other candidate has run in the Democratic primaries with the specific intent of mobilizing black voters. In 1992, Jackson had been persuaded by Democratic Party leaders, including his former campaign manager, Ron Brown, not to run and risk another four years of George Bush. In 2000, primary candidate Bill Bradley made race a much more prominent theme than his opponent, Al Gore. Bradley's failure to garner much support let alone secure the nomination was a result of many things, but two-party dynamics were certainly a part of it. Bradley confronted two major, and related, obstacles from the two-party system. First, Bradley, like Jackson before him, was faced with opposition from Democratic leaders who worried that he would distract from a November victory by pushing the party away from the national median voter. Party leaders were content with the political strategy of Bill Clinton that showed that moderate Democrats could win national elections when they avoid talking about race and other traditionally liberal topics. In providing an alternative to this strategy, Bradley was isolated and marginalized, something that manifested itself in the second major obstacle that Bradley faced – he was overwhelmed by Al Gore on issues of money and leadership support; support that is critical in mobilizing voters in early primaries.

Conclusion: The Need for Electoral Reform

The institutional forms that marginalize African-American interests, while deeply rooted, socially pervasive and both politically and judicially sanctioned, are not insurmountable. In the past fifty years the US has made great strides in rectifying racial inequality by changing laws and ridding the government of explicitly racist institutions. These improvements have come through concerted efforts not just of civil rights groups, labour organizations and political activists, but also through the main-stays of American government – its judicial, legislative and executive branches. After a hotly contested election, the public mood appears ripe for supporting reform movements and many alternatives will remain on the table in the aftermath of the divisive 2000 election.[48] The Supreme Court's endorsement of Equal Protection in voting ('the idea that one group can be granted greater voting strength than another is hostile to the one man, one vote basis of our representative government')[49] may be just the added spark necessary to embolden these reform movements.

Certainly an important first step is a commitment to Equal Protection through meaningful dialogue and an institutionalized voice for racial minorities in the political process. But for meaningful dialogue to take place there needs to be an incentive for party leaders to begin and engage in it. As I have argued in this chapter, such dialogue will only occur in an electoral system that allows for more than two voices and encourages at least some of these others to be non-white. Most democracies around the globe have electoral systems designed to provide more inclusive representation. In recent years, the UK and now the US are seeing in-creasing pressure from political dissenters to do likewise. One alterna-tive being promoted in the US is the instant run-off in presidential elections where voters can support a third-party candidate without facing the prospect of their last choice getting elected. This would not only allow for candidates such as Ralph Nader and Pat Buchanan to get more votes, but enable candidates promoting a diversity of values to run sub-stantive campaigns and mobilize specific groups of voters without the fear of being marginalized as a 'spoiler'. This would be a relatively easy reform to institutionalize and yet could have deep and longstanding significance. Given the historical legacy of legal racism and its aftermath in America, such a small reform is a vital first step.

NOTES

Many thanks to Kerstin Carlson, Tom Kim and Corey Robin for their ideas and constructive criticisms.

1   See David Cole, *No Equal Justice: Race and Class in the American Crimi-nal Justice System* (New York: New Press, 1999), ch. 4; Randall Kennedy, *Race, Crime, and the Law* (New York: Vintage Press, 1997), ch. 9.
2   Alison Mitchell, 'The 2000 Campaign: The Texas Governor; Response Polite as Bush Courts the NAACP', *New York Times*, 11 July 2000, p. A1.
3   Jim Moret and John King, 'Vice President Reluctant to Join Debate on Capital Punishment', CNN, 21 June 2000, transcript #00062109V23.

4   For just a couple of examples from the national press, see Mireya Navarro and Somini Sengupta, 'Contesting the Vote: Black Voters; Arriving at Florida Voting Places, Some Blacks Found Frustration', *New York Times*, 30 Nov. 2000, p. A1; Gregory Palast, 'Florida's "Disappeared Voters": Disenfranchised by the GOP', *The Nation*, 272, no. 5 (5 Feb. 2001), p. 20.

5   When Gore was asked at a news conference about whether black votes were discounted, he responded, 'Well, I am very troubled by a lot of the stories that have been reported about a roadblock on the way to one precinct, questions raised about various activities there. I do not have any personal or firsthand knowledge of those events. But whenever there are problems of that kind alleged, they are deserving of attention . . . They are not part of the ongoing court action'; quoted in 'Contesting the Vote; Gore's Remarks at White House News Conference', *New York Times*, 6 Dec. 2000, p. A28.

6   Michael Crowley, 'Why Feminism Wins Elections; Why Blacks Want Gore to Keep Fighting', *New Republic*, 18 Dec. 2000.

7   I have argued elsewhere as to why the marginalization of African Americans in the political system is unique, even among racial minorities; see Paul Frymer, *Uneasy Alliances: Race and Party Competition in America* (Princeton: Princeton University Press, 1999), ch. 7.

8   The importance of institutionalizing a voice for minorities in the political system has been aptly discussed by Lani Guinier, *The Tyranny of the Majority* (New York: Free Press, 1994); Will Kymlicka, *Multicultural Citizenship: A Liberal Theory of Minority Rights* (New York: Oxford University Press, 1995); Iris Marion Young, *Justice and the Politics of Difference* (Princeton: Princeton University Press, 1990); Melissa S. Williams, *Voice, Trust, and Memory: Marginalized Groups and the Failings of Liberal Representation* (Princeton: Princeton University Press, 1999).

9   In fact, the nation's most widely read daily newspaper, *USA Today*, recently supported an 'instant run-off' for presidential elections. 'Under it, voters rank the candidates 1, 2, 3 in order of preference. Voters thus could support both a Nader and a Gore, both a Buchanan and a Bush, or any other combination. If a candidate wins a majority of first-preference votes, the count is over and that candidate wins. If not, the last-place finisher is eliminated. Ballots cast for that candidate are counted for voters' next choice, until someone has a clear majority. Australia and Ireland have used the system for decades': 'Spoiler Free Elections', *USA Today*, 5 Feb. 2001.

10 *Bush v. Gore*, 121 S. Ct. 525 (2000).

11 This is not a recent phenomenon. See Alexis de Tocqueville's discussion of race in the final chapter (ch. 10) of *Democracy in America*, ed. J. P. Mayer (Garden City, NY: Anchor Books, 1969).

12 Dianne M. Pinderhughes, *Race and Ethnicity in Chicago Politics* (Urbana: University of Illinois Press, 1987), p. 261.

13 On the importance of race in the writing of the Constitution, see Derrick Bell, *And We Are Not Saved* (New York: Basic Books, 1987), ch. 1. On its importance in the creation of the modern-day social welfare state, see Robert C. Lieberman, 'Race and the Organization of Welfare Policy', in Paul

E. Peterson (ed.), *Classifying by Race* (Princeton: Princeton University Press, 1995); Jill Quadagno, *The Color of Welfare: How Racism Undermined the War on Poverty* (New York: Oxford University Press, 1994); Douglas S. Massey and Nancy A. Denton, *American Apartheid: Segregation and the Making of the Underclass* (Cambridge: Harvard University Press, 1993); George Lipsitz, *The Possessive Investment in Whiteness: How White People Profit from Identity Politics* (Philadelphia: Temple University Press, 1998), chs 1–2.

14 See Frymer, *Uneasy Alliances*, ch. 2; John H. Aldrich, *Why Parties? The Origin and Transformation of Party Politics in America* (Chicago: University of Chicago Press, 1995), chs 3–5.

15 See Arend Lijphart, *Democracy in Plural Societies* (New Haven: Yale University Press, 1977).

16 See Anthony Downs, *An Economic Theory of Democracy* (New York: Harper and Row, 1957), p. 120.

17 See Thomas Byrne Edsall with Mary D. Edsall, *Chain Reaction: The Impact of Race, Rights, and Taxes on American Politics* (New York: W.W. Norton, 1991).

18 See Katherine Tate, *From Protest to Politics: The New Black Voters in American Elections* (Cambridge, Mass.: Harvard University Press, 1993).

19 Most notably, see Guinier, *Tyranny of the Majority*; Bell, *And We Are Not Saved*; Tate, *From Protest to Politics*; Ronald W. Walters, *Black Presidential Politics in America: A Strategic Approach* (Albany: State University of New York Press, 1988); Clarence Lusane, *Race in the Global Era: African Americans at the Millennium* (Boston: South End Press, 1997); Hanes Walton Jr, *Black Political Parties* (New York: Free Press, 1972); Dianne Pinderhughes, 'Political Choices: A Realignment in Partisanship among Black Voters?', in National Black Urban League, *The State of Black America* (New York: National Black Urban League, 1984).

20 See Frymer, *Uneasy Alliances*, ch. 6.

21 Nelson W. Polsby, *The Consequences of Party Reform* (New York: Oxford University Press, 1983), p. 147.

22 Byron E. Shafer, *Quiet Revolution: The Struggle for the Democratic Party and the Shaping of Post-Reform Politics* (New York: Russell Sage Foundation, 1983), p. 252.

23 See Paul Frymer and John David Skrentny, 'Coalition-Building and the Politics of Electoral Capture during the Nixon Administration: African Americans, Labor, Latinos', *Studies in American Political Development* (spring 1998).

24 See Martin Shefter, *Political Parties and the State: American Historical Perspectives* (Princeton: Princeton University Press, 1994); Alan Ware, *The Breakdown of Democratic Party Organization, 1940–1980* (New York: Oxford University Press, 1984); Polsby, *Consequences of Party Reform*.

25 Downs, *An Economic Theory of Democracy*.

26 Stanley B. Greenberg, 'Report on Democratic Defection', report to the Democratic Party, 15 Apr. 1985, p. 13.

27   See Peter J. Boyle, 'The Rise of Kweise Mfume', *New Yorker*, 1 Aug. 1994.
28   Of course, this balancing act was not persuasive with black voters, as he was summarily rejected by more than 90 per cent of black votes nationwide and in his home state of Texas. In fact, Bush received a smaller percentage of the black vote (8 per cent nationally) than any Republican candidate since 1964.
29   304 U.S. 144 (1938).
30   On employment, see Paul Burstein, *Discrimination, Jobs, and Politics: The Struggle for Equal Employment Opportunity in the United States since the New Deal* (Chicago: University of Chicago Press, 1985). On voting, see Steven F. Lawson, *Black Ballots: Voting Rights in the South, 1944–1969* (New York: Columbia University Press, 1976).
31   See *United Steelworkers v. Weber*, 443 U.S. 193 (1979). For discussion of the Court's interpretation of the affirmative action provisions, see William N. Eskridge Jr, *Dynamic Statutory Interpretation* (Cambridge: Harvard University Press, 1994), ch. 1.
32   See John Hart Ely, *Democracy and Distrust* (Cambridge: Harvard University Press, 1980).
33   *Arlington Heights v. Metropolitan Housing Corp.*, 429 U.S. 252 (1977). On necessary intent for proving discrimination in school segregation, see *Milliken v. Bradley*, 418 U.S. 717 (1974); for proving employment discrimination, see *Washington v. Davis*, 426 U.S. 229 (1976).
34   *Adarand Constructors, Inc. v. Pena*, 575 U.S. 200 (1995).
35   See J. Morgan Kousser, *The Shaping of Southern Politics: Suffrage Restriction and the Establishment of the One-Party South, 1880–1910* (New Haven: Yale University Press, 1974).
36   42 U.S.C. §1971(e).
37   See Lani Guinier, 'The Triumph of Tokenism: The Voting Rights Act and the Theory of Black Electoral Success', *University of Michigan Law Review*, 89 (1991), p. 1077.
38   This problem was exacerbated because of the unique identity of southern white Democratic voters. Unlike national Democrats, southern white Democrats identified with the party largely because of historical attachment stemming from the Democratic Party's support of the South at the time of the Civil War. As a result, these voters were a lot more conservative than the rest of the Democratic Party on issues not specific to civil rights, but also economics, crime prevention and defence. Thus, when black voters in the South were faced with a candidate choice of a black Democrat versus a white Democrat, the choice was not simply about the colour of the candidate but about that candidate's ideology. See Kenny J. Whitby, *The Color of Representation: Congressional Behavior and Black Interests* (Ann Arbor: University of Michigan Press, 1997).
39   *Thornburg v. Gingles* 478 U.S. 30 (1986).
40   509 U.S. 630, at 657 (1993).
41   See *Adarand Constructors, Inc. v. Pena*, 575 U.S. 200 (1995).

42   See *Miller v. Johnson*, 515 U.S. 900 (1995); *Bush v. Vera*, 517 U.S. 952 (1996), and *Shaw v. Hunt*, 517 U.S. 899 (1996).

43   See Robert Singh, *The Congressional Black Caucus: Racial Politics in the US Congress* (Thousand Oaks: Sage, 1998); David T. Canon, *Race, Redistricting, and Representation: The Unintended Consequences of Black-Majority Districts* (Chicago: University of Chicago Press, 1999); Frymer, *Uneasy Alliances*, ch. 6.

44   See Walton, *Black Political Parties*; Walters, *Black Presidential Politics*.

45   520 U.S. 351 (1997).

46   Ibid., at 367. Also see *Rutan v. Republican Party of Ill.* 497 U.S. 62, 107 (1990), 'the stabilizing effects of such a [two-party] system are obvious.' *Davis v. Bandemer*, 478 U.S. 109, 144 (1986), 'there can be little doubt that the emergence of a strong and stable two-party system in this country has contributed enormously to sound and effective government.' *Branti v. Finkel* 445 U.S. 507, 532 (1980), 'broad-based political parties supply an essential coherence and flexibility to the American political scene.'

47   *Arkansas Educational Television Commission v. Forbes*, 523 U.S. 666 (1998); *California Democratic Party v. Jones*, 530 U.S. 567 (2000).

48   On the power of public moods to lead to legislative reform, see David R. Mayhew, *Divided We Govern: Party Control, Lawmaking, and Investigations 1946–1990* (New Haven: Yale University Press, 1991), ch. 6.

49   *Bush v. Gore* at 531, quoting *Moore v. Ogilvie*, 394 U.S. 814, at 819 (1969). Also see Lani Guinier, 'A New Voting Rights Movement', *New York Times*, 18 Dec. 2000, p. A27.

4

'If You're Disgusted with Us, I Don't Blame You': Television and American Politics Today

Robert Mason

Introduction: 7–8 November 2000

At best, the mistake was an embarrassment for broadcasters. At worst, it threatened to jeopardize the democratic process. On election night in 2000, 7 November, it was shortly after 8 p.m. on the east coast when the American television networks broke important news. According to their projection of the final result, based on exit polls and early indications from the official counts, their journalists announced that Al Gore would win Florida. For both candidates, Florida was a make-or-break state. Gore looked likely to become the next president. Dan Rather of CBS called Bush's prospects 'shakier than cafeteria Jell-O'.

Less than two hours later, the television reporters confessed that they had spoken too soon. The networks' pollsters now decided that either Gore or George W. Bush might win Florida. Rather swiftly apologized. 'If you're disgusted with us,' he said, 'frankly, I don't blame you.' Everything soon changed yet again. At 2.20 a.m., the networks called Florida for Bush; they announced that Bush was consequently the winner of the presidency. By this point, Gore knew that he could not win without Florida. He therefore telephoned Bush with his congratulations and prepared to deliver his concession speech. On his way to deliver it, Gore received word of the latest from Florida; Bush's lead was not so comfortable, after all. Instead of giving his speech, Gore called Bush back to retract the concession. At 4 a.m., the networks announced that Florida's votes in the Electoral College were again in doubt. Like their counterparts at a number of other newspapers, journalists at the *New York Times* found that their front page projecting a Bush win was out of date; 115,000 copies were pulped. The race was by no means over. There would, of course, be many weeks yet before headlines about Bush's victory were at last true.

In the aftermath of the 2000 miscall, the networks reviewed their use of exit polls. The work of Voter News Service, a polling operation funded jointly by major news organizations, was placed under scrutiny. The investigations attracted relatively little public attention, absorbed instead by the judicial wrangling about which candidate would receive Florida's presidential votes in the Electoral College. Some thought that the networks' competitive desire to make projections of the result deserved much more scrutiny. There has long been a suspicion – denied by broadcasters and unsubstantiated by most analysts – that early calls depressed the level of voter turnout in the west, where polls were still open, potentially distorting the outcome of elections. In 2000, it was only 5 p.m. on the Pacific coast when Rather and his counterparts at other networks said that Gore was the likely winner. Claiming that the networks were generally quicker to call states favouring Gore than those favouring Bush, Representative Billy Tauzin (R-LA) argued that the effect was to discourage some Republican supporters in the west from voting.[1]

The events of election night were a particularly vivid example of the key political role played by the mass media. Even the candidates themselves were relying on the broadcasters for authoritative reporting of the election's outcome. The events were also an inescapable example of journalistic carelessness, driven by the commercially competitive desire to broadcast the results as soon as possible – well before those results were final. 'I was appalled,' said academic Alex S. Jones on the day after the election. 'These institutions have a huge responsibility; people count on them, and they made a terrible blunder.'[2]

The twists and turns of this election night were a surprise to everyone. But the apparently irresponsible actions of the broadcasters were no surprise to many observers of the American media. There is no disagreement that the media have weighty responsibilities within a democracy, to promote an informed citizenry and to act as a 'watchdog' against governmental abuses. In the American case, there is, however, disagreement about the success enjoyed by media organizations in meeting these responsibilities. Indeed, many argue that Americans have significant reason to blame journalists and media owners for inadequate coverage of political life.

This chapter surveys some recent contributions to the scholarly debate about the relationship between politics and the media in the United States, concentrating on television, and it illustrates them with information about developments in this relationship over the past decade. The survey suggests that there is much evidence in support of the irresponsibility thesis. It also suggests that little is likely to change. The primary reason is commercial. 'With limited demand for first-rate journalism, most news organizations cannot afford to supply it,' observes Robert Entman, 'and because they do not supply it, most Americans have no practical source of the information necessary to become politically sophisticated.'[3]

The Commercial Imperative

There are two principal charges against American journalism. First, as Entman suggests, it is argued that it offers an inadequate amount of information about politics.[4] Second, the nature of much coverage fails to encourage healthy debate about politics; it even promotes cynicism about politics rather than engagement with the political process.[5] Studies suggest that many ordinary Americans, as well as experts, share these concerns.[6] In looking at the media in the United States and at the persuasiveness of these claims, the most important medium is television. In 2000, three-quarters of Americans cited television – whether network, local or cable – as their primary source of campaign information.[7]

The first charge is the easier to investigate. Coverage of politics is relatively marginal to American television. Recent developments have not changed this marginality. Three major networks – ABC, CBS, NBC – include news and political interviews within breakfast shows during the morning, and run half-hour news programmes during the early evening. Thanks to increased competition, network evening news, having once reached a large audience, now achieves ever-declining ratings; by 2000, no more than 30 per cent of Americans regularly watched.[8] Beyond the morning shows and the evening news, the networks offer few other outlets for political reporting. The flagship of network political coverage is the discussion and interview programme, with ABC, CBS, NBC, and their more recent rival Fox, all screening a version on Sunday mornings. Such programmes enjoy influence, often featuring news-making comments by politicians on the significant issues of the moment, but they attract few viewers.

More news can be found on non-commercial public television (PBS), which features in-depth analysis, and on twenty-four-hour cable channels, notably CNN, plus MSNBC and the Fox News Channel – both new arrivals of the 1990s. Again, few are watching. One estimate of the keen audience for politics on television is only 2 million, a small proportion of the population and the electorate.[9] (Well over 100 million people voted in the presidential election of 2000.)

Within their news broadcasts, the major networks devote relatively little attention to politics. Extensive attention to politics is not generally seen as a way to maintain audience share in an intensely competitive market; many observers believe that, as competition has increased, the serious content of these broadcasts has decreased.[10] This lack of attention remains true even as elections approach. During the two months of the fall campaign, the three network news broadcasts devoted a total of 805 minutes to campaign coverage, an average of four minutes each night on each programme. The total remained low even though the contest between Gore and Bush was the most competitive race for the presidency for many years.[11]

It is to local television stations that many Americans turn for news. Each network is a loose collection of local stations, some of which it owns, but others of which are independently owned. Most stations offer several hours of news each day, but reports about politics do not feature prominently in these programmes. They are an important source of income for most stations, and their managers tend to decide that political coverage does not bring in so many viewers and therefore so much advertising revenue. An analysis of a Los Angeles news programme in the early 1990s, for example, found that it devoted a disproportionate amount of time to crime – a quarter of its news coverage in total – thus crowding out many important local issues.[12] In 2000, a station in Chicago, WBBM, initiated a high-profile revamp of its late evening news, stressing serious coverage of important events and issues. But the experiment did not work. The effort to bring substance to local news lasted less than a year, disappearing before election day, a victim of falling ratings.[13] Commercial considerations seem to rule out a more serious approach to mass-audience news on television.

Even campaigns fail to attract much-attention. During California's gubernatorial contest of 1998, a study of its coverage by local television news found that it amounted to an average of just 72 seconds each night on each station during the last month of campaigning.[14] The campaign of 2000 witnessed an effort to foster more political coverage at local stations. Its results will be discussed later; they do little to alter the overall picture of inattention to electoral politics.

But it is not inattention alone that shapes the way in which American journalism treats politics. The second main charge by critics against American journalism involves a number of common practices that influence political coverage adversely. Shanto Iyengar, for example, writing in 1991, points out that most television reports are 'episodic' rather than 'thematic'. That is, they focus on events and personalities rather than longer-range social, economic and political developments. Coverage of terrorism on television, for example, is much more likely to feature news of a hijacking or bombing, rather than analysis of the reasons for terrorist activity. An 'episodic' approach, Iyengar argues, usually discourages viewers from holding politicians accountable for problems and from expecting a political solution. 'Thematic' news, by contrast, usually does encourage such connections. The format of television news, according to this analysis, therefore diminishes the medium's democratic role.[15]

Another critic is Mark Rozell. He sees special problems in the coverage of Congress; a journalist's sense of a good story is offended by the careful deliberations that characterize the institution. Reporters, he points out, often present lengthy congressional debate, an essential feature of the institution, as negative inactivity. Coverage tends to focus on personalities, scandals, conflict within Congress and between the legislative and executive branches, rather than on policy and on congressional processes. On this basis, Rozell assigns to journalists much of the responsibility for public disaffection with Congress.[16]

According to other commentators, journalists often develop a cosy relationship with politicians and other policy-makers, a cosiness which can undermine the effectiveness of the media as a public 'watchdog'. A particularly compelling example is the Savings and Loans crisis of the 1980s. An economic downturn at the end of the decade precipitated disaster among Savings and Loans institutions – the equivalent of UK building societies – because many had pursued risky and sometimes even illegal diversification of their activities. The federal government had a legal responsibility to underwrite the losses of investors; this responsibility cost the country hundreds of billions of dollars. While the problem developed, media organizations were almost completely silent on the issue – until the crisis finally hit. Bartholomew Sparrow identifies a deference among journalists that contributed to this oversight. On the whole, reporters rely on their sources within the policy community for information; if no one within that community notices a problem, then nor do the journalists. There is, moreover, a consensus among journalists about what is news; it is difficult for an individual reporter to break this consensus.[17]

The way in which journalists cover campaigns attracts special criticism. In the eyes of many analysts, their crimes are numerous, and they add up to a corrosive scepticism directed at politicians that feeds public cynicism. Thomas Patterson traces the problem to a shift in the approach of journalists to politicians that took place in the late 1960s and early 1970s. Rather than reporting policy proposals in a straightforward way, they concentrated instead on investigating electoral strategy. Rather than describing the statements of candidates, they subjected these statements to scrutiny, showing how they were calculated to win votes. By 1992, more than 80 per cent of campaign reports in the *New York Times* looked at the activities of candidates in terms of strategy.[18] Similarly on television, many campaign stories are devoted to the 'horse race', dominated by information about the latest findings of pollsters, as well as by discussion of the candidates' strategies to improve their placing in the race – as opposed to relaying their statements and reporting their policy proposals to the electorate.

Despite the criticism that news organizations faced as a result of this research, early analysis suggests that the 2000 election showed little improvement. During the fall campaign, a slightly higher proportion of reports on network news dealt with the substance of politics than in presidential elections of the 1990s, but the figure remained low – 40 per cent, as opposed to 33 per cent in 1992 and 38 per cent in 1996. Indeed, reports were even more likely to investigate the 'horse race'. As many as 71 per cent of reports fell into this category, indicating that even when news programmes looked at policy proposals and at the candidates' qualifications for office, the journalists presented this information within the context of strategic calculation.[19] Their assessment of commercial considerations prevented the organizations from running fuller coverage or from emphasizing policy matters at greater length. 'We probably all could have done a few more stories on issues', commented Bob Schieffer, a reporter for CBS, surveying early campaign reporting in July 2000. 'It's very hard to get people interested in these issue stories, I must say.'[20]

Not all scholars share the view that media coverage encourages public cynicism about politics. Pippa Norris, for example, challenges the existence of any causative connection between a change in the nature of political journalism and a rise in discontent about the political process. She points out that while distrust in government increased during the late 1960s and early 1970s, it then remained roughly stable. Public cynicism did not, therefore, emerge as the result of an increasingly sceptical approach among journalists to politics. Norris also points out that the consumers of news in the United States are not only better informed about politics, but they are also no more cynical about politics than those who do not watch or read the reports of journalists.[21]

Work conducted by Lawrence Jacobs and Robert Shapiro lead them to make a different criticism of Patterson. A key recent trend of American politics, they argue, is the dominance of the opinion poll. But in avidly consuming poll data, politicians do not change their position on issues to meet the preferences of voters, except at election time. Their position on issues is not responsive to soundings of public opinion, but reflects their own political ideas and those of their active supporters. Instead, they use polls to understand how to sell their policies in ways that are acceptable to the electorate. The conclusion of Jacobs and Shapiro is that strategy is everything in modern politics; it is therefore entirely appropriate for journalists to probe tactics and political game plans for hidden goals and intentions. The media should be cynical, because politics is cynical.[22] An attraction of the thesis is its apparent success in offering a persuasive picture of how contemporary politicians behave. According to Dick Morris, who worked for him as a poll analyst, Clinton used soundings of public opinion in exactly the way described by Jacobs and Shapiro: to understand how to sell his policies, rather than to decide their nature.[23]

Samplings of public opinion in 2000 lent some weight to both schools of thought. On the one hand, coverage fails to impress many Americans. According to a poll conducted shortly after election day, only 28 per cent of respondents thought that the reporting of the campaign was good. There was, therefore, dissatisfaction with the coverage of journalists; the extent of the respondents' negativity does, however, almost certainly reflect disappointment with the confusion caused by the miscalls of election night. On the other hand, most voters – as many as 83 per cent of the same sample – were nevertheless sure that they were sufficiently informed about the presidential contest to make the right choice. The perceived inadequacies of the media did not result in any crisis of democracy, according to the voters themselves.[24]

The critics have not yet succeeded in persuading news organizations to change their coverage, with two notable exceptions. The first is the trend towards 'civic journalism' or 'public journalism' that began in the 1990s as the result of concern about the quality of political coverage. Civic journalism sought to place control of campaign debate in the hands of voters, rather than those of politicians or journalists, and to emphasize issues, rather than the 'horse race'. Typically, newspapers, sometimes in conjunction with local broadcasters, commissioned polls and convened focus groups to identify a 'citizen's agenda'. The idea began during the contest for the governorship of Kansas in 1990, when the *Wichita Eagle* ran such a project, called 'Your vote counts'. It was claimed that turnout was higher and the electorate better informed in areas served by the *Wichita Eagle* than in other parts of the state.

In 1994, a charitable foundation established the Pew Center for Civic Journalism, which awards grants to newspapers and broadcasters in order to encourage projects 'to close the gap between people's lives and public discourse'. The experiment spread to many other areas. Despite its lofty aims, civic journalism does not lack its critics. They challenge some of the claims about the success of civic journalism in promoting democratic participation. More fundamentally, they see its ideas as inconsistent with detachment and objectivity, as embodying a form of political bias.[25] The overall impact of civic journalism therefore remains unclear. Despite the inclusion of television stations in some of its projects, the movement – whether successful or not – remains concentrated within print journalism.

The second effort to change coverage of politics involved television exclusively. As the 2000 campaign approached, a government commission issued a recommendation for reform to improve political coverage on American television within a voluntary framework. The voluntary nature of the initiative meant that it escaped constitutional scrutiny and political controversy, but also that its effectiveness was limited. The Advisory Committee on the Public Interest Obligations of Digital TV Broadcasters, convened by the White House and informally known as the Gore Commission, issued a report in December 1998 recommending that broadcast television stations should air five minutes of 'candidate-centered discourse' each evening during the last thirty days of the campaign. The recommendation revealed the influence of television's critics, who are anxious that broadcasters should offer more extensive political coverage but also that they should avoid the 'horse race' model of campaign reporting. The emphasis of 'candidate-centered discourse' is the debate on the issues, not strategy.

Despite the involvement of commercial broadcasters in the Gore Commission, the results of the recommendation were by no means impressive. Only 7 per cent of local television stations agreed to aim for the five-minute target as the election approached. There was little success in reaching the target. According to one survey, the average time for candidate-centred discourse on such stations was little more than two minutes per night. The figure for stations that did not make the commitment was rather less than one minute. Among the stations surveyed, the worst case was KWTV; its viewers in Oklahoma City saw an average of two seconds of candidate-centred discourse each night. There was, overall, no significant change in campaign coverage – either in terms of its volume or of its type – although the few stations that aimed to reach the targets covered the campaign somewhat more effectively than their rivals.[26] The impact of the recommendations on the content of network news programmes was no better.[27]

Bias

It is an inescapable facet of the relationship between media and politics that journalists face accusations of bias from time to time. Most observers of the American media do not, however, see much evidence of political bias. Although there are more liberals within journalism than among the population as a whole, professional ethics of objectivity and balance transcend any desire to express personal views. Moreover, the industry's commercialism generally acts as a further obstacle to overt bias; bias is not a sellable commodity on the whole.[28]

Still, many voters see things differently and suspect liberal bias. A report during the 2000 campaign suggested that a majority of Bush supporters perceived media bias against their candidate, while a third of Gore supporters acknowledged favourable treatment of theirs. Content analysis of news stories suggested a somewhat different picture. Early coverage on television of Bush's candidacy was generally positive, while Gore's problems on the campaign trail gained attention. When the fall campaign began in earnest after the conventions, the advantage was switched: more reports looked at Bush's weaknesses, while Gore fared better. As the campaign progressed, nevertheless, things changed again. Towards election day, Bush won the more positive coverage. Overall, network news treated the candidates in a roughly similar fashion, more negative than positive. Sixty per cent of comments evaluating Gore on television news were negative during the fall, compared with 63 per cent of those evaluating Bush.[29]

Journalists defended their treatment of the candidates as accurately reflecting their fortunes; negative comments did not show bias, but simply reacted to lack-lustre campaigning. The defence is persuasive. But for conservative critics it was not convincing enough. Journalists were generally much readier, they claimed, to seize on any missteps by Bush and to overlook those by Gore. A key example cited was press reaction to a subliminal message in a Republican advertisement; it included the word 'rats' for a fraction of a second. Negative coverage of this incident was extensive, and some claimed that there would have been rather less attention to it if the Gore campaign had produced the ad.[30] Some liberals, by contrast, suspected that journalists treated Bush too kindly; they harboured doubts about his ability to be President, but thought that those doubts were neither adequately aired nor comprehensively investigated by the mass-audience media.[31]

In view of the content analysis of network news reports, more compelling than claims of liberal bias among journalists is the observation that American journalism exhibits a certain bias against the political process in general. Both candidates were the object of more negative than positive comment on the evening news. In this, the campaign of 2000 was similar to its recent predecessors. Some scholars have noted that journalistic analysis usually leads to adverse criticism; when journalists scrutinize rather than describe the activities of candidates they highlight their negative elements – where rhetoric outstrips reality, where one promise contradicts another, where spending plans do not add up.[32] Whether or not these negative comments feed public cynicism with politics remains open to debate, but the work of some scholars suggests that they do. The experiments of Joseph Cappella and Kathleen Hall Jamieson, for example, offer particularly strong evidence for exactly such a link.[33] This is why some scholars advocate a shift in journalistic practice towards the provision of candidate-centred discourse – so that voters can hear directly from politicians, free from the commentary of reporters.

Conventions and Debates

Two important events of the television campaign are the party conventions and the presidential debates. They are a rare opportunity for the candidates to speak directly to the voters, and, according to surveys, they often succeed in making viewers better informed about the campaign. Over time, however, the fortunes of conventions and debates as television events are evolving in rather different ways.

The conventions, where the parties meet to make their official choice of presidential candidate, were once the location of serious political exchange. Reforms of the nomination process in the early 1970s undermined their significance, shifting the arena of decision from the convention to primary elections. But television played an important role in their transformation, too. From the start of political television fifty years ago, broadcasters were anxious to show the colourful political confrontations of conventions to their viewers. Party managers increasingly wished to play down difference and to use these televised events as a free commercial for their cause. In 2000, the Republicans, for example, in nominating George W. Bush, were anxious to distance themselves from the controversially combative conservatism of the 1990s and to emphasize their inclusiveness and social compassion.[34]

As television changed the nature of conventions, so television lost its enthusiasm for broadcasting them. Although full events are now available on cable and online, a long-term trend towards less coverage on network television has continued. On some nights, NBC and CBS featured the convention as one report among others on magazine programmes. The ploy was still not enough to keep viewers watching. An edition of 'Dateline NBC' during the Republican convention saw its audience almost halved when it moved from a report on nursing homes to the proceedings in Philadelphia.[35]

While conventions continue their decline, the health of debates remains good. They were created for television, first appearing in 1960 and returning in 1976, since when presidential debates have taken place during each campaign. In 2000, the three debates between Bush and Gore received 46.5 million, 37.6 million and 37.7 million viewers respectively. The debates allowed many voters to hear the candidates talk about the issues at some length. Whether the debates changed any minds is less clear. Analysis of previous elections suggests that debates sometimes change public opinion; the perceived winner of a debate tends to gain a few percentage points of support.[36] In 2000, many observers agreed that the principal contribution of the debates was to challenge the widespread suspicion that Bush was not weighty enough for the presidency.[37] If so, given the evidence of previous presidential campaigns, the debates may well have played at least some role in his victory.

The 'New Media'

A key debate of the last decade has focused on the impact of the so-called 'new media' on American politics. The category is wide, encompassing a number of quite different phenomena. What unites them is their distinction from conventional network news, the half-hour broadcasts from ABC, CBS and NBC in the early evening. Until the 1990s, these programmes – together with special coverage of political conventions and presidential debates – were the principal televised forum in which electioneering was played out. When alternative fora of communication emerged in the 1990s, there was some optimism that they might energize the dialogue between candidates and voters. By 2000, that optimism seemed rather misplaced.

Talk of the new media arrived in 1992, largely because of the ways in which Bill Clinton and Ross Perot, the third-party candidate, fought their campaigns. For both, the new media seemed important. When damaging revelations emerged about Clinton's past, his appearances on talk shows played an important role in improving his public image and in offering a platform for his message.[38] Perot launched his candidacy on a talk show, CNN's 'Larry King Live', and he waged his campaign largely through such appearances and through thirty-minute commercials. He avoided traditional press conferences and conventional, harder-edged news programmes.

There was no novelty to such appearances in 2000. The talk show is now an essential appointment of a presidential campaign. Gore and Bush visited shows including King's and Oprah Winfrey's daytime programme. They also engaged in banter with late-night hosts Jay Leno and David Letterman. Indeed, the campaign of 2000 saw television comedy about politics elevated to fresh prominence. Organizations including the *New York Times*, CBS and the AP news agency all tracked television humour about politics, while a research group, the Center for Media and Public Affairs, continued a long-term project counting jokes. This interest was bolstered by poll figures, which suggested that many Americans – more than a quarter in total and almost a half of those under thirty – found out campaign information from late-night comedy.[39] Moreover, the shows were a valuable method for the candidates to reach out to voters, especially because of the lack of airtime afforded them on network news. When Al Gore appeared on CBS's 'Late Show with David Letterman' in September, for example, he had more minutes of speaking time than he did on all three evening news programmes during the whole of that month.[40]

In 1994, two years after the apparent emergence of the 'new media', there was another new medium – an old one discovering fresh prominence. Talk radio grew between the late 1980s and the mid-1990s, by which time it accounted for about 15 per cent of the radio audience. It relied heavily on discussion programmes, featuring call-in contributions from listeners; some that became particularly successful were overtly conservative. The most prominent among the talk-radio hosts was Rush Limbaugh, whose show was broadcast by over 600 stations and reached as many as 20 million Americans each week by 1994. Objectivity was no ambition of this political entertainment. Limbaugh subjected Bill Clinton to unceasing attack, while praising the plans of Newt Gingrich and the Republicans. He 'may be the most consequential person in political life at the moment', said William Bennett, the former Secretary of Education, in 1993. 'He is changing the terms of debate.'

In 1994, exit polls suggested that talk-radio listeners were much more likely to vote for Republicans than voters as a whole. In the Texas gubernatorial contest of that year, for example, George W. Bush won 69 per cent of talk-radio listeners.[41] Any causative link between listening to talk radio and supporting Republican candidates is questionable, however. Callers to Limbaugh's show became known as 'ditto-heads' for their method of signalling agreement with the host's statements. It would be unsurprising if many within the larger audience were 'ditto-heads', not changing their minds because of the shows, but choosing to listen to Limbaugh and others – including Ronald Reagan's son, Michael, and Watergate criminal G. Gordon Liddy – because of ideological agreement with their content.

By 1996, the newest of the new media was the internet. In that year, 6 per cent of Americans said that they received daily news from the World Wide Web. The internet's arrival as a major medium was greeted with enthusiasm by some as promising to offer voters interactive means by which they could become more actively involved in political exchange. One of the enthusiasts was Clinton, who called the internet 'our new town square'. Senator John Ashcroft (R-MO) said that the age of the internet 'redefines the way citizens can communicate and participate in our democracy' and '[provides] new avenues for people to be involved in changing government'.[42]

There is no question that use of the internet spread during the 1990s with unusual rapidity. By 2000, about two-thirds of Americans had access to the internet at home or at work.[43] Eighteen per cent said that they went online for campaign news at least sometimes.[44] But the impact of the internet on politics has hardly yet lived up to the expectations of Clinton and Ashcroft. In the eyes of internet enthusiasts, Usenet news groups, offering an open opportunity for discussion, were especially promising as a new possibility for political exchange, but they soon proved especially disappointing. An early scholar of the internet, Richard Davis, finds that the quality of debate is low. Within each news group, participants tend to share similar views, and they pander to each other's prejudices. Any disagreement is usually met with insults rather than reasoned counterargument. A news group about abortion offers one example. 'I am presently pro-life,' wrote a contributor, 'but I would consider changing my position if the pro-choice people would agree to be aborted retroactively.'[45]

Nor has the internet provided an opportunity for newcomers to challenge the dominance of established media organizations and to create a different voice within American journalism. Instead, existing broadcasters and newspapers have adapted to the arrival of the internet, and their websites are the most successful. At the start of 2001, the sites reporting the highest number of monthly hits were MSNBC.com, a joint venture between NBC News and Microsoft (9.8 million), CNN.com (7.7 million), and NYTimes.com (3.4 million). The sites tended to offer similar content to that which the parent organization was broadcasting or printing.[46] The internet has therefore made little difference so far to the structure of journalism in the United States, even if it is a different medium of news dissemination.

Commercials

Candidates have relatively few opportunities to appear on television programmes, but they have many to air commercials within programmes. In 1998, for example, the fall campaign for California's governorship attracted news coverage amounting to 27 hours in total on television stations across the state. In the same period and about the same race, Californian stations featured 190 hours of commercials.[47] Commercials are an immensely significant forum for candidates to present their case to the electorate. In the absence of truly effective coverage of politics for a mass audience, they generally play an important role in disseminating information about candidates, especially among voters who do not follow politics closely.

At the presidential level, commercials are, however, a regionally unequal forum. Unsurprisingly, campaigns concentrate their media spending on important states where the outcome looks in doubt. In many parts of the United States, therefore, television viewers rarely see the candidates' commercials. In others, commercials become a constant part of the television diet. During 2000, the Gore and Bush campaigns targeted fewer than twenty states. For example, they ran thousands of advertisements in Philadelphia, in search of the precious Electoral College votes of Pennsylvania, but very few in New York City, which was safely Democratic.[48]

Particularly controversial are 'attack' advertisements. Rather than make out a case in favour of a candidate, these advertisements launch an attack on his or her opponent. They are controversial because their tone apparently feeds public cynicism with the political process; they do not spell out a positive vision for future policy-making but a negative characterization of an opponent, often in personal terms. Attack advertisements are by no means a recent phenomenon. The most famous example of all is a commercial run by Lyndon Johnson's presidential campaign of 1964. It tried to encourage fears that Barry Goldwater, Johnson's Republican opponent, was a 'trigger-happy' politician, unfit to run America's foreign policy. Known as 'the daisy ad', the commercial showed images of a girl counting the petals of a daisy; the picture then faded into the mushroom cloud of a nuclear explosion. In 2000, a pro-Bush group aired a revised and updated version of the same advertisement, criticizing Gore's proposals for foreign policy.[49] The reaction to the commercials, both in 1964 and in 2000, reveal one reason why politicians use them. Attack ads are more likely to gain press attention than positive commercials, thus providing a larger audience for the initial investment.

Still, historical antecedents do not diminish concerns about the impact of attack ads. In recent years, these concerns have gained some impetus from empirical work by political scientists. Stephen Ansolabehere and Shanto Iyengar argue that such commercials succeed in souring the tone of political discussion with destructive consequences. Their study of contests for the US Senate in 1992, for example, found a relationship between the atmosphere of a campaign, as played out in television advertisements, and the level of voter turnout. A positive campaign encouraged voters to participate in the election; it added a few percentage points to turnout. A negative campaign, by contrast, increased citizen dissatisfaction with politics and politicians; it pulled voter turnout down by a couple of points. Ansolabehere and Iyengar posit that some candidates are aware of this effect and that, if they calculate the move is favourable to their chances, they make a conscious decision to turn negative in order to turn voters away from the polls.[50]

The claims of Ansolabehere and Iyengar are not uncontroversial, and the scholarly debate remains open. Steven Finkel and John Geer placed three decades of presidential campaigning under similar scrutiny, and reported no similar relationship between the tone of a campaign and the level of voter turnout. They argue that the passion of an intensely fought contest – as represented by attack ads – might well lead to increased interest in politics and in issues, rather than the opposite.[51] Digging deeper into America's history, it becomes apparent that aggressive, low-level rhetoric has always been a feature of electoral politics. In the nineteenth century, for example, political candidates often engaged in insubstantial exchanges and even personal abuse. Television did not, therefore, create this kind of campaigning, but simply offered a more effective means for its dissemination.

Most observers agreed that the commercials of the presidential campaign in 2000 presented fewer grounds for concerns than those of other recent contests. The commercials of both candidates generally avoided any personal criticism of the opponent, although the Bush campaign sometimes ran advertisements encouraging the suspicion that Gore was prone to exaggerating his record. When the commercials engaged in attack, it concerned the issues. According to Gore ads, Bush designed policies to favour business at the expense of ordinary Americans, and he did not care about environmental damage. 'After seventeen years in the oil business, George W. Bush ran for governor,' said one, 'then passed laws to let big polluters regulate themselves.' According to Bush ads, Gore was ready to increase funding of wasteful programmes. He would waste the nation's budget surplus. 'Al Gore plans to spend it all and more,' one commercial alleged. 'Gore's big-government spending plan threatens American prosperity.' Such issue-oriented attacks still represented a minority of the television campaign, which concentrated instead on the candidates' claims about their own strengths. A study during the campaign suggested that less than a third of Gore's advertisements fell into this category and less than a fifth of Bush's. In 2000, therefore, network coverage of the candidates was more negative than the commercials.[52]

A particularly significant implication of the centrality of commercials, whether negative or positive, to electoral politics is financial. Their cost to candidates is enormous. Indeed, in 1998, political commercials were estimated to account for 10 per cent of all television advertising.[53] Those seeking major office spend almost two-thirds of their campaign budgets on this form of communication.[54] The reliance on advertising to reach the electorate therefore plays a significant role in driving the need for money in American politics.

Reform is difficult to achieve. The First Amendment, which provides constitutional protection for the freedom of speech, constrains any quest for reform-minded regulation. It would, for example, prevent the government from restricting the access of candidates to paid television time. Constitutional considerations do not, however, rule out all possible reform initiatives; they do not, therefore, explain their failure. Elected politicians have usually proved unwilling to change a system they have mastered. In 1998, for example, Clinton proposed that the broadcasting regulator, the Federal Communications Commission, should create new rules to provide for free or reduced-cost time for candidates. Congressional Republicans reacted with hostility to the proposal, and any momentum for reform retreated to the Gore Commission's voluntarism.[55]

In recent years some special concern has emerged about the growth of issue advocacy advertisements or 'issue ads'. The growth is spectacular; according to estimates, in 1996 the spending on this form of advertising was between $135 and $150 million, but in 2000 it rose to over

$500 million. Issue ads are distinguished from campaign commercials because they do not directly advocate the election of a candidate for office. They may, however, comment favourably or unfavourably about a candidate. Consequently, the distinction between 'issue ads' and 'advocacy ads' – as perceived by the viewer – might even be unnoticeable during a campaign. But the distinction as to the manner in which these commercials are funded is crucial. Money spent on issue ads in support of a candidate – whether by a party, union or lobbying organization – is free from any federal regulation of campaign expenditure and from any disclosure requirements.[56] A first step to regulation was reached in April 2001, when a campaign finance bill co-sponsored by John McCain (R-AZ) and Russell D. Feingold (D-WI) passed the Senate; it included a controversial provision to prevent outside groups from running a commercial referring to a federal candidate as an election approached.[57]

Conclusion

When they subject the coverage of the 2000 campaign to deeper scrutiny, scholars who write of media irresponsibility are unlikely to find reason to modify their arguments. Television coverage was not substantially different from before. It dwelt on strategy at the expense of issues, and it often adopted a sceptical stance towards the claims of candidates. Moreover, there was relatively little coverage of politics within mainstream news programming. It was necessary to hunt out detailed coverage, and most Americans did not.

The central problem that undermines the quality of political coverage is one very difficult to tackle; it is the commercial imperative that faces news organizations in an intensely competitive environment. Although the marketplace creates niches in which in-depth coverage can flourish, those niches are ignored by the mass audience. Media developments of recent years have subjected these organizations to still further competition, and it therefore becomes less rather than more likely for mass audience journalism to achieve greater substance.

NOTES

The author would like to thank Paul Martin and Rob Singh for their helpful comments about this essay.

1 Eric Schmitt, 'Counting the Vote: House Republicans', *New York Times*, 17 Nov. 2000, p. A32.

2 Peter Marks and Bill Carter, 'The 2000 Elections: The Network Predictions', *New York Times*, 9 Nov. 2000, p. B1.

3 Robert M. Entman, *Democracy without Citizens: Media and the Decay of American Politics* (New York: Oxford University Press, 1989), p. 17.

4 Bartholomew Sparrow, *Uncertain Guardians: The News Media as a Political Institution* (Baltimore: Johns Hopkins University Press, 1999), pp. 73–104.

5 See, notably, Thomas E. Patterson, *Out of Order* (1993; New York: Vintage, 1994).

6 Marion R. Just, Ann N. Cigler, Dean E. Alger, Timothy E. Cook, Montague Kern and Darrell M. West, *Crosstalk: Citizens, Candidates, and the Media in a Presidential Campaign* (Chicago: University of Chicago Press, 1996), pp. 155–7.

7 'The Tough Job of Communicating with Voters', Pew Research Center for the People and the Press, 5 Feb. 2000 (www.peoplepress.org/jan00rpt2.htm, accessed 17 Apr. 2001).

8 Howard Kurtz, 'Online News: The . Coming Thing', *Washington Post*, 12 June 2000, p. C1.

9 Stephen Hess in 'A Brookings Forum: How the Television Networks Covered the 2000 Presidential Campaign', Brookings Institution, 13 Nov. 2000 (www.brookings.edu/comm/transcripts/20001113.htm, accessed 22 Feb. 2001).

10 Andie Tucher, ' "You News" ', *Columbia Journalism Review* (May–June 1997) (www.cjr.org/year/97/3/you.asp, accessed 21 Mar. 2001).

11 Data compiled by the Center for Media and Public Affairs and the Brookings Institution, cited in Stephen Hess, 'Hess Report on Campaign Coverage in Nightly Network News: Week 9 Data', n.d. (www.brookings.edu/GS/Projects/HessReport/week10.htm, accessed 22 Feb. 2001).

12 Franklin D. Gilliam Jr, Shanto Iyengar, Adam Simon and Oliver Wright, 'Crime in Black and White: The Violent, Scary World of Local News', in Shanto Iyengar and Richard Reeves (eds), *Do the Media Govern? Politicians, Voters, and Reporters in America* (Thousand Oaks: Sage, 1997), pp. 289–92.

13 Jim Rutenberg, 'Chicago News Experiment is Calling it Quits', *New York Times*, 31 Oct. 2000, p. A18.

14 Martin Kaplan and Matthew L. Hale, 'Television News Coverage of the 1998 California Gubernatorial Election', working paper Institute of Government Studies, University of California, Berkeley, 2000, p. 5 (cain.berkeley.edu/IGSWorkingPapers/WP2000-6.pdf, accessed 25 Apr. 2001).

15 Shanto Iyengar, *Is Anyone Responsible? How Television Frames Political Issues* (Chicago: University of Chicago Press, 1991).

16   Mark J. Rozell, *In Contempt of Congress: Postwar Press Coverage on Capitol Hill* (Westport: Praeger, 1996).

17   Sparrow, *Uncertain Guardians*, pp. 153–61, 170–5.

18   Patterson, *Out of Order*, pp. 72–4.

19   Hess, 'Hess Report on Campaign Coverage'.

20   Howard Kurtz, 'On TV, Covering "The Issues" From A to Zzzzzz', *Washington Post*, 3 July 2000, p. C1.

21   Pippa Norris, *A Virtuous Circle: Political Communications in Post-industrial Societies* (New York: Cambridge University Press, 2000).

22   Lawrence R. Jacobs and Robert Y. Shapiro, *Politicians Don't Pander: Political Manipulation and the Loss of Democratic Responsiveness* (Chicago: University of Chicago Press, 2000).

23   Dick Morris, *Behind the Oval Office: Winning the Presidency in the Nineties* (New York: Random House, 1997), pp. 10–16, 83–8, 164–6.

24   Andrew Kohut, 'Low Marks for Poll, Media', *Columbia Journalism Review* (Jan.–Feb. 2001) (www.cjr.org/year/01/1/kohut.asp, accessed 10 Feb. 2001).

25   Michael Schudson, 'The Public Journalism Movement and its Problems', in Doris Graber, Denis McQuail and Pippa Norris (eds), *The Politics of News: The News of Politics* (Washington DC: CQ Press, 1998), pp. 132–49.

26   Martin Kaplan and Matthew Hale, 'Local TV Coverage of the 2000 General Election', Norman Lear Center Campaign Media Monitoring Project, Annenberg School for Communication, University of Southern California, Feb. 2001, pp. 1–3 (entertainment.usc.edu/publications/campaignnews.PDF, accessed 11 Apr. 2001).

27   Erika Falk and Sean Aday, 'Are Voluntary Standards Working? Candidate Discourse on Network Evening News Programs', Annenberg Public Policy Center of the University of Pennsylvania, 20 Dec. 2000 (www.appcpenn.org/Candidate_Discourse/2000-general-report-final.htm, accessed 22 Apr. 2001).

28   It should be noted that commercial considerations can sometimes generate as well as discourage bias. On occasion, the influence of advertisers has changed the news agenda of a network. And media corporations participate directly in the political arena to lobby in favour of their own interests. Sparrow, *Uncertain Guardians*, pp. 73–104.

29   Hess, 'Hess Report on Campaign Coverage'.

30   Howard Kurtz, 'Are the Media Tilting to Gore?', *Washington Post*, 25 Sept. 2000, p. A1.

31   Howard Kurtz, 'Will the "Slow" Candidate Win the Big Race?', *Washington Post*, 26 Oct. 2000, p. C1.

32   S. Robert Lichter and Richard E. Noyes, *Good Intentions Make Bad News: Why Americans Hate Campaign Journalism*, 2nd edn (Lanham: Rowman and Littlefield, 1996).

33   Cappella and Jamieson compared the attitudes of people exposed to critical coverage of an issue with those exposed to straightforward reports on the same subject. They found that the former group exhibited markedly more political cynicism. Joseph N. Cappella and Kathleen Hall Jamieson,

Spiral of Cynicism: The Press and the Public Good (New York: Oxford University Press, 1997), pp. 110–69.

34 Richard L. Berke, 'Republicans Open Convention, Emphasizing Unity', *New York Times*, 1 Aug. 2000, p. A1.

35 Bill Carter, 'Plunging Ratings Touch Off Debate on Why Public is Losing Interest', *New York Times*, 3 Aug. 2000, p. A27.

36 Thomas M. Holbrook, *Do Campaigns Matter?* (Thousand Oaks: Sage, 1996), pp. 98–124.

37 Richard L. Berke, 'Debates Put in Focus Images and Reality', *New York Times*, 19 Oct. 2000, p. A29.

38 Samuel L. Popkin, 'Voter Learning in the 1992 Presidential Campaign', in Iyengar and Reeves, *Do the Media Govern?*, pp. 173–8.

39 Dana Milbank, 'Tracking Laughs is No Joke in Election Year', *Washington Post*, 19 Oct. 2000, p. C1.

40 'Journalists Monopolize TV Election News', Center for Media and Public Affairs, 30 Oct. 2000 (www.cmpa.com/pressrel/electpr10.htm, accessed 22 Feb. 2001).

41 Howard Kurtz, *Hot Air: All Talk, All the Time* (1996; New York: Basic, 1997), pp. 228–95.

42 Richard Davis, *The Web of Politics: The Internet's Impact on the American Political System* (New York: Oxford University Press, 1999), p. 21.

43 Joel Schwartz, 'Who Says Surfers are Antisocial?', *New York Times*, 26 Oct. 2000, p. G10.

44 Pew Research Center for the People and the Press, 'Internet Election News Audience Seeks Convenience, Familiar Names', 3 Dec. 2000 (www.people-press.org/online00rpt.htm, accessed 18 Apr. 2001).

45 Davis, *Web of Politics*, pp. 149–67, quotation at p. 162.

46 Howard Kurtz, 'Online Media: Old News?', *Washington Post*, 21 Feb. 2001, p. C1.

47 'Ticker', *Brill's Content*, Apr. 1999, p. 128.

48 Peter Marks, 'Dearth of Ads Makes Race in Kansas a Snooze', *New York Times*, 27 Oct. 2000, p. A26.

49 Leslie Wayne, 'Infamous Political Commercial is Turned on Gore', *New York Times*, 27 Oct. 2000, p. A26.

50 Stephen Ansolabehere and Shanto Iyengar, *Going Negative: How Attack Ads Shrink and Polarize the Electorate* (New York: Free Press, 1995).

51 Steven E. Finkel and John G. Geer, 'A Spot Check: Doubt on the Demobilizing Effect of Attack Advertising', *American Journal of Political Science*, 42 (1998), pp. 573–95.

52 Peter Marks, 'Campaigns Set a Brisk, Focused TV Pace', *New York Times*, 17 Oct. 2000, p. A1.

53 Dan Morgan, 'A Made-for-TV Windfall', *Washington Post*, 2 May 2000, p. A1.

54 Just et al., *Crosstalk*, p. 63.

55 Charles Lewis, 'Media Money: How Corporate Spending Blocked Political Ad Reform and Other Stories of Influence', *Columbia Journalism Review*

(Sept.–Oct. 2000) (www.cjr.org/year/00/3/mediamoney.asp, accessed 11 Feb. 2001).

56   Kathleen Hall Jamieson, Lorie Slass and Erika Falk, with assistance from Natalia Gridina and Nicole Porter, 'Issue Advertising in the 1999–2000 Election Cycle,' Annenberg Public Policy Center of the University of Pennsylvania, Feb. 2000 (www.appcpenn.org/issueads/1999-2000issueadvocacy.pdf, accessed 4 Apr. 2001).

57   Alison Mitchell, 'Campaign Finance Reform Bill Passes in Senate, 59–41; House Foes Vow a Fight', *New York Times*, 3 Apr. 2001, p. A1.

5

The Rehnquist Court's Partial Revolution

Paul Martin

Introduction

The activities of the federal courts have long been controversial: the courts have, since *Marbury v. Madison*,[1] had powers of constitutional adjudication which render them, in some senses, politically supreme. When the courts have used those powers intensively and systematically, especially where they have used them to override the policy-making of institutions with a greater degree of democratic legitimacy, then the position of the federal courts themselves has become an issue of political controversy and dispute. When the Supreme Court set about overturning key elements of the New Deal in the 1930s, or when it significantly expanded the rights of criminal defendants thirty years later, the court itself became a significant national political issue. Above all, in the 2000 presidential election, the Court's decisive move to end recounting of disputed Florida ballots appeared likely to ensure considerable political notoriety.

Yet controversy does not necessarily surround the federal courts. In recent years, the Supreme Court has often been characterized by relative political quiescence. The Rehnquist Court has come to decide only around half as many cases each year as the Burger Court did, apparently with the direct intent of reducing its political visibility. Moreover, in many areas its decisions have engaged only partially in the sort of conservative judicial counterrevolution advocated by influential groups such as the Federalist Society.[2] While throughout the Clinton years the Supreme Court has retained a majority of Reagan–Bush appointees (O'Connor, Kennedy, Scalia, Souter, Thomas and, as Chief Justice, Rehnquist), that majority has not, for the most part, wiped out the liberal gains of the Warren and early Burger Court eras. Rather, it has grappled with particular elements of that liberal jurisprudence, sometimes with significant effect. Some of the key substantive liberal rulings of the postwar years have survived, in attenuated form at least. The authentically radical activism of the Rehnquist Court has been substantially confined to one particular area, that of federalism, and with the very considerable exception of *Bush v. Gore*,[3] this activism has attracted remarkably little public attention.

This chapter focuses on the ideology and output of the Rehnquist Court.[4] The argument made is that conservatives on and around the Court have not been 'extremists' frustrated by 'moderates'. Rather, on some major issues the conservative coalition on the Court has broken apart because of two quite separate, and often opposed, conceptions of 'conservatism' which come into conflict in certain types of case. Where, on the other hand, the two separate conceptions have run parallel to each other, the conservative majority has been entirely able to pursue a radical agenda with little trace of 'moderate' influence.

In ensuing sections, then, this chapter considers first the issue of how to think about the Court's behaviour, and second the history and expectations of the Rehnquist Court. Third, it assesses specific Rehnquist Court decisions in some detail. Finally, from these cases an attempt is made to draw some broad conclusions about the nature of the conservative majority on the Court, and to analyse and predict more recent and future developments in the same light.

Thinking about the Rehnquist Court

Decision-making

A major issue in the study of the Supreme Court in the 1990s has been the extent to which it is driven, in its decision-making behaviour, by each of a range of variables. In the process of deciding a case, the Justices make a range of quite distinct decisions,[5] including the decision to hear the case;[6] deciding which issues in the case need to be settled; voting on the merits in case conference after oral argument; assigning a majority opinion author; deciding whether to write an opinion, and if so deciding what to write in that opinion; deciding whether to join an opinion, and if so which opinion to join.

Essentially there are three contenders for an explanatory theory. *Attitudinalism* holds that relatively simple accounts of Justices' personal political preferences give accurate predictions of observed behaviour over time. Segal and Spaeth is the classic account of this behavioural analysis;[7] for much of the last two decades of the twentieth century the attitudinalist explanation was dominant. The account, however, has had two recent challengers. The first, the *strategic* account, holds that while preferences of the aforementioned sort are highly significant, relationships between the Court and other institutions, and relationships among the Justices, significantly moderate those initial preferences.[8] The second, an *institutionalist* account, revolves around the idea that both the institutional structure of the Court and its procedures, and the nature of law as itself an institution provide significant limits to the power of Justices simply to implement their own preferences in law.[9]

It is not the purpose of this essay to attempt to resolve the dispute among these three models of Court behaviour. Rather, we need simply note that all three accounts revolve around the idea that it is the legal policy preferences of Justices, at some suitable level of complexity, which provide the starting point for decision-making in cases. The decisional landscape of the Court is composed of the preferences of those on it; as personnel change, so does the outcome of cases.

The make-up of the Rehnquist Court

In many ways, the Rehnquist Court might be expected to be extremely conservative. Of the twelve Supreme Court appointments since the 1968 presidential election, only two have been made by a Democrat. Republican presidential candidates in and since that presidential election have been committed to, minimally, higher levels of restraint by the Court in its engagement with public policy, and, maximally, to sweeping changes in federal jurisprudence in pursuit of conservative political goals. Especially in the period since the election of Ronald Reagan, committed to the latter policy, Republican nominations to the Court have at least implicitly involved 'litmus tests' on issues such as abortion and the death penalty. Of the relatively liberal Court majority of seven Justices which decided *Roe v. Wade* (1973), for example, five have had replacements expected at the time of their appointment to hold substantially more conservative views on the issue,[10] while only one of the two dissenters was replaced by a Justice expected to hold more liberal views.[11]

Notably also, perhaps, the seven and a half years since the arrival on the Court of the last of President Clinton's nominees, Justice Breyer, represents the longest period without a change in Court membership since the eleven and a half years between the arrival of Gabriel Duvall in

November 1811 and the death of Brockholst Livingston in 1823.[12] The Rehnquist Court, then, has been an exceptionally stable court in terms of precisely the sort of individual preferences referred to in the preceding section.

Revolutionary Failure? The Rehnquist Court and 'Values'

For the New Right as a whole, a particular bugbear was a set of issues in which the Court had engaged in substantive liberal policy-making in the 1960s and 1970s. Most notoriously, this set included abortion, but was not limited to that: among others, it included some decisions about racial discrimination and most (or all) concerning gender discrimination; the rights of criminal defendants; the administration of the death penalty; and School Prayer. Clearly not all these issues mattered to the same extent to all political conservatives, but it is reasonable to see these issues as the core, perhaps the most controversial, of those that made (and continue to make) judicial politics an issue of central importance for the resurgent conservative movement. How far, then, has the Rehnquist Court 'delivered' on each of these 'value' issues? To assess this, let us consider two key areas: cases concerning abortion rights; and cases concerning the rights of criminal defendants.

Abortion

Rehnquist himself, as an Associate Justice, had been one of two dissenters when a privacy-derived abortion right was found;[13] he joined dissent again from the Burger Court's rejection of parental- and spousal-notification requirements;[14] he joined majorities permitting state and federal government not to fund the provision of abortion for the indigent;[15] and he had dissented from later Burger Court decisions invalidating stricter abortion regulations of various kinds, such as parental and spousal notification requirements and mandatory waiting periods.[16]

When first the Rehnquist Court considered abortion regulation in 1989,[17] the addition of three Reagan appointees to the Court appeared for a time to have ensured a major advance for conservatives: a majority including Rehnquist, White, Scalia, Kennedy and O'Connor appeared ready to so strictly limit *Roe* that states would be able to engage in almost any rational regulation of abortion, even if the effect of that regulation was to enforce such burdens on the provision and use of abortion rights that no abortions would in fact be provided.[18] A relic of this possibility remains a separate opinion in *Webster*, written by Justice Blackmun (author of the *Roe* judgment) which concludes that the prospects for abortion rights were not good: 'the signs are very evident and ominous, and a chill wind blows' (492 U.S. 490 at 560). Nonetheless, the Chief Justice was able to muster only a plurality behind an opinion radically restricting abortion rights, and *Webster* set no clear path for the future.

Thus, when the issue came before the Court again in 1992,[19] the replacement of two of the strongest supporters of the *Roe* decision, Justices Marshall and Brennan, by two Bush appointments, Justices Thomas and Souter, appeared to give even more reason to think that this core part of the Reagan–Bush judicial agenda would at last be achieved. However, the Court in *Casey* instead decided, by a bare majority, to restate the basic holding of *Roe* that there existed a privacy-based right to abortion, while permitting more intrusive regulation of that right by states than *Roe* had. Three Reagan–Bush appointees (Justices O'Connor, Kennedy and Souter) took the rare step of jointly writing the majority opinion arguing that *Roe* must be upheld on the basis of *stare decisis*.[20] Thus, even with the two original dissenters from *Roe*, and the addition of five Justices nominated by presidents for whom overturning *Roe* was a significant judicial priority, the Rehnquist Court simply refused to fulfil the wishes of conservatives. On the other hand, abortion rights supporters could hardly be triumphant. *Casey* was decided by a bare majority, as Blackmun's concurring opinion stated clearly: 'I fear for the darkness as four Justices anxiously await the single vote necessary to extinguish the light' (505 U.S. 833 at 923). Moreover *Casey* significantly increased the capacity of states to engage in regulation of abortion provision, upholding record-keeping, parental consent, 'informed consent', and twenty-four-hour waiting period requirements. Nevertheless, *Casey* was a stinging defeat for judicial conservatives, and their anger is well expressed in Scalia's infuriated dissent, which compares the decision to that in the *Dred Scott* case[21] which precipitated the Civil War.

Changing Court membership under Clinton, replacing a *Roe* opponent (Justice White) with a *Roe* supporter (Justice Ginsburg), appeared to solidify the decision in *Casey*, and the locus of conflict concerning abortion began to move away from the simple issue of abortion rights. In doing so it did not offer much greater comfort to conservatives. The Court unanimously held that abortion clinics could proceed with cases against anti-abortion protest groups under the RICO anti-racketeering law,[22] and in a series of cases moved to allow restrictions on the ability of anti-abortion groups to protest outside and around clinics;[23] and it has held that state attempts to ban so-called 'partial birth' abortions violate the 'undue burden' test set out by O'Connor in *Casey* and are therefore unconstitutional.[24] In summary, then, far from overturning the core holding of *Roe*, the Rehnquist Court has actively moved to protect the exercise of that right in important ways.

Defendants' rights

The record of the Rehnquist Court in cases concerning the rights of criminal defendants – in particular those rights introduced or extended under the Warren Court – is also mixed. It is true that in some areas of the law the Court has engaged in significant retrenchment; in other areas, Warren Court precedents regarded as controversial in their day have been resoundingly upheld. In yet other areas, the Court has tinkered but not overturned.

Again, Rehnquist's own work on the Court had left little doubt of his sympathy for law enforcement officials as against criminal defendants. Twice before he became Chief Justice he was the author of important opinions restricting the right to challenge police searches under the Fourth Amendment.[25] In some ways, the Rehnquist Court has pursued that agenda. It has not abandoned entirely the 'exclusionary rule' preventing the use in court of evidence obtained by searches in contravention of the Fourth Amendment.[26] But it has, for example, held that evidence should not be excluded where it results from an arrest that itself results from a clerical error by a state court official;[27] that the exclusionary rule does not apply to evidence used in parole hearings.[28] It has further held that even minor legal violations can constitutionally result in a warrant-less search or arrest,[29] and that such searches can be made on the basis of an anonymous tip sufficiently corroborated by minimal observations of behaviour, although not on the basis of an anonymous tip alone.[30]

However, although the Burger and Rehnquist Courts accepted the constitutionality of police road checkpoints performing essentially random searches against illegal aliens and drink driving,[31] the latter Court was unwilling to extend that protection to checkpoints engaged primarily in the interdiction of illegal drugs.[32] Moreover, the Court found that evidence from a programme of compulsory drug-testing of pregnant women in a state hospital was unconstitutionally obtained.[33] The Court also recently upheld the liberal landmark *Miranda* decision, requiring that a warning of a suspect's constitutional rights be given before statements made in interrogation could be used in evidence, with an opinion written by the Chief Justice himself.[34] As with the abortion cases, although the Rehnquist Court has somewhat narrowed the constitutional protections afforded criminal defendants by its more liberal predecessors, it has not done so uniformly, and it has not overruled most of the basic holdings on which those constitutional protections are based.

A True Revolution: Nine Key Federalism Decisions and One Red Herring

From the New Deal period onwards, the Supreme Court's decisions in cases concerning the constitutional balance of power between state and federal institutions are widely held to have favoured the latter. In interpreting the Commerce Clause, the Court favoured an expansive vision of interstate commerce as encompassing almost all forms of activity. For example, Title II of the Civil Rights Act of 1964, which desegregated public accommodations, was held to be constitutional as applied to a motel because its business depended in part on interstate travellers, and as applied to a restaurant because its business depended in the purchase of some items of food through interstate commerce.[35] While the Burger Court struck down an item of congressional legislation based on the Commerce Clause in 1976 in an opinion written by Rehnquist, it explicitly overruled that case less than ten years later.[36] While reading the Commerce Clause expansively, the post-New Deal Supreme Court also encouraged the growth of federal power by other means. It eroded earlier definitions of the Tenth Amendment as preserving state power;[37] it decided that the Fourteenth Amendment had applied some provisions of the Bill of Rights to the states as well as the federal government, a process known as incorporation;[38] throughout its federalism decisions, it allowed Congress to set limits on the extent to which the Eleventh Amendment protected the states from suit in federal courts.

In the years since 1995, a series of Supreme Court decisions has reversed much of this process in a series of cases, almost all of which have been decided by the same majority of five Justices (Rehnquist, O'Connor, Scalia, Kennedy and Thomas) against spirited dissents from the remainder. It is difficult to overstate the radicalism of these decisions: the Supreme Court's federalism decisions since the New Deal have been the basis for the construction of the modern American state, and the Rehnquist Court's decisions have the capacity not merely to amend the relationship between centre and periphery, but also, and thereby, radically to restructure the capacities of the United States polity. It is worth considering in some detail each step in the Rehnquist Court's development of a new jurisprudence of federalism.

United States v. Lopez[39] arose from the federal conviction of a Texas high school student under the Gun Free School Zones Act of 1990. The Act made it an offence to possess a firearm in a school zone; Congress had relied on the authority of the Commerce Clause to confer the capacity to regulate firearms which were both circulated by interstate commerce, and played a part, in schools, in the interstate commerce of illegal drugs. However, Rehnquist's majority opinion in *Lopez* found that the Act had gone far beyond Congress's regulatory powers. The majority held that the Commerce Clause should not be a 'general police power of the sort retained by the states': mere possession of a weapon did not 'arise out of . . . a commercial transaction, which viewed in the aggregate, substantially affects interstate commerce'. The Gun Free School Zones Act was, therefore, an unconstitutional extension of congressional powers beyond those enumerated in the Constitution.

While *Lopez* was a significant demonstration of the attachment of the majority to doctrines of state sovereignty, a single pro-state decision might, like *NLC v. Usery*, have been sidelined over time. But the Court did not stop at *Lopez*. Its next important federalism decision, *Seminole Tribe v. Florida*,[40] continued down a similar path. The Indian Gaming Regulatory Act of 1988 was a congressional attempt to engage in some regulation of Native American casino operation across the states. States were required to negotiate in good faith with tribes towards the production of a Tribal–State compact concerning gambling, and tribes were given the power to initiate federal lawsuits if this process broke down. When Governor Lawton Chiles of Florida refused to negotiate with the Seminole Tribe, they employed this power. The majority opinion, again written by Rehnquist, considerably extended the Eleventh Amendment protection of states from suit in Federal Court. The Eleventh Amendment was held to imply a doctrine of the sovereign immunity of states such that Congress simply could not make 'the state of Florida capable of being sued in Federal Court' except in enforcement of the Fourteenth Amendment. The relevant part of the Indian Gaming Regulatory Act was, therefore, unconstitutional, and the Seminole Tribe's suit was dismissed. In dissent, Justice Stevens called the decision a 'shocking . . . affront to a co-equal branch of our Government', while Justice Souter took the (now highly unusual) step of reading out in full, when the decision was announced, a long, detailed dissent arguing with some elegance that the doctrine of sovereign immunity was historically unlikely to have been the original intent of the framers.

The third case in three terms in which the Rehnquist Court used its developing commerce clause, Eleventh Amendment and Fourteenth Amendment jurisprudence to strike down a significant piece of congressional legislation over the states was *City of Boerne v. Flores*.[41] Congress had passed the Religious Freedom Restoration Act in 1993 in response to a 1990 Supreme Court decision holding that the criminalization of peyote use by a state did not infringe the free exercise of religion where (as with the Native American church) the ingestion of peyote was undertaken with a sacramental purpose.[42] The RFRA sought to reinstate the test used by the Supreme Court prior to 1990, under which the free exercise of religion was infringed where religious practice was substantially burdened by legislation which was not the least restrictive means of fulfilling a compelling state interest,[43] and to apply that test to federal, state and local law of all kinds. Congress sought to achieve this aim under the enforcement clause of the Fourteenth Amendment. The Catholic Archbishop of San Antonio brought a case in Federal District Court arguing that the City of Boerne's historic landmark regulations, which had resulted in denial of a building permit to expand a historic church building, violated the RFRA.

The majority opinion, written by Justice Kennedy, found that the RFRA was not in pursuit of the enforcement of the right to free exercise of religion: instead it had attempted, in restating the *Sherbert* principles, to redefine that right itself. Moreover, Kennedy argued, Congress had simply failed to provide any factual account of current religious discrimination, of the sort that had been provided with the passage of the Voting Rights Act of 1965, sufficient to make its actions narrowly tailored to a 'remedial or preventative' enforcement. Instead, the RFRA engaged in 'intrusion at every level of government, displacing laws and prohibiting official actions of almost every description and regardless of subject matter'. The RFRA was therefore held unconstitutional, and congressional power to enforce Fourteenth Amendment-derived rights was significantly limited.

The announcement of decisions in three cases on the same day provided the next significant step for the new concept of federalism.

Alden v. Maine[44] resulted from an attempt by a group of probation officers to sue their employer, the State of Maine, under the federal Fair Labor Standards Act of 1938, for violating overtime provisions set out in that act. When the case was dismissed in Federal District Court because of the Supreme Court's decision in *Seminole Tribe*, the probation officers attempted to use other provisions of the FLSA which provided them with a right to sue their employer in state court. The Maine Supreme Judicial Court held that the sovereign immunity doctrine advanced in *Seminole Tribe* must extend also to the ability of Congress to make states capable of being sued in their own courts. Kennedy's majority opinion upheld the Maine decision: 'The powers delegated to Congress under Article I of the United States Constitution do not include the power to subject non-consenting states to private suits for damages in state courts.' The relevant parts of the FLSA were found to be an unconstitutional infringement on sovereign immunity. Thus, Congress could not require states to be sued by their citizens in Federal Court (under *Seminole Tribe*); but this requirement could not be evaded by holding states accountable in state courts under the same federal laws used by citizens to sue states in Federal Court before *Seminole Tribe*.

The other two cases decided the same day were closely related to each other: *Florida Prepaid Postsecondary Education Expense Board v. College Savings Bank* and *College Savings Bank v. Florida Prepaid Postsecondary Education Expense Bd.*[45] Both cases arose out of the intellectual property owned by a New Jersey chartered bank, the College Savings Bank, in the form of patents and trademarks concerning its financing methods. An entity created by the State of Florida, the Florida Prepaid Postsecondary Education Expense Board, used a similar financing method to the College Savings Bank, and meanwhile used the trademarks of College Savings Bank in its advertising literature.

In the first case, College Savings Bank relied on Congress's 1992 amendments to the patent laws (the Patent Remedy Act) which expressly abrogated (removed) the states' sovereign immunity in patent infringement suits. The bank therefore sued the Florida state entity, the Prepaid Postsecondary Education Expense Board, for patent infringement. A majority opinion by Rehnquist held that under *Seminole Tribe* and *City of Boerne*, Congress could only abrogate sovereign immunities as a remedial matter where a widespread pattern of transgression of the Fourteenth Amendment had been identified. No such pattern had been shown, and the Patent Remedy Act was therefore unconstitutional inasmuch as it abrogated the sovereign immunity of the state government.

The Trademark Remedy Clarification Act, similarly, gave companies and citizens the right to sue state entities for false and misleading advertising using their trademarks. The bank had therefore also sued the board under the TRCA, and the majority's reasoning was applied to this case in an aggressive opinion by Justice Scalia (who accused the dissenters in the case of having previously had their criticisms 'set forth in other opinions in a degree of repetitive detail that has despoiled our northern woods'). Predictably, the Court held that State of Florida had neither voluntarily given up state sovereign immunity, nor was the abrogation of state sovereign immunity a valid enforcement of the Fourteenth Amendment; and therefore the TRCA involved an unconstitutional infringement on the sovereign immunity of the state. In doing so the Court expressly overruled the older precedent of *Parden v. Terminal Railway Co.*,[46] in which it had been held that a state entity engaged in interstate commerce had engaged in a 'constructive waiver' of its Eleventh Amendment immunities.

Having, in 1999, thus established a radically new perspective on the extent of Eleventh Amendment immunity, through a series of cases, the Rehnquist Court continued to apply and develop that perspective. In *Kimel v. Florida Board of Regents*,[47] Kimel was one of a number of state employees in universities and prisons who claimed that their employer had discriminated against them on the basis of age in various ways. A large number of such cases was consolidated to provide a test of the question of whether the Age Discrimination in Employment Act of 1967, as subsequently amended, could abrogate state sovereign immunity under the enforcement clause of the Fourteenth Amendment. Justice O'Connor's majority opinion found that ADEA was 'disproportionate to any unconstitutional conduct that could conceivably be targeted by the Act'; moreover, in passing the Act, O'Connor held that Congress had not produced evidence to show that states as employers were engaging in unconstitutional age discrimination. On the basis of the precedents set in *Seminole Tribe* and *City of Boerne*, O'Connor held that 'the ADEA's purported abrogation of the States' sovereign immunity is accordingly invalid.'

The case of *United States v. Morrison*[48] concerned (as had *Lopez*) congressional power to regulate individual rather than state conduct. The federal Violence Against Women Act provided a federal civil remedy for the victims of gender-motivated violence, including rape. A case was brought under the Act against Morrison and Crawford by a fellow student whom they had raped, but was dismissed in Federal District Court on the grounds that Congress lacked constitutional authority to create such a civil remedy. When appealed to the Supreme Court, Rehnquist's majority opinion was in agreement. Although (unlike in *Lopez*) Congress had, in enacting VAWA, collected considerable evidence to show that gender-motivated violence was widespread, that it had considerable effects on at least some of its victims, and that these effects had economic consequences relevant to interstate commerce. Rehnquist's opinion argued that this data was irrelevant: he extended the logic of *Lopez* to reject the claim that Congress might 'regulate noneconomic, violent criminal conduct based solely on that conduct's aggregate effect on interstate commerce'. Thus, 'gender-motivated crimes of violence are not, in any sense of the phrase, economic activity.' Rehnquist also found an alternative rationale for the relevant portions of VAWA, also invoked by Congress: the claim that it was needed to enforce the Fourteenth Amendment where widespread bias existed in state justice systems against the victims of gender-motivated violence. Again, congressional hearings had produced a considerable volume of evidence in support of the empirical claim. Relying on the *Civil Rights Cases* and *United States v. Harris*,[49] Rehnquist argued that the Fourteenth Amendment was simply inapplicable to action by private individuals not acting under colour of state law. Thus VAWA could not be constitutionally used against Morrison and Crawford under the Fourteenth Amendment. Finding neither Commerce Clause nor Fourteenth Amendment grounds for sustaining the relevant parts of VAWA, Rehnquist held that Congress had exceeded its powers in establishing a federal civil remedy.

In *University of Alabama v. Garrett*,[50] the Court returned to some of the issues raised in *Kimel*. The question was whether the abrogation of states' Eleventh Amendment immunities in the Americans with Disabilities Act of 1990, in allowing state employees to sue in federal court, was based on appropriate constitutional authority. Rehnquist's majority opinion held that it was not. He applied what he called 'now familiar principles' to decide that the Fourteenth Amendment required only a minimal rational-basis test of any discriminatory action against the disabled by the state: the states 'could quite hard headedly – and perhaps hardheartedly – hold to job-qualification requirements which do not make allowance for the disabled'. Although Congress had made legislative findings showing considerable levels of discrimination against the disabled, it had not shown, Rehnquist went on, that there was a pattern of irrational discrimination. Thus congressional action to enforce the Fourteenth Amendment had not been shown to be necessary, and the relevant parts of the ADA were unconstitutional.

A further significant case with a federal component deserves some mention here, although in significant ways it does not quite belong with the cases examined above. In *Bush v. Gore*,[51] the same five-Justice majority as in all the above cases bar *City of Boerne* effectively ceased recounts in Florida in the disputed presidential election of 2000. The intellectual plausibility of that opinion is well examined elsewhere.[52] What is relevant here is that the majority found in the Fourteenth Amendment a new right to equality of recount methods, with no reasoning to link that right to the particulars of, for example, presidential elections. In essence they then overruled the Florida Supreme Court on a matter of Florida law, apparently thereby expanding federal control over matters of state authority.

Evaluating the Rehnquist Court

In summary, what has the Rehnquist Court done in federalism terms, and why does its activity in federalism issues seem so much less restrained than its engagement with other, politically controversial, topics such as abortion and the rights of criminal defendants?

To answer the first question, the Court has brought about an abrupt change in the character of relations between the federal government and the states, or more specifically the US Congress and the states. In fact it is the issue of specifically congressional authority which may explain why the majority in *Bush v. Gore* was willing to engage in the regulation of what had been regarded as a state prerogative: this Court does not believe that its own authority over the states needs cutting back, although the specific partisan circumstances of *Bush v. Gore* make it difficult to believe that a line of Court action enforcing the right to equal recount methods will descend from the case.

But the Rehnquist Court does clearly believe that the authority of Congress over the states needs to be cut back quite significantly. The extent of decisions over a period still less than six years is remarkable: nine major pieces of congressional legislation found to be in part or in whole unconstitutional, either because they infringe on the proper policy-making domain of the states (*Lopez*, *Morrison*), or because they run aground on the increasingly monolithic doctrine of sovereign immunity (*Seminole Tribe*, *City of Boerne*, the College Savings Bank cases, *Alden*, *Kimel* and *Garrett*). Although there are therefore two different kinds of case involved, there is a great deal in common in the majority's reasoning across all cases. Firstly, of the nine cases all were decided by a bare majority of five votes to four, and all bar one by the *same* bare majority of five votes to four. Secondly, the cases emphasize the specific and limited enumeration of federal powers in the Constitution. Thirdly, the cases apply expansive readings to parts of the Constitution, like the Eleventh Amendment, which provide grounds for limiting the powers of the federal government. Fourthly, while the cases admit that the Commerce Clause and Fourteenth Amendment provide grounds for congressional action, they set strict factual standards for the operation of both. Fifthly, the cases show an increasing willingness to second-guess the factual findings of Congress concerning legislation it wishes to enact: while *Lopez* and *City of Boerne* emphasize the lack of supporting evidence for the legislative claims, by *Morrison* and *Garrett* the Court engages in criticism of the kind of evidence Congress had found in hearings. As Breyer wrote in dissent in *Garrett*, the Court had reviewed 'the congressional record as if it were an administrative agency record' rather than the findings of the Court's co-equal branch of government: in his view, 'Congress reasonably could have concluded that the remedy . . . constitutes an "appropriate" way to enforce this basic equal protection requirement. And that is all the Constitution requires.' Of course, it remains unclear how far the Court will take its federalism jurisprudence. Notably, although many of these decisions set rules which appear to threaten the constitutionality of elements of the Civil Rights Act of 1964 and the Voting Rights Act of 1965, as amended, the Court majority has constantly been careful to distinguish legislative behaviour in these cases from the supposedly diligent work of the Congress in 1964 and 1965. As Rehnquist put it in *Garrett*, 'The ADA's constitutional shortcomings are apparent when the Act is compared to Congress' efforts in the Voting Rights Act of 1965 to respond to a serious pattern of constitutional violations.' Possibly the Court's ultimate intention is to draw the boundaries of acceptable congressional action specifically at those cases; it would almost certainly take further personnel change on the Court to reveal whether any members of the majority wish to go further.

The second question, of explaining apparent 'moderation' in some fields of decision-making and 'extremism' in others, is clearly more difficult; a comprehensively satisfactory answer would require access to the papers of the current Justices, something unlikely to be forthcoming for many years. What can be said, though, is that the Rehnquist Court's more mixed decisions on the issues of abortion and criminal defendants' rights represent in part a greater variety of decision coalitions. Some Justices – Rehnquist himself, much of the time – are consistently conservative in almost all of their opinions and joinders. But where the decision coalition is different from that seen in the federalism cases, the outcome is often more moderate. In *Casey*, for example, two of the Justices from the federalism majority joined Justices from the federalism minority. Indeed it is those two Justices – O'Connor and Kennedy – whose commitment to the federalism decisions appears to be absolutely steady in ways in which their commitment to other issues cared about by many conservatives is not.

It makes little sense to claim that O'Connor and Kennedy are simple 'moderate' conservatives, when they appear to be just as wholehearted in pursuit of a radical, programmatic change in the structure of American governance as are Rehnquist, Scalia and Thomas. Nor does it help here to think of O'Connor and Kennedy as simply *stare decisis* conservatives compared to the latter group's programmatic conservatism: the Court's recent federalism decisions are far more programmatically than precedentially motivated. Rather, I think, we need to think about two different types of conservative aim. One model, that followed by Rehnquist, Scalia and Thomas, appears to mandate both radical institutional change and the achievement of significant conservative victories on 'values' issues such as abortion. It may even be that, for these Justices, radical institutional change is simply one further part of that set of conservative victories, although Rehnquist's personal belief in states' rights goes at least as far back as the controversial memorandum he wrote, as a law clerk, for Justice Jackson in the *Brown* case, arguing for the retention of *Plessy*'s separate-but-equal criterion.[53] But O'Connor and Kennedy, although clearly not liberals on issues such as abortion and defendants' rights, appear to have been from time to time uneasy with the idea that the Court should uproot settled social expectations, even where those expectations result from prior liberal judicial decisions. This unease seems to be combined with a strong view that it is not, either, for Congress to uproot the settled policies and expectations of the states without exceptionally good reason. This combination of beliefs is inaccurately described as 'moderation': it makes more sense to say that O'Connor and Kennedy, swing votes much of the time on this Court, represent a conservatism of a structural more than substantive sort.

NOTES

The author would like to thank Marc Stears for his thoughtful responses to an early draft of this paper.

1   5 U.S. 137 (1803).
2   See www.fed-soc.org/ for that group's comprehensively conservative/ libertarian approach to the role of law and judges in the United States.
3   121 S. Ct. 525 (2000).
4   To do so is not to overestimate the importance of the Supreme Court at the expense of state and lower federal courts. Indeed each of the latter has its own distinctive questions, and its own explanatory literature. Useful overviews of the entirety of American courts systems are provided by John Boatner Gates and Charles A. Johnson, *The American Courts: A Critical Assessment* (Washington DC: Congressional Quarterly, 1991); Lawrence S. Baum, *American Courts: Process and Policy*, 2nd edn (Boston: Houghton-Mifflin, 1990): Robert A. Carp and Ronald Stidham, *Judicial Process in America*, 4th edn (Washington DC: CQ Press, 1998).
5   See for example the separate examination of such issues in Jeffrey A. Segal and Harold J. Spaeth, *The Supreme Court and the Attitudinal Model* (Cambridge: Cambridge University Press, 1993).
6   H. W. Perry, *Deciding to Decide: Agenda Setting in the United States Supreme Court* (Cambridge: Harvard University Press, 1991).

7   Segal and Spaeth, *The Supreme Court*.
8   Lee Epstein and Jack Knight, *The Choices Justices Make* (Washington DC: CQ Press, 1998). See also Walter F. Murphy, *Elements of Judicial Strategy* (Chicago: University of Chicago Press, 1964).
9   Cornell Clayton and Howard Gillman, *Supreme Court Decision-Making: New Institutionalist Approaches* (Chicago: University of Chicago Press, 1999); Howard Gillman and Cornell Clayton, *The Supreme Court in American Politics: New Institutionalist Interpretations* (Lawrence: University Press of Kansas, 1999).
10 Burger's vote effectively replaced by Scalia's; Brennan replaced by Souter; Stewart by O'Connor; Marshall by Thomas; Powell by Kennedy. Conversely, Blackmun and Douglas were replaced by Breyer and Stevens, both at least equally sympathetic to *Roe*.
11 White replaced by Ginsburg. Rehnquist, of course, remains on the Court.
12 Interestingly, it was during these years that the Marshall Court was most critically engaged in reshaping the structure of governance in the United States.
13 *Roe v. Wade*, 410 U.S. 113 (1973).
14 *Planned Parenthood of Missouri v. Danforth*, 428 U.S. 52 (1973).
15 *Maher v. Roe*, 432 U.S. 464 (1977); *Harris v. McRae*, 448 U.S. 297 (1980).
16 *Akron v. Akron Center for Reproductive Health*, 462 U.S. 416 (1983); *Thornburgh v. American College of Obstetricians and Gynecologists*, 476 U.S. 747 (1986).
17 *Webster v. Reproductive Health Services*, 492 U.S. 490 (1989).
18 Edward Lazarus, *Closed Chambers: The Rise, Fall and Future of the Modern Supreme Court* (Harmondsworth: Penguin, 1999), pp. 373–424.
19 *Planned Parenthood of Southeastern Pennsylvania v. Casey*, 505 U.S. 833 (1992).
20 That is, the upholding of prior precedent, even where the precedent is suboptimal on other grounds.
21 *Scott v. Sandford*, 60 U.S. 393 (1857).
22 RICO refers to the Racketeer Influenced and Corrupt Organizations section of the 1970 Organized Crime Control Act, 18 USC §§ 1961–8. The case was *National Organization for Women v. Scheidler*, 510 U.S. 249 (1994).
23 *Madsen v. Women's Health Center*, 512 U.S. 753 (1994); *Schenk v. Pro-Choice Network of Western New York*, 519 U.S. 357 (1997); *Hill v. Colorado*, 120 S. Ct. 2480 (2000).
24 *Stenberg v. Carhart*, 120 S. Ct. 2597 (2000).
25 *Rakas v. Illinois*, 439 U.S. 128 (1970); *Rawlings v. Kentucky*, 448 U.S. 98 (1980).
26 *Boyd v. United States*, 116 U.S. 616 (1886); *Weeks v. United States*, 232 U.S. 383 (1914); *Mapp v. Ohio*, 367 U.S. 643 (1961).
27 *Arizona v. Evans*, 514 U.S. 1 (1995).
28 *Pennsylvania Board of Probation and Parole v. Scott*, 524 U.S. 357 (1998).
29 *Whren v. United States*, 517 U.S. 806 (1996); *Atwater v. City of Lago Vista*, 120 S. Ct. 2715 (2001).

30   *Alabama v. White*, 496 U.S. 325 (1990); *Florida v. J.L.*, 120 S. Ct. 1315 (2000).
31   *United States v. Martinez-Fuerte*, 428 U.S. 543 (1976); *Michigan Dept. of State Police v. Sitz*, 496 U.S. 444 (1990).
32   *City of Indianapolis v. Edmond*, 121 S. Ct. 447 (2000).
33   *Ferguson v. City of Charleston*, 120 S. Ct. 1239 (2000).
34   *Miranda v. Arizona*, 384 U.S. 436 (1966); *Dickerson v. United States*, 120 S. Ct. 2326 (2000).
35   *Heart of Atlanta Motel v. United States*, 379 U.S. 241 (1964); *Katzenbach v. McClung*, 379 U.S. 294 (1964).
36   *National League of Cities v. Usery*, 426 U.S. 833 (1976); *Garcia v. San Antonio Metropolitan Transit Authority*, 469 U.S. 528 (1985).
37   *Darby v. United States*, 312 U.S. 100 (1941).
38   *Palko v. Connecticut*, 302 U.S. 319 (1937).
39   514 U.S. 549 (1995).
40   517 U.S. 44 (1996).
41   521 U.S. 507 (1997). Unusually in this set of cases, Justice Stevens joined the majority and Justice O'Connor dissented, although the opinion coalitions were otherwise identical to those in the previously mentioned federalism cases. In the same term, in *Printz v. United States*, 521 U.S. 98 (1997), the Court held that aspects of the federal Brady Handgun Violence Prevention Act requiring local law enforcement officers to conduct background checks on firearms purchasers were unconstitutional. It did so by the usual federalism majority, but the reasoning adopted in this case rested on Tenth Amendment grounds, with a concurrence by Thomas suggesting an alternative reasoning on Second Amendment grounds. Neither reasoning has been significantly developed by the Court since *Printz*, and the prospects for development of Tenth and Second Amendment jurisprudence by the conservatives on the Court remain unclear.
42   *Employment Division of Oregon v. Smith*, 494 U.S. 872 (1990).
43   *Sherbert v. Vermer*, 374 U.S. 398 (1963).
44   527 U.S. 706 (1999).
45   527 U.S. 627 (1999); 527 U.S. 666 (1999).
46   377 U.S. 184 (1964).
47   120 S. Ct. 631 (2000).
48   120 S. Ct. 1740 (2000).
49   109 U.S. 3 (1883); 106 U.S. 629 (1883).
50   Not yet reported: the case was No. 99–1240 (2001).
51   121 S. Ct. 525 (2000).
52   See: Ronald Dworkin, 'A Badly Flawed Election', *New York Review of Books*, 11 Jan. 2001; Ronald Dworkin and Charles Fried, 'A Badly Flawed Election: An Exchange', *New York Review of Books*, 22 Feb. 2001; Linda Greenhouse, 'Bush Prevails', *New York Times*, 13 Dec. 2000, p. A1.
53   *Brown v. Board of Education*, 347 U.S. 483 (1954); *Plessy v. Ferguson*, 163 U.S. 537 (1896).

6

The Presidency and Congress: A Trifocal Approach

Nigel Bowles

Introduction

This chapter discusses a categorization of forces which shape the political opportunities and constraints in the political relationship between the presidency and Congress. That relationship is the pivot on which federal politics and government turn. Being pivotal, the relationship attracts much interest – from federal politicians and bureaucrats, from foreign governments, and from scholars. The subject occupied (and at times preoccupied) the Constitution's framers at Philadelphia; it has often dominated the thinking of influential Washington politicians, anxious to advance their interests against their political opponents; and it has formed the subject of much scholarly writing by political scientists and constitutional lawyers. Among scholars just as among the public, interest in the subject has risen as crises in relations between presidency and Congress have erupted – as they did during the Korean and Vietnam wars, and during the impeachment hearings and trial of President Clinton – and it has fallen as crises have abated.

In this essay, I indicate the three broad approaches which scholars have hitherto taken to the subject before sketching out a different way of thinking about relations between the presidency and Congress. I then show how that different approach can be used to examine two cases of those relations during Clinton's administration: the creation of the World Trade Organization (WTO) as a successor to the General Agreement on Tariffs and Trade (GATT) in 1994, and the granting of Normal Trading Relation (NTR) status to China in 2000. The two cases are chosen because the President's own policy position on them was clear and stable.

Few other cases in Clinton's presidency meet the criteria of clarity and stability. Bill Clinton's presidential politics were mostly a calculated study of haze and ambiguity: for example, Clinton embraced the cause of welfare reform, but acquiesced in the Republican Congress's abandonment of welfare; he advanced health care reform, but abandoned it and adopted deficit reduction as his defining policy stance.[1]

He was, however, consistent in paying a close, continuing and detailed attention to opinion polls – commissioning, receiving and examining a poll on average once per week in his second term. There is no precedent in modern presidential politics for a president stitching polling so finely into the politics of his decision-making. While polling data did not necessarily determine his policy choices, they powerfully informed them and always shaped their presentation. He devoted time each week with senior staff to studying the results and reflecting upon their implications. The President supplemented that professional attention to public opinion with exquisite political sensitivities, as Dick Morris, one of his early polling advisers, told the *Washington Post*:

> In a room he will instinctively, as if by canine sense of smell, find anyone who shows reserve toward him, and he will work full time on winning his approval and affection. America is the ultimate room for Clinton. For him a poll helps him sense who doesn't like him and why they don't. In the reflected numbers he sees his shortcomings and his potential, his successes and failures.[2]

Even by comparison with other presidents and with the most exceptional congressional politicians, Clinton's political instincts and abilities as President were extraordinary. They served him well in doing what he did best: turning political adversity to his advantage.

The Existing Approaches

Scholars writing on political relations between the presidency and Congress have adopted three broad approaches to the subject.

The first approach is of constitutional law, a parent discipline to political science in a country where most questions of politics and policy come before the courts for clarification or settlement. Constitutional doctrine and discourse frame American politics and political life, especially with respect to the charged subject of relations between presidency and Congress. That being so, the approach of constitutional scholars such as

Louis Fisher and Edward Corwin to the subject provides a necessary point of reference for others approaching the subject differently.[3] In other words, even for those writers for whom it is not the primary frame of reference, constitutional law is foundational. It is concerned with the rules and understandings of the boundaries and interactions between the two branches; with the vast growth of the federal government's regulatory roles since the late nineteenth century, and with their positive and normative implications. The approach is neither settled nor dull, but lively and important: what presidents may and may not do, where the boundaries of congressional and presidential powers might be thought to lie, and what courts may and may not do in relation to the two elected branches are questions to which constitutional scholars have made decisively important contributions.

Constitutional law is for the United States partly a set of foundational assumptions about values and authority. It is also an arena within which American judges, politicians and citizens reconsider and develop the complex relationship between their constitutional language and their values. That general claim applies to the constitutional law of relations between presidency and Congress where boundaries have never been settled and resist simple drawing. Yet an approach to the subject focusing purely upon constitutional law risks leaving unexamined the texture of politics – of ambition and calculation about opportunities for power and constraints upon achieving it.

The second approach is that of presidential leadership of Congress. Some who have contributed to the field have done so in celebration of the presidency's possibilities (at least when the White House was occupied by politicians of whom they approved). The approach is dominated by historians, but has also attracted some political scientists. Among the most influential works are James MacGregor Burns's studies of Franklin Roosevelt's presidency;[4] Fred Greenstein's account of Eisenhower's administration;[5] and Lou Cannon's study of Reagan.[6] Others have viewed such leadership more sceptically, as Arthur Schlesinger did in *The Imperial Presidency*, which he wrote in anguished response to what he thought was the abuse of presidential power in foreign affairs under Lyndon Johnson and Richard Nixon.[7]

The third approach is that of the separationist school, whose members include David Mayhew, Charles Jones and Richard Neustadt.[8] These scholars regard presidential leadership as one aspect of the broader context of political relations between the presidency and Congress: they argue that the American federal system is not presidential but separated. Jones is explicit on the point: 'The President is not the Presidency. The

Presidency is not the government. Ours is not a Presidential system.'[9] To that extent, these scholars regard the extraordinary legislative productivity of the first three years in office of Franklin Roosevelt and Lyndon Johnson, and the first year in office of Ronald Reagan, as misleading indications of how American government works: in a system of separated powers, these passages of presidential–congressional history are wholly exceptional political events. Mayhew shows that presidency and Congress produce as much legislation (and as much important legislation) when each branch has a different partisan majority as when the two branches are in the hands of parties with the same label. And Neustadt, contrary to what is commonly supposed, actually argued that as a political institution, the presidency is not strong but weak. Indeed, Neustadt thought that point central to his argument, the 'underlying theme of *Presidential Power*'.[10] President Clinton's political struggles with a Congress controlled by his partisan opponents from 1995 to 2001, and President Bush's difficulties with an evenly divided Senate thereafter, comprise familiar contours of modern federal politics. Those politics can be characterized as separated because of the rarity with which presidential mandates may plausibly be claimed; the scattering both of authority and power throughout the federal system; the buttressed power of minorities in Congress and elsewhere to resist majorities; and the logic of the system as pointing to negotiation, compromise and bargained agreement between politicians elected at different times from constituencies of different sizes to formally separate institutions.

Any perspective upon the presidency and Congress which neglected the implications of formal separation for presidents seeking to translate campaign promises into law would certainly be misleading. Yet a separationist perspective which took insufficient account of the presidency's unmatched and unmatchable potential to frame (and reframe) policy questions, to form agendas, to identify a rank ordering of national priorities and to command the attention of a national audience would be incomplete.

I now offer an alternative trifocal categorization of forces which shape the political opportunities and constraints in the political relationship between the presidency and Congress. The first category is constitutional authority; the second, parties, electoral cycles and coalitional forces; and the third, political power. It cannot possibly displace any of the three traditional frameworks, but it does afford a different approach which highlights aspects of the subject that otherwise risk being missed.

Authority

The first category comprises those forces of authority which derive from the Constitution and which in turn underpin political opportunities and constraints. Such constitutional forces are stable and predictable (although some presidents with no prior experience of federal government and politics find themselves frustrated by what they belatedly discover to be the severity of the constitutional constraints upon the presidency). The most important of these forces are the presidency's and Congress's bases of constitutional authority as laid down in Articles I and II.

Article I of the Constitution grants Congress extensive formal authority. Yet Congress is not supreme. Supremacy belongs to the Constitution. Limits on Congress's authority are, according at least to Amendments 1–10, 13, 14, and 15, tight. Congress may invade neither those rights which the Constitution specifies nor others which, over the course of 200 years of constitutional debate and development, it has been held to imply. While some federal constitutional law grants certain (and, as it has turned out, heavily expandable) authority to Congress, other provisions limit that authority – not least by protecting the rights of minorities. Since all Americans are members of at least one minority group, that characteristic of the US Constitution has powerful substantive and symbolic importance.

Article II establishes and limits *presidential* authority. The Constitution grants to a president certain exclusive areas of authority through his powers of legislative recommendation and his qualified veto; in the authority of chief executive by which he exercises limited power to direct the departments and agencies of government where Congress does not specify otherwise; by his authority of Commander in Chief of the Armed Forces; by his implied power of chief diplomat; and by his authority to pardon which, with the single exception of cases of impeachment, is unqualified. However, Articles I and II read together divide authority over legislation, the implementation of policy, and its oversight. These two Articles give no charter for the exercise of unbridled presidential power.

Viewed from where the President sits and works in the Oval Office, the bicameralism which Article I of the Constitution establishes makes the legislature at the eastern end of Pennsylvania Avenue more complicated, and often seemingly more awkward, to deal with than a unicameral legislature might. At its simplest, dealing with two sets of autonomous legislative politicians in formally independent institutions doubles the work load of the President and his legislative liaison staff. However, viewed from the perspective of party leaders in Congress, bicameralism appears often to constrain the legislature in engagements with the executive, not least by permitting the White House to play off one chamber against the other in the politics of attempting to pass, obstruct or amend legislation.

Authority in American politics is limited and contested, and power is scattered not only between but within separated institutions of government. How are power and authority expressed in relations between the presidency and Congress? 'Power' is defined here as a politician's (not an institution's) capacity and will to achieve intended effects; it is, accordingly, a measure of what a politician *can* do, and is examined more fully below under the heading of the third factor of contingency. 'Authority' is defined here in two distinct senses, each of which contrasts sharply with the definition of 'power'.

The first definition of authority is that which a politician or an institution *may* or *may not* do under the provision of constitutional or public law; it is, in other words, an expression not of 'power' but of 'powers'. This sense of authority we may understand as 'constitutional authority' – but that does not imply that the content of such constitutional authority is settled or defined. Who has authority to do what, and in respect of what, are questions that are typically contested, open to dispute, uncertain, fluid, or in the process of development or redefinition. To that extent, the United States Constitution's grants of constitutional authority are no more unambiguous or fixed than are grants of such authority in other democracies. What is essential, however, is that we signify authority as having a legal foundation of a constitutional or legal kind. A second sense of authority, 'moral authority', is quite distinct from constitutional authority and is discussed below under the heading of power. I now need to develop my claim about constitutional authority's extent.

Article II shows that the President's authority is narrowly drafted. Some instances of that authority are also incomplete, even where they appear not to be. For example, although the President is Commander in Chief, Congress competes with him to define that authority's scope, particularly with regard to defence policy-making, the deployment of force abroad, engagements with hostile powers, and the vastly contentious subject of secrecy in foreign and security policy. What constitutional law actually is in these cases is not settled, cannot be settled, and ought not to be settled in a liberal democracy. The Constitution fosters difference, enjoins dispute, resists tidy closure. Courts, Congress, presidency, journalists, academics contest constitutional provision case by case. The questions are complex and inherently uncertain. If they were simple, their solutions would be straightforward; as it is they are anything but simple, and their solutions (if solutions there be) are anything but straightforward.

A second example shows that in respect of the legislative process, authority is not only contested but – in practice – necessarily shared. The President's power to recommend measures to Congress and to veto bills place him temporally and politically at the beginning and at the end of the process of law-making. However, they make him no less dependent upon a bicameral legislature institutionally separate from him to determine the content of authorizing and appropriating legislation. Congress is not bound as a matter of constitutional law to take the slightest notice of a president's recommendations. However, it has no option but to take full account of his vetoes, as Clinton demonstrated after the Republicans gained control of the House and Senate from January 1995: having vetoed no bills passed by the Democratic-controlled Congress in his first two years in office, he did so repeatedly thereafter to establish for himself a record with which key Democratic constituencies and middle-American voters alike would be pleased.[11]

In fact, a president's authority is wider than either of these examples might suggest because a president is not confined in his actions to doing that which Congress expressly permits. He has his own prerogatives, though presidents and Congresses typically disagree (and often publicly quarrel) about their extent. Two forms of authority which presidents have assumed are presidential proclamations, and executive orders. The latter are better known than the former, much more frequently issued and usually more far-reaching.[12] In fact, executive orders are best understood as secondary symptoms of the presidency's underlying forces of authority – not only its prerogative powers set out in the Constitution but those powers which Congress delegates to the President by statute. The Supreme Court is quite clear on this point: an executive order may neither supersede a statute nor 'override contradictory Congressional expressions'.[13] That, indeed, was precisely the point on which the Supreme Court struck down President Truman's executive order issued at the height of the Korean War that the steel plants be seized. The Court decided that he had no constitutional authority to issue the order (his Article II authority as Commander in Chief did not extend to a general power to seize property) nor had Congress written any law conferring authority upon the President or any Cabinet Secretary to do so.

By contrast with the President's own, Congress's authority is broad. What Congress may *not* do is mostly indicated in certain amendments to the Constitution as indicated above. What it may do beyond these restrictions is now vast and extensive. Since 1937, the Supreme Court has acceded to interpretations of the interstate commerce clause which have greatly expanded Congress's constitutional authority and, hence, its regulatory reach. In 1789, the framers intended the language of Article I, Section 8 strictly to limit Congress's authority. In 2001, notwithstanding the efforts of some conservative Supreme Court Justices in the last decade of the twentieth century to restate and enforce more limited understandings of the interstate commerce clause, that language has little restrictive force and none for which a majority on the Court has succeeded in identifying a stable constitutional principle. If Congress wishes to regulate commercial or para-commercial activity, the Constitution as it is now interpreted will rarely prevent it from doing so. Since the middle of the twentieth century, liberals have had great political success in using the interstate commerce clause to extend federal regulation to protect the rights of minorities, women and the disabled. Social conservatives, many of whom protest that extension of federal regulation into such areas is unconstitutional, themselves enthusiastically seek to extend federal regulation into questions of ethics and criminal justice. Neither side has shown itself especially aware of the apparent contradiction in its own stance on the question of constitutional principle.

The presidency is not the executive branch. It is only a small part of the executive branch. Excepting the presidency itself, the executive branch is created by Congress in the form of public law. None of the departments, agencies, and commissions ('agencies' for short) which comprise the bureaucratic part of the executive branch are created by the Constitution. Nor (and this is the decisive contrast with most other Western polities) does the executive create them by will: instead, Congress creates in law. The executive branch is defined in public laws each of which Congress writes, each of which it votes upon, and most of which have a limited life. Accordingly, each executive agency has a legal personality in this sense: its jurisdiction flows from its existence in *authorizing* laws. These laws do what their name indicates: they authorize the existence, jurisdiction, purpose and programmes of the agency or commission in question. Funding for programmes is a separate matter but it, too, is a question of law. Funding decisions are made in *appropriating* law, written by Congress, by which public funds are appropriated to finance those programmes and their administration. That is how Congress designs and shapes the executive branch: it does so autonomously, on its own constitutional authority. Whatever its purpose, whether it seeks to expand and sustain certain agencies and programmes, or to curtail and restrain others, it expresses its will in law.

Approached in this way, the key to understanding political relations between the presidency and Congress appears to depend upon identifying where constitutional authority lies and over what areas of public policy it is exercised. Much of that authority lies in or with Congress. Yet such an approach misleads, for the story of the federal government since the creation of the Interstate Commerce Commission in 1887 has been of Congress's repeated willingness (and need) to delegate authority to the executive branch by creating agencies and commissions to deal with specific public policy problems. From one perspective, Congress has in its building of the executive branch by accretion of agencies and programmes in public law exercised its authority, and thereby demonstrated its centrality to federal government and to public policy. That is certainly what Congress did from the end of the Federalist era to the beginning of the Progressive era at the end of the nineteenth century, during which period it directly controlled domestic departments in policy formation and implementation. Even during that period, Congress regarded the Departments of State, War, and Navy differently, recognizing the Constitution as having vested special constitutional authority and political responsibilities for the conduct of their business in the executive. However, Congress deemed heads of domestic executive departments to be responsible primarily to it rather than to the President and accordingly oversaw the (then rather few) domestic departments with special attention. Its powers over interstate commerce, for example, were exercised directly and not through the intermediary regulatory commissions of which the Interstate Commerce Commission was the first federal example in 1887.

From a different perspective, what Congress has repeatedly done by its creation of executive branch agencies and delegation of authority to them is implicitly to recognize its own institutional limitations. The pre-Civil War model of running parts of the United States government direct became unworkable long before the federal government began to acquire a significant regulatory role at the beginning of the twentieth century. Commercial and environmental regulation, extensive welfare programmes, a monetary policy created and executed by a central bank, a large federal fiscal role, and civil rights programmes required bureaucratic agencies autonomous in their operations and decisions from Congress. Only through executive agencies having specific purposes identified in authorizing legislation could public policy be reliably, fairly and evenly implemented free of direct congressional interference. Efficiency and effectiveness in implementing public policy required the energy, expertise and flexibility which could come only from executive agencies enjoying discretion in how public laws were to be interpreted and implemented but which Congress itself could not supply. The counterpart of such discretion is a principal-agent problem: Congress cannot reliably ensure that its legislative purpose will be reflected in agencies' own decisions and rule-making. There is no formal solution to this problem: Congress has to adjust to it by establishing oversight mechanisms. The cyclicality of authorizing and appropriating legislation offers Congress some chance of influencing the implementation of policy. But every intelligent Senator and Representative knows that Congress's delegation of authority to executive agencies makes comprehensive oversight impossible. That is not a happy circumstance for Congress. But nor is it entirely reassuring for the President since his influence over agencies is, at best, incomplete, and exercised (if at all) indirectly through his political appointees.

Parties, Electoral Cycles and Coalitional Forces

A second category of forces shaping the political opportunities and constraints in the political relationship between the presidency and Congress comprises the asynchronous electoral cycles and different electoral rules which Articles I and II establish, and the complexities of coalition building both for the purposes of winning elections and for the winning of votes in Congress afterwards.

With the exceptions allowed by Article IV, Section 3 of the Constitution, the Senate's constituency boundaries are fixed in perpetuity. By contrast, state assemblies change the boundaries of most House constituencies after each decennial census. The President's singular constituency is national. The Senate is divided into senators of three different classes, each class having an electoral cycle of six years but subject to election at the same time, so producing a legislature approximately one-third of whose members is subject to election in every even-numbered year. The House runs to a short election cycle of two years – just 730 days. The presidency has a four-year term with a constitutional limitation of a maximum of two terms. The significance of these differences is that they buttress both bicameralism and separation of powers, and so form parameters within which the politics of relations between the presidency and Congress are played out. Each of the three players – House, Senate, President – operate on different electoral cycles. As their political time-frames differ, so too do their perspectives upon politics and policy. For example, in November 2000 Hillary Clinton was elected to the US Senate as George W. Bush was elected to the presidency: neither will again run for those offices at the same time. A person newly elected to the House 2000 has entirely different electoral horizons: she will be running in her third election when the presidential election of 2004 takes place. The non-coterminous nature of federal elections symbolizes the separation of powers and bicameralism, and deepens the significance of both.

That has been particularly so since 1968 because the commonest outcome of American federal elections has been divided government by which one of the three elective institutions lies in different partisan hands from the other two. Bicameralism and separation of powers do not entail this peculiarly American form of coalition building, but do make it possible. There is much debate both about why divided government has emerged since 1968, and about what its consequences are for legislative productivity. The best analysis of the data about the latter issue is that there is no causal relationship between such partisan division and legislative output, whether measured by the quantity or quality of legislation.[14] There is good evidence that American voters approve of divided government, but little that many deliberately choose it. Byron Shafer's argument on the point is powerful:

> The public had not necessarily chosen 'divided government'; it merely became more comfortable with it through experience. What this public did prefer was its own modal policy positions. As long as the active members of *both* political parties were opposed to these positions, that public was destined to find split partisan control of national government to be a useful resolution, and these party activists were effectively dedicated to helping the public find it.[15]

The scattering of power which the combination of bicameralism and separation of powers facilitates, and which divided government expresses, is underpinned by contrasting procedural and organizational rules between the two chambers which Article II permits, and by the cultural differences which in part flow from those different rules. The House's roots in local issues and cultures, and the Senate's in state politics and cultures, make party leaders' task of effecting collective action all the harder. The constraints upon congressional leaders seeking to build majorities, whether to support a president of their own party or to oppose a president of the other party, are reinforced by the politics of individual calculation which localism not only fosters but requires for a Congress member's electoral survival and political advancement.

The notion of coalitional forces refers to the social sources of opportunity and constraint which arise from factors unrelated to the structure or constitutional order of the presidency or Congress, but over which individual politicians have no control. They are not entailed by the structure or culture either of the presidency or of Congress but are contingent in their application: they arise from factors external to government, but have heavy implications for it. Among these social sources of opportunity and constraint are party and ideology, and social and socioeconomic cleavages. In combination, they shape not only the character of government institutions but the processes and ends of policy-making. For example, the House and Senate are both divided not just by structural characteristics (whether of a constitutional kind, as described above, or of a contingent-endogenous kind as described below) but by ideological, regional, racial, and ethnic cleavages and interests. To the extent that such divisions, many of them cross-cutting, inhibit party leaders in their task of building coalitions of support or opposition to the President on major bills, they are (by definition) themselves constraints. However, from different perspectives, such divisions may and do provide the building-blocks of opportunity for the formation of broader coalitions, whether based around or across party. That is true for party leaders in Congress, attempting to build majority coalitions of their own or minority coalitions sufficiently large to disrupt presidential initiatives. It is also true for presidents seeking to build coalitions of support for their legislative initiatives, nominations or treaties. Both implications were apparent during Clinton's presidency, as explained below.

Political Power

By political power, the third category, I refer to the will and capacity of politicians to shape the patterns of political relations between presidency and Congress to their advantage. The proposition is simple: that individual politicians' actions matter. The much more complex questions to which this deceptively simple (though contentious) proposition gives rise are those of how they matter, why, and under what circumstances. These questions can be established only by considering particular cases, because the forces bearing upon each case of interaction between presidency and Congress are infinitely variant. They matter for the pattern and content of political relations between the two branches, regardless of whether politicians intend the consequences that their actions have. To make this claim is not to imply that nothing else matters: as the other two categories show, authority, parties, electoral cycles, and coalitional forces also matter. Yet it is politicians who create institutions, whether large and complex structures of government such as the United States Congress, or procedural rules by which (for example) a House committee orders its business of overseeing executive agencies and in drafting legislation. Most politicians typically operate within the framework of the institutions of which they are members. When they retire from the presidency or Congress or are defeated in running for re-election, the institutions which politicians leave look and operate much as they did when the politicians in question were first elected to them. Even if politicians wished it otherwise, they cannot as a matter of practical politics alter most aspects of the institutions to which they are elected and in which they work: most democratic institutions are stable – at least in the short term. Part of a constitutional order created in the late eighteenth century, the US presidency and Congress are particularly stable institutions.

Yet within the stability of these institutions, it is politicians who in different proportions and at different points in their careers have purposes, ideals, ambitions and intentions.[16] There are no political relations between presidency and Congress except in so far as politicians seize opportunities to create those areas of politics within the constraints of the rules of the institution to which they belong. Whether their purposes are lofty or base, what politicians do, when and how they do it, and the inferences which other politicians draw from their actions about their motives, are the stuff of politics. It is impossible to make sense of politics within the White House or within Congress, or of relations between the two institutions, except by examining how politicians act in them, through them, and beyond them in addressing voters and listening to them.

A support to power is the quality of 'moral authority', noted earlier. By it I mean that combination of qualities attaching to a politician by reason of the public's estimation of her or his behaviour or record in office. Politicians would not sensibly claim moral authority, not least because to do so would be to undermine the claim's plausibility: to claim it would be to destroy it. Moral authority is synonymous not with public support but, rather, with 'prestige' or 'standing': it is a reputational measure, an index of the public's (or, as is more often the case, publics') view of a politician. It is attributed to a politician by the public or publics, a quality which the public may recognize a politician as having.

Moral authority is therefore not only conceptually distinct from constitutional authority, but usually in political practice independent of it. Whereas constitutional authority is a prerequisite to political action in a law-governed political system, moral authority is a resource for politicians to draw upon in order to enhance their power. What difference can moral authority make? It is not a trump card in politics: being thought to have the quality does not confer power upon a politician to shape the patterns of political relations between presidency and Congress to her advantage as she will. In part, that is because voters will disagree: at any one time, some will regard a politician as having the quality and others will not. Voters will also disagree in the intensity of their estimations of politicians. As a resource upon which a politician may draw, moral authority is, however, an asset to be prized. To lack it is not to be without power. Opinion polls do not typically measure moral authority but there is little doubt that it was not a quality which the American public ever thought President Clinton to have had in abundance; there is equally little doubt that in 1998–9 during the depths of the Monica Lewinsky scandal only a minority thought him to have any moral authority at all. Yet even without it, Clinton enjoyed majority support: he was not admired, but he was supported. Given the sheer tawdriness of his personal life and his constant search for campaign money, that was a remarkable political accomplishment.

As Clinton's case suggests, moral authority is not the sole power resource upon which politicians may draw. As Richard Neustadt has explained in *Presidential Power and the Modern Presidents*, a president's other power resources are his 'professional reputation' among decision-makers in Washington; and his 'human qualities', by which Neustadt meant his 'sense of purpose', his 'feel for power', and his 'self-confidence'. He thought that the third (self-confidence) was 'fashioned from experience and temperament' and shaped the first two.[17] Neustadt's framework is useful not just for thinking about the bases of a president's power, but of other politicians, including those 535 legislators on Capitol Hill with whom a president must deal if he is to make the separated system work for him. However, those 535 legislators are also attempting to make the separated system work for them. Examples drawn from President Clinton's trade policy show how some of them went about doing so.

Applying the Framework to Clinton's Trade Policy

Introduction

President Clinton pursued a free trade policy from his first year in office to his last. In his first, he won Congress's approval for the North American Free Trade Agreement (NAFTA) which created a free trade area between the United States, Canada and Mexico and which had been negotiated under George Bush's presidency. In his second year, he

secured congressional approval for the major Uruguay Agreement establishing a new trade regime. In his final year in the White House, he sought
and won Congress's approval for China to be granted permanent Normal
Trading Relations (NTR), so paving the way for China's admission to
the World Trade Organization (WTO) which the Uruguay Agreement
had created. All three cases illustrate the importance of authority, coalition building, and the creative power of politicians in Congress and the
White House. All also show the constraints upon and opportunities
before a president and congressional leaders faced with divisive policy
questions.

Constraints upon Democratic presidents in international trade tightened considerably between approval of the Kennedy Round in 1962 and
of the Uruguay Round in 1994, not least because of the loss of many
southern Democrats, internationalist by conviction and economic interest. The increased proportion of America's total output accounted for
by international trade during those thirty-two years, and the vastly
heightened exposure to foreign competition of certain of its key (mostly
unionized) industries, such as vehicle, steel, textile and civil aircraft manufacturing, transformed the constraints upon and opportunities available
to presidents of both parties. For Democrats, the constraints became
especially apparent – as Clinton's politically painful but necessary
dependence upon Republican congressional majorities for trade liberalization showed. Republican presidents, by contrast, gained more
freedom for manoeuvre as the congressional GOP's support for free trade
grew in the second half of the twentieth century. In 1993, labour's opposition to NAFTA centred on the supposed threat of Mexican labour to
American job security and wage rates and the anticipated willingness of
American business to export capital to Mexico. In 2000, labour's opposition centred upon similar supposed threats from cheap Chinese labour.
In these cases and in the creation of the WTO in 1994, environmentalists found ample reason for alarm. The constraints upon congressional
politicians closest to those causes tightened accordingly, not least because
all three groups are important sources of organizational and financial
support to Democratic candidates in congressional and presidential
elections.

Among Republicans, opposition to China being granted NTR came
from two factions. The most vocal was from religious groups hostile to
the Chinese government's policies on abortion and religious freedom.
Republican candidates in many districts and states could not afford to
ignore these groups because of the sophistication of their political organization, the intensity of their dedication to conservative politics, and
their high propensity to vote. The second group was composed of older

anti-communist voters who had consistently opposed closer links with China since the 1949 communist revolution. Even in combination, these groups did not comprise a majority among Republicans – but their opposition was intense and not readily susceptible to bargaining.

Uruguay Agreement

The setting   The Uruguay Agreement of 124 states provided for the reduction of tariff barriers by an average of 38 per cent for industrial economies, so lowering the tariff barrier to an average of 3.9 per cent from 6.3 per cent; for the establishment of the World Trade Organization (WTO) in Geneva with the power to oversee and enforce multilateral trade agreements; for the reduction of various non-tariff barriers to trade; and for the expansion of GATT rules to cover such economic sectors as agriculture, services and intellectual property.

Authority   Article I, Section 8, of the US Constitution grants authority over trade law to Congress: 'The Congress shall have power to lay and collect . . . duties [and] to regulate Commerce with foreign nations.' President Clinton had ample warning from history to take that authority seriously because the Senate had in Truman's administration refused to support an organizational secretariat (the International Trade Organization) for GATT. However, in 1974, Congress passed a Trade Act which included provisions for 'fast-track' implementing authority by which trade agreements would be subject to two votes on the floors of the House and the Senate – and so either approved or not in the form that the President submitted them – and considered under a strict timetable. Congress's motive was that it recognized that trade agreements would otherwise be vulnerable to attempts by Congress members and senators to modify them in accord with their own particular economic or political interests, as had often been the case before. Congress commonly decides voluntarily to limit its own authority in this way, implicitly acknowledging its own institutional weaknesses in considering trade agreements which a majority of its members know intellectually to be in the national interest but which a minority of its members have the political incentive to modify in damaging ways. Although Clinton repeatedly failed during the remainder of his presidency to persuade a Republican-dominated Congress to reauthorize fast-track procedures, Congress's consideration of the Uruguay Round agreement was subject to them.

While the 1974 Trade Act's fast-track rules permitted each chamber only an up or down vote on the bill without amendments, they permitted each committee chair with jurisdiction over the bill to take up to forty-five days to consider it. As chairman of the Senate Commerce Committee, Senator Hollings (D-SC) announced on 28 September 1994 that he would exploit that rule and hold the bill in his committee for the full permitted period – well after 7 October, the planned date of Congress's adjournment in preparation for the mid-term congressional elections in November and for which members would wish to campaign intensively for the month before they took place. Hollings's move privately infuriated his free-trade colleagues, but they could not complain that he was unentitled to do what he did: he had invoked his authority to publicize his opposition to the agreement. Senator Pat Moynihan invoked his authority as chairman of the Senate Finance Committee, too. But he did so to publicize his support for the bill, and quickly saw it through his committee to the Senate floor by a 19–0 vote. In the House, much more tightly bound by rules than is the Senate, the Ways and Means Committee voted 35–3 in favour of the bill just one day after Clinton had submitted it to Congress on 27 September.

Hollings's move forced Majority Leader George Mitchell and Minority Leader Bob Dole (about to exchange their posts following the Republicans' gaining of a majority in the mid-term elections) to schedule a two-day lame-duck session beginning 30 November, solely for debate and a vote on the GATT bill. Working under the fast-track procedures, the House duly passed HR 5110 on 29 November by 288 to 146; the Senate followed two days later with a vote of 76–24 in support.[18]

Parties, electoral cycles and coalitional forces   Clinton secured congressional approval of the Uruguay Agreement at a time of rapid partisan change in Congress. Between Hollings's decision to hold the bill in the Commerce Committee at the end of September and the short lame-duck session of Congress from 28 November to 1 December, the Republicans won major victories in the House and Senate mid-term congressional elections, giving them nominal control of both chambers for the first time since 1954. It was a hugely consequential event, not least (much as it was generally unanticipated at the time) for enabling President Clinton to develop and master the considerable political skill of outwitting his major partisan opponents, Senator Bob Dole, Majority Leader of the US Senate, and Congressman Newt Gingrich, Speaker of the House of Representatives. In the short term, however, the elections did not weaken the President's prospects of securing approval of the Uruguay Agreement, which drew majority support both from Democrats and from Republicans in the House and the Senate. At the margins, Hollings's delay to the bill in his committee might actually have increased the majorities in support since among those voting were no fewer than eighty-five outgoing House members (one-fifth of the House's total membership), and ten senators who were retiring or had been defeated.

Power Without his two victories on major trade legislation (NAFTA in 1993, and the Uruguay Agreement in 1994), Clinton would have had no major legislative achievement in his first two years in office. As it was, the two trade measures which he sponsored fuelled the long period of growth in the American economy that coincided exactly, if fortuitously, with his period in office. The Uruguay Agreement posed fewer tactical difficulties for Clinton than NAFTA had done. The tabloid headline threat that NAFTA would cause the seepage of American jobs to Mexico, though insufficient to derail the agreement in Congress, had considerable force within the Democratic Party. The Uruguay Agreement did not raise the same fears.[19] Faced with no single identifiable threat, opponents from labour unions found it altogether harder to rally supporters and stir anxieties: the dilemma of one opponent, Rep. Marcy Kaptur (D-OH), a strong supporter of labour unions, was illustrated by her being unable to offer a stronger argument to her constituents than the assertion that the Uruguay Agreement had no value for them: 'Working people in America, there is nothing in this GATT for you and your family.'[20] It was scarcely a call to arms.

The political difficulty of labour supporters was further illustrated by the support which House Majority Leader Richard Gephardt (who had firmly opposed NAFTA) gave, while the political difficulty of Clinton's anti-free trade opponents was illustrated by Gingrich's support for the agreement. Even at the height of his power following the GOP's congressional victories in November, Speaker-elect Gingrich joined Gephardt in writing to President Clinton on 16 November reaffirming their 'strong support'.[21] During the lame-duck session, both Speaker Foley (who had been defeated in his bid for re-election from his District in Washington) and Minority Leader Bob Michel (who had not run for re-election) supported the agreement in the last speeches which they each made from the floor.

In the Senate, Bob Dole proved harder to pin down: he was carefully manoeuvring himself into position to run for the Republican presidential nomination in 1996. Accordingly, Ross Perot's opposition to the extent of the WTO's powers gave him pause since that maverick independent candidate for the presidency in 1992 was in 1994 preparing for a further bid in 1996 by waving the flag of American sovereignty at his opponents. In its final form, the agreement provided for the United States to withdraw from the WTO if it so chose following a finding from a panel of US judges that the WTO had acted arbitrarily against US interests in three cases. Congress could then propose a joint resolution instructing the President to withdraw from the WTO; that joint resolution would have to be signed into law or enacted over the President's veto to take effect. This convoluted and improbable chain of events gave Dole the cover he needed in public to claim that his anxieties about American sovereignty had been met. It also gave him the cover which he badly needed to fend off attacks from Perot. In fact, just as Dole's pressure upon Clinton had been tactical, so was Clinton's concession to Dole since the agreement specified that Congress would have the right to review quinquennially the United States's membership of WTO.

Dole also attempted to extract an undertaking from the White House to support revisions to capital gains tax rules in exchange for his support of the agreement. But, as the White House independently knew, Dole lacked key interest group support and was acting as he did because of his concern about the threat from Congressman Jack Kemp to his bid for the Republican nomination in 1996. The President made no concession to Dole because he calculated (correctly) that Dole would support the agreement without it. As he often did, Clinton calculated correctly those concessions that he needed to make and those that he did not: Dole publicly supported the agreement, and strove to ensure maximum Republican support for it in the Senate.[22] Under adverse partisan circumstances, and following an undistinguished legislative record during his first two years in office, Clinton's securing of congressional approval for the Uruguay Agreement was a powerful indication of his resourcefulness and a hint at the formidable capacity for political recovery which he repeatedly displayed in the six years that remained of his presidency.

Normal trade relations with China

Authority The Trade Act of 1974 authorized the President to grant most-favoured nation (MFN) status (renamed 'normal trade relations', or NTR, by an amendment in 1998) to certain communist states for only twelve months at a time and then only on condition that the state concerned had adopted free emigration practices acceptable to the US. That clear expression of Congress's statutory authority constrained the President to work within narrow parameters (as Congress had intended), giving him some room for his own choice-making but no freedom of fundamental policy decision (as Congress had also intended). American trade policy towards China during Clinton's presidency took the form it did in part because of the 1974 law; that was especially the case with respect to the question of whether China should be granted MFN/NTR status and, if so, under what conditions. The President had no authority over the matter: Congress did, and debated the question every year. Representatives and Senators with special political interests in trade with China used the annual debates to advance them. The salience of MFN renewal rose after the Chinese government massacred peaceful protesters in Tiananmen Square, Beijing, in 1989. MFN was further politicized by broader tensions between the Republican White House under President Bush (who during Richard Nixon's presidency had served as Ambassador to China) and a Democratic Congress. In 1991–2, Bush overcame congressional resistance to the renewal of China's MFN status only because Senate opponents lacked the votes to override the President's veto of a bill which renewed constraining conditions of which he disapproved.

The Tiananmen massacre gave human rights interest groups the opportunity to attract the attention not just of those members of Congress receptive to their criticisms, but those who had not previously accorded them special significance. Moreover, the subject of human rights became especially powerful in American politics because the cause attracted such a broad coalition of supporters across party lines. Liberals, accustomed to using a rights language in arguing about politics and policy, found support not only from their usual supporters on the left who had principled objections to China's violations of human rights and use of prison labour in manufacturing goods for export to the United States (which in any case constituted a violation of US customs law), but also from corporate interests whose profits were threatened by such low-priced imports. Similarly, liberals' longstanding protests at China's brutal oppression of ethnic Tibetans were matched not only by the objections of social conservatives to China's restriction of Tibetan religious freedom, but by the alarm expressed by national security conservatives about China's threat to Taiwan's security, China's weapons exports to countries unfriendly to the United States, and the risk which China's extensive espionage posed to America's nuclear security.

Parties, electoral cycles and coalitional forces   Clinton sought towards the end of his second term in office to make China's NTR status permanent. He did so while facing Republican majorities in both the House and the Senate, and in his final term: the constitution prohibited him from running for the presidency in 2000. He had no prospective power to protect in 2001, merely an ambiguous reputation to shore up. Moreover, many Republicans were not only opposed to President Clinton's social values but detested him personally with an intensity towards a president unknown in Washington politics since Richard Nixon had incurred the hatred of many congressional Democrats. It was not a promising combination of circumstances. However, Clinton's own position on NTR was clear, as were his private calculations about where his own political interests lay. Notwithstanding his public reservations about the externalities of free trade when a candidate for the presidency in 1992, Clinton adopted in office a clear and stable position in favour of trade liberalization – both in general, and with China in particular. It was a stance that it was easier for him to adopt in times of strong employment and output growth than it would have been under less favourable economic circumstances.

The Senate presented significant obstacles to Clinton. Among the opponents were senators such as Jesse Helms who was institutionally well placed to combine the limited constitutional authority of his chairmanship of the Senate Foreign Relations Committee with his significant political power as a leading conservative and anti-communist, and with his unusually tenacious political capacity to engage in protracted debate to obstruct the legislation. Among other resourceful opponents were Senator Robert Byrd, a highly experienced conservative Democrat and former Senate Majority leader; Senator Ernest Hollings, another conservative Democrat whose sponsoring of various amendments to undermine the bill arose primarily from his being constrained to defend the textile and agricultural interests of his state (South Carolina) against cheaper foreign imports, whether from China or elsewhere; Senator Paul Wellstone, a liberal Democrat who sought to defend the interests of organized labour; Senator Robert Smith, an environmentally sensitive Republican from New Hampshire; Senator Russell Feingold, a Wisconsin Democrat; and Senators Fred Thompson and Robert Torricelli, a moderate Republican and Democrat respectively, who attempted to add a clause to the bill providing for the imposition of sanctions upon Chinese companies if they were found to be exporting weapons of mass destruction.

Of the eighteen amendments which were offered to the China NTR bill in the Senate, these senators proposed the most important thirteen. Senator Wellstone sought to amend the President's legislation because he objected to China's use of prison labour in the manufacture of internationally traded goods and to make the granting of NTR conditional upon China's compliance with requests for information regarding the numbers of persons arrested or detained for organizing or attempting to organize independent trade unions.[23] Senator Hollings attempted by two amendments to require the President to report annually from 2001 on the balance of trade with China in soyabeans and cereals; and to direct the Securities and Exchange Commission (a federal regulatory agency with jurisdiction over the financial sector) to require businesses to disclose foreign investment information.[24] Senator Helms offered amendments to delay normal trading relations with China until the President certified to Congress that China had taken specific steps to end its abuse of human and religious rights; to urge China to end its practices of forced abortion and sterilization; and to encourage American businesses trading with Chinese companies to adopt a code of conduct reflecting American democratic values.[25] Senator Byrd offered an amendment to provide for import relief in the event of a market disruption (a device to protect US companies).[26] Senator Smith offered amendments to monitor China's cooperation in eliminating the harvesting and transporting of organs for profit from executed prisoners; to scrutinize China's implementation of laws protecting human health and the environment; and to monitor China's accounting for prisoners of war and for soldiers missing in action from the Korean and Vietnam wars.[27] Senators Thompson and Torricelli offered an amendment to provide for sanctions against China in the event of it making any sales of weapons of mass destruction;[28] and Senator Feingold offered an amendment to establish a congressional-executive commission to make recommendations to the House and the Senate about the US's trade relationship with China.[29]

Senators made their decisions within the constraints and opportunities of parties, electoral cycles, and coalitional forces described earlier. The multiple issue divisions to which the China trade question gave rise and which were revealed by the amendments offered to the President's bill imply that party, the building-block of congressional coalitions, was of little use either to the President or to his congressional opponents. The voting figures show that this was so on the amendments: Republican opposition to the President's position (that is, support for the non-free trade option) in the thirteen votes listed above varied between one and twenty-four votes (the latter vote being on Helms's abortion amendment). The median such Republican vote among the thirteen was nineteen. In other words, the median anti-free trade amendment to the bill attracted one-third of Republican senators. Democratic opposition to the President's position (that is, support for the non-free trade option) in the thirteen votes listed above varied between five and nineteen. The median such Democratic vote among the thirteen was eleven. In other words, the median anti-free trade amendment to the bill attracted slightly fewer than one-quarter of Democratic senators. Support for amendments to the bill was marginally stronger among Republicans than among Democrats.

Yet the final vote on the President's bill was 83–15, a far greater victory for the free-trade forces than might have been inferred from the support for the amendments to it. It was also a remarkably bipartisan outcome: opposition to the bill was evenly divided between the two parties – eight Republicans and seven Democrats voted against.[30] Despite the appearance from votes on amendments of anti-free trade sentiment, Senate support for the principle of the China bill itself had always been substantial. The difference between the Senate's support for amendments to the bill (a median figure of nearly one-third of senators) and that for the bill as a whole (less than one-sixth of senators) is both large and significant. The difference is explained by senators' appreciation that they have not just the authority but the opportunity and the incentive to advertise to constituents and interest groups their support for amendments (especially those amendments that they know will be defeated and for which they will not later have to take responsibility). When it comes to the weighty question of the bill itself, however, members of the Senate and the House are less susceptible to sectoral pressures and more susceptible to an appeal to the national interest. President Clinton had the opportunity and the moral authority to make such an appeal on behalf of an important principle and commercial opportunity. Even two of those senators who actually offered amendments to the bill (Torricelli and Thompson) voted for the bill on the floor. Clinton's own power was mightily assisted by external resources: the fight to secure passage of the bill drew intensive lobbying support from corporate interests, especially those in high-tech industries who anticipated large commercial gains from expanded trade with China.

Power Instead of a single opponent and a single line of cleavage, there were several opponents with the potential to prevent the emergence of a majority for the President's position on the bill. Yet a resourceful president may relish taking on multiple opponents, not least because he might be able in conjunction with supporters in Congress and among key interest groups to play them off against each other. Clinton was precisely such a resourceful president: he and his staff collaborated closely with the dominant business interest groups whose members stood to gain from a normal trading partnership with China. Once the House had passed the bill, that collaborative effort was expressed in the President's unyielding opposition to all amendments which senators offered to the bill. Together with his allies in the Senate majority and minority party leaderships and in major corporations (which supported the bill because they knew that expanded trade with China was in their and their shareholders' interests), the President defeated all eighteen amendments. He had once again correctly calculated how to achieve the objective he had set himself.

The President had no authority to prevent senators offering the amendments. Senators' use of their unquestioned resource of authority in doing so is but one example of the separation of powers at work. It is, moreover, not only authority but power that is relevant here: not only *may* senators offer amendments, they *can* offer amendments. Senators have, that is to say, the opportunity to bring their resources of authority and power to bear: it is up to them as individual politicians to calculate whether it is in their interests to offer amendments and to seek to persuade their colleagues to agree to their adoption. As individual members of a legislature where party lacks coercive power, senators do have the power and, often, the incentive to make such calculations and to act on them. Senate rules make the offering of amendments relatively straightforward (and much easier than it is for members of the House in their more rule-bound chamber where party leaders can use rules to help them form cohesive majorities). Nevertheless, having the power to offer them does not carry with it the power to constrain other senators to adopt them: all of the eighteen amendments offered were defeated. Senator Helms's amendment seeking to end forced abortions drew the most support, but even this attracted only forty-three votes.

We should not infer from their defeat that those proposing them expected them to pass: the senators in question are, in fact, too shrewd to have misled themselves in that way. Nor should we infer that the senators were politically weakened by their amendments being defeated. On the contrary, each took the opportunity to exploit his authority to offer amendments while demonstrating to supporters within the Senate and outside it that they remained true to their ideological beliefs (in the cases of Senators Wellstone and Helms); to their state's commercial interests (in the case of Senator Hollings); and to their sense of patriotism (in the cases of Senators Thompson and Torricelli). By his three amendments to support the environment, to identify himself with US prisoners of war in Vietnam and Korea, and to oppose organ harvesting from executed persons in China, the agile Senator Smith attempted to show his diverse voting constituency in New Hampshire (as well as his potential opponents) that he could by creative use of amendments to trade legislation please environmentalists, conservative patriots and concerned liberals.

All of these senators were constrained by the different politics of their different states: none was a free agent. Each was autonomous, but none was independent. Nevertheless, all showed that they could accommodate the resultant pressures and reduce the chances of their being defeated in the vote that really mattered to them: the next elections for their US Senate seats. All senators demonstrated their sensitivity to the need to take the opportunities available to them to use authority and power in office creatively in order to retain their office and to augment their power in future debates and struggles. It is not necessarily irrational for a politician to propose a step which she or he knows will be defeated: senators may have other objects in view (as Byrd, Feingold, Helms, Hollings and Smith did in the cases discussed here) which defeat might even promote. Senators may (and often do) sense that other opportunities will arise in the future as a result of their offering certain amendments to a bill today. Politically far-seeing senators may (and often do), in other words, act today in order to defend, consolidate or augment their prospects of power tomorrow.

Conclusion

This essay has explored the value of existing approaches to the subject of political relations between Congress and the presidency and proposed a new, trifocal, approach to examining it. Even after the huge partisan setback of November 1994 with a resurgent Republican Party under the leadership of a new and self-confident Speaker-elect in the person of Newt Gingrich, Clinton led (and showed himself to be leading) a cross-party majority to recover some prestige and to recraft the bases of his authority and power. For a president whose political errors in the first two years of his term gave his partisan opponents so much cause for encouragement and his partisan allies so much cause for anxiety, Clinton was fortunate to have the opportunity of pressing the case for the adoption of a trade agreement to which most congressional Republicans were themselves ideologically committed. Yet in Congress's approval of the Uruguay Agreement during its brief lame-duck session after the Republican victories of the 1994 midterms lay the seeds of Clinton's political recovery in 1995–6. Even at the end of his presidency in 2000, after the travails of the Lewinsky scandal which would have crushed a politician whose self-belief was less than complete, at a time when he had no partisan majority in either House of Congress, and as a so-called lame-duck, he led (and showed himself to be leading) a potentially divisive and contentious China trade bill through Congress. Clinton was a president with a greater capacity for recovery of his power than any of his twentieth-century predecessors.

Clinton was fortunate in his opponents. A more able Speaker than Newt Gingrich, one with a subtler understanding both of the nature and sources of authority within the political system and a finer anticipation of President Clinton's supple capacity to change course, to tack, to sniff the air for political advantage, would have promised less, have achieved more, and not been forced from the Speakership. As it was, Gingrich allowed Clinton successfully to insist in public that a set of decisions lying fully within Congress's own authority (the setting of a budget) was in fact a choice between saving the Medicare programme (as he said that he wished to do) and cutting tax rates on the rich (as, indeed, Mr Gingrich and his colleagues wished to do). From the apparent wreckage of his party's defeats in 1994, Clinton repositioned himself to where his opinion polls showed the electorate to have moved. He gradually ended his political marginalization by moving back to the centre of electoral politics, and painted Gingrich as an extremist bent upon undermining Medicare. No matter that the latter charge was substantially false: politically, it was devastating. Gingrich had allowed himself to be manoeuvred into a corner from which, as Clinton's political recovery in 1996 showed, there was to be no escape.

When the federal government shut down from 14 to 20 November 1994 following Clinton's vetoes of the bills to increase the debt limit and the continuing resolution on the budget of which he chose to disapprove, and when it shut down again following the expiry of the continuing resolution on 15 December, the public blamed not Clinton but Gingrich. In using his veto on three occasions on major bills in the course of four weeks, Clinton had used the slender reserves of his authority, under adverse partisan circumstances, comprehensively to outmanoeuvre a Speaker who only twelve months before had foolishly been hailed as a 'Prime Minister'. There is, of course, no such office in the United States. Nor, as Gingrich belatedly learned, does the Constitution permit one.

So effective were the Constitution's framers in scattering authority and power in America that presidents and Congresses continue to live with the fact and its implications. Yet despite scattering's effectiveness, the system is 'presidential' to the limited but significant extent that the presidency retains an unrivalled institutional capacity for effecting cyclical political recovery and renewal. It requires a president of Clinton's exceptional political guile and agility to define and deploy that capacity, and to make it work in the course of producing law in a legislature over which his authority is slight. And it requires such skills in a president for power to be exercised effectively over a legislature whose members have powerful partisan, ideological and personal reasons for conducting legislative politics at their own pace and in their own ways. For all its

536 elected politicians, the frustration of federal politics is that no one of them is fully in control.

NOTES

1   Charles O. Jones, *Clinton and Congress* (Norman: University of Oklahoma Press, 1999), p. 84.
2   *Washington Post*, 31 Dec. 2000.
3   Edward S. Corwin, *The President, Office and Powers, 1787–1957* (New York: New York University Press, 1957); Louis Fisher, *Constitutional Conflicts between Congress and the President* (Princeton: Princeton University Press, 1985), see also now 3rd edn (Lawrence: University Press of Kansas, 1991).
4   James M. Burns, *Roosevelt: The Lion and the Fox* (London: Secker and Warburg, 1956); James M. Burns, *Roosevelt: The Soldier of Freedom, 1940–1945* (London: Weidenfeld and Nicolson, 1971).
5   Fred Greenstein, *The Hidden-Hand Presidency* (New York: Basic Books, 1982).
6   Lou Cannon, *President Reagan* (New York: Simon and Schuster, 1991).
7   Arthur M. Schlesinger Jr, *The Imperial Presidency* (Boston: Houghton Mifflin, 1973).
8   David R. Mayhew, *Divided We Govern* (New Haven: Yale University Press, 1991); Charles O. Jones, *The Presidency in a Separated System* (Washington DC: Brookings Institution, 1991); Charles O. Jones, *Separate But Equal Branches*, 2nd edn (Chatham: Chatham House, 1999); Richard E. Neustadt, *Presidential Power and the Modern Presidents* (New York: Free Press, 1990).
9   Charles O. Jones, 'The Presidency in a Separated System', in James P. Pfiffner, *The Managerial Presidency* (College Station: Texas A and M Press, 1999), p. 334.
10 Neustadt, *Presidential Power*, p. xix.
11 *Congressional Quarterly Weekly Report (CQWR)*, 20 Jan. 2001, p. 171.
12 Fisher, *Constitutional Conflicts* (1985), pp. 128ff.
13 Ibid., p. 133.
14 Mayhew, *Divided We Govern*.
15 Byron E. Shafer, 'The Partisan Legacy', in Colin Campbell and Bert A. Rockman, *The Clinton Legacy* (New York: Chatham House, 2000), p. 29.
16 Linda L. Fowler and R. D. McClure, *Political Ambition* (New Haven: Yale University Press, 1989).
17 Neustadt, *Presidential Power*, p. 203.
18 *CQWR*, 3 Dec. 1994, p. 3470.
19 *CQWR*, 1 Oct. 1994, pp. 2763–4.
20 *CQWR*, 3 Dec. 1994, p. 3447.
21 *CQWR*, 19 Nov. 1994, p. 3348.

22 *CQWR*, 26 Nov. 1994, p. 3405.
23 Senate Votes 238 and 246, *CQWR*, 16 Sept. 2000, pp. 2162 and 2163.
24 Senate Votes 247 and 250, *CQWR*, 16 Sept. 2000, p. 2163.
25 Senate Votes 239 and 243 and 244, *CQWR*, 16 Sept. 2000, p. 2162.
26 Senate Vote 240, *CQWR*, 16 Sept. 2000, p. 2162.
27 Senate Votes 241 and 248 and 249, *CQWR*, 16 Sept. 2000, pp. 2162 and 2163.
28 Senate Vote 242, *CQWR*, 16 Sept. 2000, p. 2162.
29 Senate Vote 245, *CQWR*, 16 Sept. 2000, p. 2162.
30 Senate Vote 251, *CQWR*, 23 Sept. 2001, p. 2234.

7

The Politics of Power-Sharing: The Case of Welfare Overhaul

Fiona Ross

Introduction

For many British observers, one of the most enthralling puzzles of the US political system is that it functions even quasi-effectively while dispersing power so extensively. Although American institutions actually concentrate power in a number of important ways, for example via a winner-takes-all electoral system for most offices and two-party system, the structural mechanisms for diffusing power, notably the separation of powers, checks and balances, bicameralism and federalism, are often perceived to be overriding impediments to effective governance. America's brand of institutional pluralism provides numerous actors with multiple opportunities to petition government and oppose, delay and dilute policy initiatives. While all institutional arrangements lock in the status quo, the accessibility of America's political architecture often seems to encourage a politics of incrementalism at best and a politics of gridlock at worst.

This familiar portrait of the US policy process, however, is in some respects crude. Multiple points of access to governmental institutions do not necessarily result in policy stalemate (and an increase in access points does not automatically increase policy incoherence as a direct linear relationship would assume). *Where* access points are institutionally located affects the types of actors that are likely to exert influence over government policy. In the case of welfare retrenchment, access points are most likely to foster deadlock where they encourage the mobilization of left-wing interests. The two institutional factors that are largely responsible for the presence of powerful leftist interests, the multiparty system and mechanisms for integrating trade union movements, are not found in the United States. In some instances, the separation of powers, bicameralism and federalism may even enhance leaders' retrenchment capabilities. With respect to welfare overhaul, federalism has proved to be a particularly useful resource for imposing cuts and avoiding electoral blame because voters generally lay blame at the level of service provision.[1] Indeed, the interaction between the location of access points, dominant actors and specific policy proposals conditions the impact of institutional power-sharing more than the mere presence of accessible political structures.

Compounding the institutional fragmentation of power in the United States, of course, is the division of partisan power between the executive and legislature for twenty-six of the last thirty-two years. Despite the fact that America's decentralized parties have rarely counteracted the institutional differences wrought through the separation of powers, the recurrence of divided government has led commentators to deride the legislative process in terms of 'deadlock', 'gridlock', 'stalemate' and 'drift'.[2]

Yet in much the same way as descriptions of institutional power-sharing are often rough around the edges, accounts of partisan power-sharing frequently lack nuance. In an attempt to challenge the conventional wisdom regarding the negative effects of divided government, David Mayhew argued a decade ago that partisan power-sharing does not hamper the effectiveness of the legislative process.[3] Irrespective of party label, the President and Congress must cooperate in order to produce the legislative successes that substantiate the credit claiming of electoral politics. On face value, Mayhew's argument is more compelling if voters are intentionally policy balancing when they split their ballot papers.[4] If voters are signalling a preference for policy moderation when they split-ticket vote, the electoral incentives for bipartisanship are that much greater than if divided government results from random or non-intentional factors such as high rates of congressional incumbency.[5] A recent study by Gerand and Lichtl finds evidence that voters with high levels of political knowledge do split their ballots with the intent of policy balancing.[6] While these purposive voters may constitute a minority of split-ticket voters, the authors rightly point out that it takes very few votes to swing electoral outcomes and create divided government.[7] Consequently, this select group of strategic voters might be expected to provide incentives for executive–legislative cooperation under split-party control.

Mayhew's claims have, of course, evoked a number of challenges. Examining all legislation produced between 1945 and 1994, Howell et al.

argue that Mayhew's results are a statistical artefact and that divided government reduces *landmark* legislation by close to 30 per cent.[8] The authors claim that the effect of divided government on legislative productivity depends upon whether legislation is judged to be critical at the time of passage or retrospectively. Contemporaneous assessments are associated with much lower levels of legislative productivity under divided government, whereas retrospective evaluations produce inverse effects. According to Howell et al., Mayhew's bundling of the two types of evaluation falsely leads him to conclude that divided government has no impact on the passage of highly significant legislation. Of some interest, however, the authors do concede that divided government has little impact on the quantity of *important* (but not *landmark*) bills that are approved and that it actually increases the production of *trivial* legislation by approximately ninety-seven laws per session.[9] The latter would appear to constitute a 'substitution effect': while the politics of divided government discourage the delivery of highly significant legislation, the credit-claiming politics that Mayhew makes note of encourages legislative productivity, resulting in a host of less time-consuming minor measures.[10]

Edwards et al. also find that the effects of divided government are more complex and qualified than the standard 'gridlock' argument allows.[11] Focusing their analysis on important bills that failed under conditions of divided and unified government, the authors' report that the President opposes more legislation under divided government for the obvious reason that he is less likely to agree with initiatives put forward by his partisan opponents in Congress. Moreover, he can prevent such bills from being enacted into law by exercising his veto power. The majority party in Congress may even be tempted to send the President legislation he will be loath to sign in the hope of cornering him into a veto. Senate majority leader Bob Dole attempted to use this strategy with the Clinton administration over welfare reform in 1996. However, the President must achieve a legislative record. Consequently, he does not support less legislation under divided government and, owing to the fragility of partisan support in Congress, split party control makes scant difference to whether lawmakers accept or reject legislation he supports.

If we consider the above points together, the politics of institutional and partisan power-sharing are rather more subtle and contingent than the terms 'deadlock', 'stalemate' and 'gridlock' suggest. However, to gain a fuller understanding of the effects of power-sharing, it is useful to look beyond the issue of legislative productivity and presidential success scores to examine its impact on the politics of the legislative process; that is, the politics of compromise, delay, failure, revision and approval. Most studies investigating the effects of power-sharing, like those cited above, examine a large number of legislative initiatives and quantify the productivity of the legislative process under conditions of divided and unified government or assess presidential success scores (which typically tally the number of initiatives on which the President and Congress voted the same way). Yet as Howell et al. suggest: 'It may be . . . that during periods of divided government, what would otherwise be extremely innovative, and therefore landmark, legislation is compromised down into the lower echelons of legislative significance.'[12] Likewise, Edwards et al. concede, 'We have not addressed the complex issue of the dilution of legislation through interbranch bargaining, nor have we discussed the years of delay that divided government may cause for legislation that does eventually pass.'[13]

Indeed, in many instances, including welfare reform, the President does not simply approve or disapprove of a bill. He may send the legislature a signal about the principle of an initiative and wait to see the detailed bill that Congress delivers. President Clinton repeatedly promised to 'end welfare as we know it'. He agreed with the Republican-controlled Congress on the need for fundamental welfare reform. Yet he twice vetoed overhaul legislation, arguing that it was 'tough on children and weak on work'. The third time Congress sent the President a welfare restructuring package he expressed reservations about some of its provisions yet nevertheless chose to sign the measure. The reforms that Republicans originally sought were compromised in important ways to avoid a third presidential veto. Despite these concessions, however, welfare overhaul remained a landmark legislative accomplishment.

Although we cannot draw any generalizations on the basis of a single case, an overview of a critical measure that was proposed, opposed (twice vetoed), compromised, eventually passed and later revised can help us discern some of the more intricate effects of institutional and partisan power-sharing on the politics (as opposed to productivity) of the legislative process. Welfare reform is a particularly instructive example because power-sharing occurred across levels of government as well as among federal institutions. State governors, especially Republican governors, played an important role in renewing momentum for welfare overhaul in the face of two failed attempts.

The Case of Welfare Reform

On 22 August 1996 a Democratic president working with Republican majorities in both Houses of Congress signed the dramatic Personal Responsibility and Work Opportunity Reconciliation Act (PRWORA). The PRWORA ended six decades of the federal guarantee Aid to

Families with Dependent Children (AFDC), affecting close to 14.5 million people. The $23 billion welfare programme was replaced by a block grant to the states, Temporary Assistance for Needy Children (TANF). This was the first time such a large-scale federal entitlement programme had been reduced to a block grant.[14] While dismantling AFDC formed the core of the legislation, it was not the most important element in terms of budgetary savings. Indeed, the reach of PRWORA went well beyond the 5 million families dependent on the federal entitlement – a figure that included one in seven children in America.[15] As *Congressional Quarterly* commented prior to the measure's enactment: 'The welfare debate touches on almost every aspect of federal social policy. It could change whether and how poor people enter the work force, care for their children, get free or subsidized meals, obtain health care and get fathers to contribute to their children's upbringing.'[16]

The significance of the legislation can be illustrated by recounting just a few of its provisions. The PRWORA mandated that an individual can only receive welfare assistance for five years during their entire adult lifetime (counting from its enactment). Within two years of receiving welfare, claimants must work. At state discretion this period may be reduced or abolished so that welfare recipients can be required to work immediately. Participation in community service is mandatory after two months of receiving benefits. Education, vocational training and school attendance can only replace work for 20 per cent of claimants in any state and for a maximum of one year (as adjusted in the Balanced Budget Act 1997). The PRWORA stipulated that each state must demonstrate that 35 per cent of recipients are working for a minimum of twenty hours per week by financial year 1997 (three-quarters of two-parent families for a minimum of thirty-five hours per week). This figure must rise to 50 per cent for a minimum of thirty hours per week by financial year 2002 (90 per cent of two-parent families must be working for a minimum of thirty-five hours per week).[17]

Sanctions are imposed on both individuals and states that fail to comply with the above regulations. In the case of an adult refusing to work, the family's benefit can be reduced pro rata for each day the individual is absent from their place of employment. At state discretion, the sanction may exceed the pro rata penalty to include the full denial of benefits. Medicaid coverage (a federal-state programme that provides health insurance for the poor) can be terminated for adults (but not their children) who do not fully comply with the work requirements. Sanctions are also imposed on states that are unable to meet the PRWORA's work participation requirements. The first year a state misses the federal government's target its grant will be cut by 5 per cent, followed by an additional 2 per cent cut for each year of non-compliance (up to a total of 21 per cent).[18]

The law also mandated that no person between the ages of eighteen and fifty (without children) can receive food stamps for more than three months in a three-year period. It tightened benefit eligibility criteria for a number of groups, including disabled children. The Congressional Budget Office, an independent source of budgetary advice, estimated that 300,000 children (22 per cent) would cease to qualify for Supplemental Security Income (SSI), a federal programme that also provides cash assistance to the low-income elderly, disabled and blind.[19] Legal immigrants were also hit hard by the legislation. Indeed, a large portion of the PRWORA's $54.6 billion in savings (expected by financial year 2002) derived from withdrawing benefits, such as Supplemental Security Income, from legal immigrants.

It is important to recognize that the PRWORA was not simply designed to cut the cost of federal welfare provision. Perhaps more importantly, it also legislated a conservative moral agenda. It allowed states to impose family cap policies on welfare recipients whereby children born on TANF can be excluded in the calculation of family benefits. No TANF funds can be allocated to unmarried parents under eighteen years of age without a high school education (or GED) who have a child of twelve weeks or older unless they are enrolled in an educational programme (leading to high school diploma or GED). Any parent under the age of eighteen must live in an adult-supervised setting.[20]

To place the significance of this legislation in context, it is worth recalling that just eight years earlier when the Family Support Act of 1988 was under consideration, many of the Democrats who supported the PRWORA routinely referred to workfare as 'slavefare'.[21] Moreover, prior to the GOP takeover of Congress in January 1995, even many Republicans expressed serious reservations about dismantling AFDC as an entitlement.[22] How was this critical series of welfare reforms formulated, delayed, diluted, denied, eventually passed and revised amid the institutional and partisan fragmentation that characterizes the US political system?

The Legislative Politics of the PRWORA

Two failed attempts at welfare overhaul

Welfare overhaul has been intermittently on the national agenda since the Nixon administration. In 1972, however, restructuring AFDC proved too controversial to survive the cycle of US electoral politics.[23] Twenty years later, growing public dissatisfaction with the programme, fuelled by racist stereotypes and policy experts asserting that welfare was the problem not the solution, changed the political costs of overhaul.[24] William Jefferson Clinton came to office in 1992 promising to transform welfare into 'a second chance not a way of life'. Running as a 'New Democrat', he flagged his role in shaping the Family Support Act of 1988 while governor of Arkansas and chairman of the National Governors' Association (NGA) as proof of his commitment to workfare.[25]

Yet despite promising radical overhaul of an increasingly contentious welfare system, the President's prioritization of health care reform and the administration's delay in delivering this complex plan meant that almost half the presidential term had elapsed before welfare reform received serious attention. Furthermore, although Clinton's overhaul plan responded to the public's concern that welfare recipients should work, the scheme was considerably more limited than many had hoped or feared. For example, the work mandate would only apply to those born after 1971 and the federal government would continue to assume a central role in welfare provision by creating federally subsidized jobs, training opportunities and childcare.[26] The measure received little direct pressure from the White House and it came as no surprise when it failed to emerge from the 103rd Congress.

In a sweeping victory at the 1994 mid-term elections the Republican Party took control of both Houses of Congress for the first time in forty years. The election was widely considered to be a landmark event owing to its anti-Democratic thrust (no Republican incumbents lost their seat), and because of the unusually cohesive right-wing platform on which many Republicans ran. Defying expectations, House Republicans fulfilled their electoral promise to introduce all key elements of the 'Contract with America', a ten-point agenda for the 104th Congress which included welfare overhaul, within their first hundred days in office. Welfare reform was by far the most ambitious measure listed in the Contract. With much of the budget devoted to untouchables such as defence and social security, overhaul had to produce hefty savings in order to meet the GOP's pledge to balance the budget.[27]

The House of Representatives acted on restructuring the welfare system with some speed and delivered a tough cost-cutting bill with comparative ease. Though debate was heated and predictably partisan, the lower chamber quickly passed its version of welfare overhaul on 24 March 1995.[28] However, in pursuing a 'crashing through' legislative strategy during their hundred day 'honeymoon', House Republicans explicitly eschewed a bipartisan approach and rode roughshod over the concerns of Democratic law-makers.[29] Democrats were particularly enraged that Republicans had attempted to reduce Medicaid from a federal entitlement to a block grant by lumping it together with welfare overhaul. This bundling of the two entitlements seemed to be a particularly myopic means of doing business given that any bill would ultimately require the President's signature. Infuriated by the GOPs treatment of House Democrats and their plans for Medicaid, Clinton signalled his unequivocal opposition to the bill: 'a narrow partisan majority passes a bill that is weak on work and tough on children.'[30]

Not only had House Republicans passed a bill that would clearly invite a presidential veto, it was also clear that the upper chamber would not support such a radical initiative. The more independent Republican majority in the Senate delayed their version of the bill with a protracted opening debate.[31] The family cap and the division of federal spending among the states caused a number of disagreements between moderate and conservative Republicans. Differences over the family cap were exacerbated by splits in the Republicans' religious constituency and interest group network. The Christian Coalition and the Family Research Council endorsed the House's position of preventing federal money from being used to support children born on welfare in order to cut 'illegitimacy' rates. The Catholic Conference and the National Right to Life Committee, by contrast, demanded greater leniency to avoid a surge in abortions.[32]

With respect to funding formulae, Republican senators squabbled over the allocation of $16.8 billion per annum in federal welfare spending for the following five years.[33] The key controversy boiled down to whether federal funds should be primarily distributed on the basis of a state's previous spending commitment or its rates of child poverty. Not surprisingly, this issue drew a sharp cleavage between senators from the South and West with steep population increases and low benefits and those from high-immigrant states with comparatively generous welfare assistance such as California and New York. Although the financial implications of this decision were important as far as welfare spending was concerned, the issue proved to be so divisive largely because of the precedent it would create for Medicaid, where federal spending was five times as great.[34]

In an attempt to reconcile Senate Republicans, Majority Leader and soon-to-be presidential nominee Bob Dole formulated a compromise measure. When Dole was promoting his bill he was keen to point out that it enjoyed the support of several governors from early primary states.[35] Indeed, presidential politics played an integral role in welfare overhaul from the outset. Phil Gramm, one of Dole's chief rivals for the

1996 Republican nomination from the conservative right, withheld his support, arguing that the states deserved much greater leeway in determining their welfare arrangements and that non-naturalized residents should be subject to tighter eligibility criteria for a number of benefits.[36]

While ideological differences within the Republican Party were primarily responsible for delaying Senate progress on welfare overhaul, opposition from the minority party was by no means irrelevant. Democrats were furious that Republicans had folded an issue as critical as welfare reform into the larger process of deficit reduction.[37] The Senate's slow progress on their version of welfare overhaul meant that a freestanding bill would be unlikely to get the President's signature in time for inclusion in the Reconciliation Bill.[38] As a result, the savings wrought from reforming welfare could not be counted towards the Republicans' goal of balancing the budget. Dealing with overhaul through the Budget Reconciliation Bill limited debate to twenty hours and offered protection from a filibuster – an important calculation given the Republicans' slim majority in the Senate. The downside of using reconciliation for welfare restructuring from the Republicans' perspective was that the reach of the initiative would be constrained by the Byrd Rule (which limits reconciliation to items that pertain directly to deficit reduction unless overruled by a majority of sixty votes). In other words, a free-standing welfare bill would still be required to bring about more substantial changes in the welfare system.[39]

Deprived of the opportunity to filibuster, Democrats put forward many amendments in an attempt to delay the legislation further and the party's leadership introduced an alternative bill as a focus for minority party opposition.[40] However, senior Democrats were not united in this strategy and the changes that moderate Republicans had managed to win from their conservative colleagues enticed enough Democrats to ensure bipartisan support for the legislation. Indeed, the bill that emerged from the Senate in September 1995 was inclusive and moderate compared with the House version. Clinton was quick to praise the upper chamber for its bipartisan effort but cautioned that Democratic cooperation was contingent upon conferees not capitulating to the demands of House extremists. At the same time, these so-called extremist Republicans threatened to retract their support if the Senate's bill was not toughened up in conference committee. Republican conferees succumbed to this pressure and leaned too far towards the House version to secure any measure of bipartisan support. The result was a highly partisan vote in both chambers followed by a presidential veto on 6 December 1995. After alienating Democrats in conference it was clear that Republicans would be unable to muster the necessary two-thirds majority to override Clinton's veto.[41]

It is of some importance that Clinton suffered little electoral blame for vetoing the bill. Congressional Republicans had gravely underestimated the President's political skills, particularly his ability to frame the national agenda very effectively when reacting to his partisan opponents in Congress, especially the controversial Speaker, Newt Gingrich. Clinton's portrayal of House Republicans as fanatics, intent on waging war against all manner of social programmes, seemed to resonate with the public. The GOP did not help matters when they chose to close down the federal government over budgetary conflicts with the President.

The Republican's free-standing welfare bill fared little better. This was hardly surprising given that House Republicans continued to eschew a bipartisan approach. Much like the previous effort, the reconciliation process sacrificed Democratic support by overaccommodating House Republicans.[42] Moderate Republicans in the Senate also prevaricated over whether to accept the conference report, and a number of late-day compromises had to be offered in order to rally enough votes. In the end, a concession on state control of school meal programmes and the repeal of close to 5 billion dollars worth of cuts by 2002 helped secure the necessary Republican signatures. Even then, five moderate Republicans who eventually provided enough votes for the Senate to accept the report wrote Bob Dole a letter conveying their astonishment at the severity of the bill conferees had delivered.[43]

It is noteworthy that the concessions offered in conference committee were barely adequate to secure the votes of moderate Republicans in the Senate, let alone enlist bipartisan support. The GOP's failure to provide Democratic law-makers with a stake in the measure again ensured the President would reject the bill. Matters were not helped by the fact that the NGA had been unable to muster the three-quarters majority required to provide law-makers with an official position on welfare overhaul, encouraging congressional leaders to negotiate only with Republican governors.[44] When two of the most prominent state leaders on welfare overhaul, Governor John Engler, a Republican from Michigan, and Governor Tommy Thompson, a Republican from Wisconsin, held a news conference urging President Clinton to sign the bill they waved a petition bearing no Democratic signatures.[45]

For a second time the President was successfully able to frame Republicans as extremists who were willing to punish the innocent children of welfare recipients in their quest for radical reform. The GOP was too concerned with its own internal quarrels over the party's presidential nominee to fully exploit the situation.[46] Consequently, Clinton again managed to avoid electoral blame for exercising his veto power on 9 January 1996. After the second veto, however, radical welfare reform seemed unlikely to emerge from the 104th Congress.

The third legislative attempt

In his State of the Union address on 23 January 1996, President Clinton reaffirmed his commitment to welfare overhaul and invited congressional Republicans to formulate a genuinely bipartisan plan. Clinton's interest in having a third attempt at restructuring AFDC was unambiguous. With the embarrassing collapse of health-care reform, the President had few major legislative accomplishments to flaunt in an election year – especially since congressional Republicans were threatening to weaken some of his more popular domestic initiatives, including the Earned Income Tax Credit for the working poor.[47]

Republicans, however, were ambivalent about a third attempt. GOP campaign strategists cautioned that if Clinton was afforded a further opportunity to meet his 1992 promise to end welfare, Republicans would pay the price in November. Others, including the presidential nominee Bob Dole (who had taken to calling the President 'old veto Bill'), wanted to corner Clinton into a third veto by again combining welfare and Medicaid – a condition that Clinton had explicitly rejected.[48] A further section of the party favoured sending the President a more moderate, bipartisan bill, resembling the Senate's version that he had publicly welcomed. A bipartisan effort, they reasoned, would greatly raise the political costs of a veto (exposing Clinton as the closet liberal that many Republicans believed him to be). Conversely, if the President accepted a bipartisan measure he would alienate many of his liberal allies inside and outside Congress and Republicans would still receive most of the credit for dismantling AFDC.[49]

In the midst of these competing calculations, the NGA delivered a reform proposal on 6 February 1996 that combined welfare and Medicaid overhaul.[50] This statement from the states was important in providing renewed momentum for reform. While the statement was approved by Democratic governors, dissension within the NGA was apparent from the start.[51] Reiterating Clinton's earlier objections, Democrats remonstrated against retrenching Medicaid through the back door of welfare reform. They were especially vocal in pointing out that the NGA's plan did not enjoy the degree of bipartisan support that Republican governors claimed it did.[52] On top of these grievances, House

Republicans complained that the NGA had diluted their agenda on both a moral and financial level. They particularly resented the NGA's proposal to let the states decide whether or not to use federal money to support children born on welfare. They also opposed the governors' plan to relax welfare-to-work targets and rejected their call for smaller cuts in Supplemental Security Income and food stamps, the two principal sources of budgetary savings.[53]

The NGA's proposal, however, did validate Bob Dole's preference for combining welfare and Medicaid reform. Again, this decision automatically alienated Democrats, as did packaging the bill into budget reconciliation for a second time in the hopes of avoiding a Senate filibuster and truncating debate on a highly charged matter. When Republican legislators presented the measure at a news conference on 22 May 1996 there were no Democrats in attendance.[54] The fact that Republicans had made such little effort to accommodate Clinton's concerns or even enter into consultations with the White House fuelled suspicions that the GOP intended to corner the President into a third veto.[55]

The concessions that Republican law-makers offered in the revised bill were principally aimed at appeasing the governors and moderate Republican senators rather than congressional Democrats or the President. For example, the bill adopted the NGA's position on the family cap, exemptions from work mandates were set at 20 per cent rather than 15 per cent (although the bill tightened the definition of work), and additional funds for childcare and contingencies such as recession were provided for.[56] The issues on which the governors had not explicitly staked out a position underwent little change, including the sharp reductions in social services for legal immigrants.[57]

Predictably, Clinton denounced the Medicaid reforms as a 'poison pill' that would damn welfare overhaul.[58] At the same time, however, he offered Republicans an olive branch by reaffirming his support for many of the changes contained in their revised bill. An increasing number of Republicans in the House as well as the Senate were keenly aware that if they did not offer further concessions they would sacrifice their last opportunity for major restructuring. They were also nervous that the public would again find them culpable if they sent Clinton a measure he felt compelled to veto for a third time. The President's huge lead over Dole in the polls (sometimes as high as 20 per cent), on top of the poor ratings of many GOP law-makers, put pressure on congressional leaders to reassess the merits of combining welfare and Medicaid reform.[59]

During the second week of July, the Republican leadership offered the significant concession of agreeing to separate welfare and Medicaid.[60]

This compromise was largely made possible by the fact that Bob Dole had retired from the Senate in a desperate attempt to boost his failing bid for the presidency. Abandoning the Medicaid provisions allowed many Democrats to support the bill in principle, especially in the Senate. Still, political manoeuvrings from both parties continued. A game of 'chicken' ensued as Democrats and Republicans in both legislative chambers sought to improve their bargaining power in conference.[61] While the White House welcomed the removal of Medicaid from the revised bill, the legislation did not meet with unqualified enthusiasm. Clinton continued to express doubts about the wisdom of specific provisions pertaining to legal immigrants and the cuts in food stamps. Senate Minority Leader Tom Daschle issued a warning that the President's signature was by no means assured after Jack Howard, aide to Speaker Newt Gingrich, sent his boss a memo on 15 July advising Republicans that the 'White House will sign just about anything we send them, so we should make them eat as much as we can.'[62] The uncertainty of Democratic support increased (and thus their leverage in conference) when a study by the Urban Institute was circulated on 26 July 1996, projecting that the House bill would condemn nearly 1.1 million children and 1.5 million adults to a life of poverty.[63]

Despite this exchange of threats, the electoral context (specifically, the floundering state of the Republicans' bid for the presidency and the prospect of congressional losses) helped foster a spirit of compromise rather than stalemate this time round. Conferees diluted some of the most contentious elements of the House bill with more lenient and flexible provisions from the Senate's bipartisan version, allowing congressional Democrats and the White House to find enough merit in the legislation to justify their support.[64] For example, the report specified that people between the ages of eighteen and fifty with no dependants or disability could qualify for three months of food stamps over a three-year period. The House bill would have allowed them to receive a total of three months of food stamps up to the age of fifty, while the Senate bill would have provided for four months of food stamps per year. With respect to the family cap, conferees endorsed the Senate's and the NGA's position of allowing states to choose whether to use federal funds to support children born on welfare. The House had attempted to ban the states from using federal money in this way (unless they could pass legislation exempting themselves from this restriction). On the divisive issue of Medicaid for legal immigrants, conferees adopted the Senate's position of leaving the matter to state discretion. The House had sought to disqualify legal immigrants from receiving Medicaid. House Republicans were also unable to devolve control to the states over adoption programmes, school meals, and nutritional assistance for pregnant women and children. They also failed to impose tighter eligibility restrictions on the Earned Income Tax Credit and they were forced to restore over $7 billion in proposed cuts.[65]

As these compromises suggest, Republicans included Democrats in the reconciliation process the third time round and the conference agreement attracted considerable bipartisan support. The House voted 328–101 for the report on 31 July and the Senate by 78–21 the following day. However, Republicans were anxious to keep overhaul as primarily a GOP accomplishment. When the party's leadership presented the finalized report at a news conference on 30 July Democrats were not invited.[66] Moreover, the Democratic leadership in both the upper and lower chamber continued to oppose the bill.

The President announced on 31 July that he would sign the bill but he gave little indication of his intent before this date. As noted, Clinton had strong incentives to fulfil his 1992 campaign promise to overhaul AFDC. He was acutely aware that this was his last chance to fundamentally restructure a system he believed to be broken. After announcing that he would sign the bill, he declared that AFDC 'undermines the basic values of work, responsibility and family, trapping generation after generation in dependency and hurting the very people it was designed to help'.[67] Clinton also had much to gain in electoral terms by swinging to the right. After the Democrats' disastrous mid-term results in 1994, the President needed to shed his damaging liberal persona and substantiate his claims to be a 'New Democrat' in time for the November elections.

Still, some of the President's aides argued that the compromises contained in the conference report were inadequate and that previous experience indicated Clinton could afford to veto what remained primarily a radical Republican reform.[68] Although the most offensive elements of the GOP's overhaul plan had been contained, the heart of their proposal, terminating AFDC as a federal entitlement, remained firmly in place. Liberal interest groups, including civil rights organizations and advocacy coalitions for the poor, also petitioned the President to reject the legislation.[69] The president of the National Urban League bemoaned, 'It appears that Congress has wearied of the War on Poverty and decided to wage war against poor people instead.'[70] It is also significant that the bill received scant support from the Democratic Party's minority legislators: only two out of thirty-four African Americans, two out of twelve Hispanics and nine out of thirty-one women voted for it.[71] Senator Carol Mosley Braun denounced the legislation for violating civil rights laws owing to its particularly punitive effects on African Americans, and

Senator Daniel Monnihan described it as 'the most brutal act of social policy we have known since reconstruction'.[72]

However, the only real bone of contention for the White House was whether the *non-AFDC* provisions were excessive. From the beginning of the eighteen-month debate on welfare, Clinton was willing to help abolish AFDC as a federal entitlement. When he announced that he would sign the legislation, he tried to appease his critics on the left by insisting that he did not agree with every aspect of the PRWORA, especially its impact on legal immigrants and the cuts in food stamps. He noted that his original overhaul plan would have saved $41 billion less.[73] He also promised that if granted another four years in the White House, he would reformulate some of the PRWORA's more ill-considered provisions as a matter of priority.

The possibilities for legislative revision

When Clinton promised to amend the PRWORA, he did not intend to reverse its principal conditions. Rather, his pledge was the more limited one of providing a number of supports to help people move from welfare to work with greater effectiveness, ease the law's impact on legal immigrants and restore some cuts in food stamps.[74] However, few held out any serious hope for these amendments given the fiscal and policy implications they would naturally entail. While the PRWORA's predicted savings amounted to $54.6 billion by 2002, the bulk of this sum did not come from terminating AFDC but from cuts in the areas Clinton sought to amend. The Congressional Budget Office calculated that savings from the food stamp programme would be worth in the region of $23 billion by 2002 and those from legal immigrants around $23.8 billion, although these two estimates partially overlap.[75]

The deficit-conscious mood of the country and the fact that both Houses of Congress remained in Republican hands made the President's revisions seem even less likely. In order to realize even some of these changes it was clear that Clinton would have to include his amendments in a bipartisan deal to balance the budget by 2002.[76] Perhaps even more important than the budgetary limitations and the continuing right-wing mood of the country, however, was the simple fact that there was little demand for significantly amending the PRWORA. As Mark Greenberg, a senior staff attorney at the Center for Law and Social Policy, aptly observed, 'In order to have a "fix-it bill", there has to be a strong sense that there's something that needs fixing. And probably not enough has happened yet to change the views of those who thought this was a good bill in the first place.'[77]

Yet the President proved more adept at revising the legislation than many expected, including his own aides. The White House partially circumvented Republican opposition by issuing an administrative directive requiring welfare recipients to be protected by a host of federal labour laws.[78] For example, people enrolled in workfare schemes would have to be covered by legislation such as the Civil Rights Act and the Americans for Disability Act and enjoy the same basic legal protections as other workers, including equal health and safety standards, minimum wage levels, and overtime pay regulations.

Not surprisingly, House Republicans argued vociferously that these revisions fundamentally impaired the work mandate that was so integral to the PRWORA by making it too expensive for the states to provide subsidized jobs for welfare recipients. The NGA was willing to accept that people moving from welfare to work should be paid the minimum wage but flatly refused to provide them with further benefits, such as unemployment insurance, on the grounds of cost.[79] House Republicans tried to reduce the reach of the Labor Department's directive through the budget spending bill. The directive allowed food stamps to be treated as compensation under some conditions. Therefore their value could be incorporated into calculations of the minimum wage. House Republicans took advantage of this opening and attempted to treat the cost of Medicaid, childcare and housing benefits in the same way – although they later agreed that only the value of food stamps and assistance from the federal government's welfare block grant should be included in the minimum wage.[80]

According to Clinton, however, the fair and equal protection of welfare recipients in the workplace was an ethical issue that he was unwilling to see compromised – although Republicans argued that principle was less important than the power of the labour unions who were demanding pay-backs for their support during the 1996 campaign.[81] To the surprise of many, the President triumphed on the issue of workplace regulations. He also enjoyed wins on other welfare-related matters in the budget spending bill. On the critical issue of legal immigrants, Republicans eventually accepted that people resident in the United States prior to the PRWORA's enactment on 22 August 1996 could qualify for Supplemental Security Income. While the neutrality of the NGA on the position of legal immigrants had originally helped congressional Republicans impose tough restrictions on their right to benefits, it also allowed Clinton to revise these provisions – especially since governors from politically important states with high immigrant populations, such as New York, were growing increasingly anxious about the social and financial implications of the PRWORA.[82]

The amendments that Clinton was able to extract from the GOP-controlled Congress, however, did not come free and the President had to accept a number of other cutbacks. Republicans won on several issues, including critical ones such as taxation and Medicare.[83] Moreover, the President was unable to restore most of the cuts in food stamps that he had objected to so ardently when he signed the PRWORA and that he had pledged to overturn as a matter of priority.

Conclusions

What does this overview of welfare reform tell us about the politics of institutional and partisan power-sharing? The most striking point for many British observers may be the multiple points of compromise and potential failure that afflict the American legislative process. Indeed, the terms 'gridlock' and 'deadlock' may seem highly appropriate. Compounding the frictions and inefficiencies flowing from divided government, the moderating impact of bicameralism (even where both Houses of Congress are controlled by the same party) proved to be highly significant in delaying and diluting welfare legislation. The slow pace of Senate progress on the initial bill forced overhaul to be lumped into the budget reconciliation process, a procedure which invited further opposition from the minority party and enhanced the likelihood of a presidential veto. While it is common to point out that the American parties rarely unite the institutional separation of the executive and legislature, a similar point may be made, albeit less forcefully, with respect to the two Houses of Congress. The different constituencies, electoral timeframes and procedural rules of the House and Senate often result in distinct approaches to the legislative process and divergent policy perspectives irrespective of shared party bonds. While statistical differences in presidential support scores between the two chambers are not strong, the most significant impact of bicameralism may well show up in the Senate's delaying and moderating influence on legislation rather than the more absolute measure of whether the Senate accepts or rejects bills in any different quantity from the House.

A similar point might be made with respect to the state governments. With hefty majorities at the gubernatorial level, Republican governors were initially unwilling to make the compromises necessary to build cross-party coalitions. Thus the NGA was unable to provide law-makers with a bipartisan statement on welfare overhaul until February 1996. The absence of a guiding policy statement from the states in turn sharpened partisan divisions within Congress. With the explicit exclusion of Democrats at all levels of government during the first two attempts at overhaul, a presidential veto was all but guaranteed.

However, it is also worth bearing in mind that the policy-moderating impact of bicameralism helped forge the legislative compromises that, in the final analysis, allowed landmark legislation to emerge under conditions of divided government. Moderate Republican senators were primarily responsible for softening the House bill in ways that facilitated a more inclusive approach to welfare overhaul and provided the President with a stake in the legislation. While the bipartisan efforts of the upper chamber were overridden in conference and the first two reports were passed along strict party lines, the Senate's version of the bill provided Clinton with a starting point for a third attempt at overhaul and a concrete basis for negotiation with the House.

Indeed, the effects of divided government partially depend on how successfully bipartisan coalitions are formed in the legislature. To some degree, this is contingent upon the size and cohesion of the majority party in both chambers and partisan divisions at the state level. A less cohesive and smaller majority in the legislature (more typical of the Senate) provides the dominant party with stronger incentives to offer the bipartisan compromises that are necessary to make divided government work effectively. The legislative process may be slower and more contentious under these circumstances (contrast the legislative politics of the House and Senate with respect to welfare overhaul), but they also create a more centrist governing dynamic that facilitates effective governance under split party control. The first two failed attempts at welfare overhaul sharply illustrate how law-makers' failure to build bipartisan coalitions in the House, in conference and among the states encouraged divided government to fail.

The good news for the American legislative process is that cooperation is not simply contingent upon the size and cohesion of congressional majorities. There are numerous formal and informal incentives for compromise embedded within the US architecture. The politics and institutional rules of bicameralism and federalism actually facilitate bipartisan coalition building in a number of ways. Institutionally, the Senate's looser procedural rules (and for most legislation, the threat of a filibuster) and the NGA's three-quarters majority rule provide obvious incentives for cross-party negotiation. Politically, the large electoral constituencies and high visibility of senators and governors can have a similar effect. These inducements are lower in the House. In the case of welfare overhaul, it took the more imminent pressures of the upcoming elections to compel House Republicans to accept the Senate's and the NGA's moderating influence in conference. Still, it is important to recognize that the House also has a number of institutional and political incentives to compromise *in the final analysis*: a two-year electoral cycle combined with an electorate that is hostile to the perception of political extremism and, to some extent, even blatant partisanship.

This interpretation of institutional and partisan power-sharing suggests that veto points do not necessarily accumulate in an additive way to impede policy change. Sources of institutional and partisan fragmentation do not automatically compound each other, culminating in ever greater deadlock and drift. With respect to welfare reform, strong bicameralism and federalism to some extent greased the wheels of the separation of powers and particularly divided government. As noted, the Senate was particularly important in crafting an initiative that Democratic law-makers and the President could accept. While the NGA was slow to bring Democratic governors on board, it also proved crucial in providing renewed momentum for welfare reform in the wake of two presidential vetos and in endorsing some of the Senate's more moderate provisions. While partisan divisions among the states exacerbated partisan divisions in Congress, let us not forget that the federal structure of the government provided the President with the means to wash his hands of a politically contentious welfare programme in the name of increasing state autonomy.

None of this implies that institutional and partisan power-sharing does not make for intricate bargaining politics. Reaching compromises is inevitably a politically fraught process and forging bipartisan deals can easily break down, as the first two attempts at welfare overhaul illustrate all too clearly. Strategic action is precarious where there are multiple unknowns and uncertainties – factors that surely increase with the complexity of institutions and the partisan division of power within these structures. Political gamesmanship can go badly wrong where the intent of so many players must be weighed up, where blame can be widely dispersed and where accountability can be diverted to multiple institutional locations. Under these circumstances, however, cooperation often has the highest pay-offs and while the fragmentation of institutional and partisan power encourages a politics of compromise, it does not necessarily result in either extreme incrementalism or deadlock. As a side point, it is also worth considering whether a process that relies on building bridges should necessarily be equated with an inefficient one. For example, a large number of policy stakeholders may well weaken opposition with respect to implementation. Once Clinton and his partisans in Congress had agreed to support the PRWORA, they had an interest in seeing overhaul work effectively and in limiting the scope of their revisions.

There are also reasons to suggest that a unified administration might not have been able to deliver such a landmark legislative initiative as the PRWORA. It may seem intuitive to argue that a Republican president would have been willing to support an even more far-reaching series of reforms than Clinton, perhaps restructuring Medicaid as well as AFDC in the way that House Republicans originally wanted. Likewise, Senate Republicans might have accepted a more dramatic overhaul package if pressurized by a Republican president. These assumptions, however, may be incorrect. The move away from the political centre by a unified administration can pose electoral problems. As noted above, American voters are hostile to political extremes. Republicans, especially in the House, retained control of the legislature by shedding their ideological baggage. Recall that Republican zealotry had already become a liability for the GOP in the 1996 elections even with the concessions the party offered on welfare reform and a number of other issues, including a raise in the minimum wage.

The perceived extremism of a unified Republican administration, therefore, could well have invited a much harsher backlash against radical welfare overhaul than emerged under conditions of divided government where both parties had a stake in the final reform effort. With Democrats and Republicans signed up to various elements of the PRWORA – if not necessarily the same elements – Democratic opposition inside and outside Congress was much reduced and blame was politically dispersed. Far more vocal criticism and counterframing from Democrats could have been expected had this landmark legislation been the product of a unified Republican administration, potentially transforming a broadly popular initiative into a highly divisive one.

By the same token, it seems safe to argue that a unified Democratic administration would have produced a much weaker measure than the PRWORA. Despite the President's promise to 'end welfare as we know it', it is not at all clear that Clinton would have given welfare reform the priority it required had the national mood not swung to the right after two years of Democratic governance. As the *Congressional Quarterly Weekly Report* projected:

> Another 18 months of Democratic control on Capitol Hill – on the heels of the disastrous second session of the 103rd Congress – would have meant more of the contentious rivalry between the Democratic power factions:

between competing leaderships, the White House and Congress, the states and the federal government, blacks and whites, business and labor, social liberals and social conservatives ... Continued Democratic dominance would have meant another broad assault on the health care delivery and financing system, with all the predictable fallout ... In the suburbs and other swing precincts that decided American elections, the issues of 1996 would have been high taxes, big government, social decay and intrusive public authority ... Instead the story lines of 1996 are largely about the excesses of the GOP.[84]

While these arguments are inevitably speculative, they should caution us about blindly accepting the proposition that power-sharing necessarily results in deadlock or that power concentration always provides leaders with a free hand to implement their legislative goals. In the American context of frequent elections and a public thirsty for moderation, power-sharing can produce a centrist and thus more successful governing dynamic.[85] Under these circumstances, of course, sweeping change tends to be limited to a centrist or centre-right platform and is often dependent upon a clear rejection of the status quo. Indeed, in contrast to the President's comparatively liberal plan for health care form, welfare overhaul did not have to overcome widespread support for the status quo or defeat entrenched interests with a heavy investment in existing arrangements.[86]

Taking these points together, one final matter might be raised in trying to draw lessons from the case of welfare overhaul: perhaps the basis for comparison should not simply be divided versus unified government. Inevitably most studies of split party control capture the legislative effects of a Republican president and Democratic congress. Yet if parties matter – something that most political scientists accept – then the type of divided government matters: who occupies which institutional position matters. Counterintuitively, welfare retrenchment may have been best served by having a Democrat in the White House and a Republican-led Congress. As noted earlier, Clinton had strong electoral incentives to move to the right in preparation for the 1996 elections. His clear lack of an electoral mandate in 1992 – reinforced after the whole-hearted rejection of the Democrats at the 1994 midterms – greatly undermined his incentives and authority to pursue a liberal agenda. However, unlike a Democratic president, House Democrats have fewer incentives to accept belt-tightening measures. Shielded from national and international pressures, locally oriented representatives have strong partisan, ideological, institutional, and sometimes electoral reasons to oppose the more divisive elements of a cost-cutting agenda.

By the same token, Republican members of Congress are less reluctant to tenaciously pursue programmatic cuts than Republican presidents who are politically constrained by their national electoral constituency which inevitably includes Independents and Democrats as well as Republicans. The push for radical overhaul was provided by the cohesive and zealous Republican Congress, energized after its years of minority status, by the ideological leadership of Speaker Gingrich, the influx of new members, its claim to a mandate and the security of institutional position. This leadership was accepted by the Democratic President who needed to dispense with his big-spending liberal image and attract the support of moderate conservatives.

In the final analysis, though we cannot generalize on the basis of one piece of landmark legislation, the case of welfare overhaul should alert us to three issues for further consideration when evaluating the impact of institutional and partisan power-sharing. First, we should take account of the interactive effects of different sources of power-sharing. Thus we might want to move beyond the assumption that veto players accumulate in an additive fashion to render the legislative process ever more inefficient. In the case of welfare overhaul, strong bicameralism in particular allowed landmark legislation to emerge under conditions of divided government. Secondly, we should be open to the possibility that power-sharing can produce positive governing dynamics in terms of blame avoidance, political centrism and multiple stakeholding. Third, the impact of power-sharing is contingent on other non-institutional factors, not least the short-term political and electoral context, the saliency of the issue, and, in the case of AFDC, Clinton's considerable political skills in framing the welfare debate.

NOTES

1   Centralized institutions allow voters to draw clear linkages between leaders and policy and thus provide fewer opportunities for blame avoidance. If voters do not care for government actions, they are in no doubt as to who is responsible. See Paul Pierson, *Dismantling the Welfare State: Reagan, Thatcher and the Politics of Retrenchment* (Cambridge: Cambridge University Press, 1994); Kent R. Weaver, 'The Politics of Blame-Avoidance', *Journal of Public Policy*, 6 (1986), pp. 371–98. Moreover, while forcing contentious measures through the legislative process is institutionally possible in centralized systems such as Britain, non-negotiated settlements on divisive issues often lack legitimacy and are prone to invite the backlash that was so evident in the case of New Zealand during the early 1990s (in terms of sweeping institutional change, voter flight to new parties further to the left and right, and rising levels of political disillusionment).

2   See James MacGregor Burns, *The Deadlock of Democracy* (Englewood Cliffs: Prentice-Hall, 1963); James MacGregor Burns, *Cobblestone Leadership: Majority Rule, Minority Power* (Norman: University of Oklahoma

Press, 1990); Gary W. Cox and Matthew D. McCubbins, 'Divided Control of Fiscal Policy', in Gary W. Cox and Samuel Kernell (eds), *The Politics of Divided Government* (Boulder: Westview Press, 1991): James L. Sundquist, *Constitutional Reform and Effective Government*, rev. edn (Washington DC: Brookings Institution, 1992).

3   David R. Mayhew, *Divided We Govern: Party Control, Lawmakings and Investigations, 1946–1990* (New Haven: Yale University Press, 1991).

4   Morris Fiorina, *Divided Government* (New York: Macmillan, 1992); James C. Gerand and Marci Glascock Lichtl, 'Explaining Divided Government in the United States: Testing an Intentional Model of Split-Ticket Voting', *British Journal of Political Science* (2000), pp. 173–87.

5   John Petrocik, 'Divided Government: Is It All in the Campaign?', in Cox and Kernell, *Politics of Divided Government*.

6   Gerand and Lichtl, 'Explaining Divided Government in the United States', p. 186.

7   Ibid., p. 187.

8   William Howell, Scott Adler, Charles Cameron and Charles Riemann, 'Divided Government and the Legislative Productivity of Congress, 1945–94', *Legislative Studies Quarterly*, 25, no. 2 (May 2000), pp. 285–312, at p. 302.

9   Ibid., pp. 300–2.

10 Ibid., p. 300.

11 George C. Edwards, Andrew Barrett and Jeffrey Peake, 'The Legislative Impact of Divided Government', *American Journal of Political Science*, 41, no. 2 (Apr. 1997), pp. 545–63.

12 Howell et al., 'Divided Government', p. 303.

13 Edwards, Barrett and Peake, 'Legislative Impact', p. 562.

14 *Congressional Quarterly Weekly Report* (*CQWR*), 3 Aug. 1996, p. 2191.

15 *CQWR*, 23 Sept. 1995, p. 2911.

16 *CQWR*, 25 Feb. 1995, p. 614.

17 See *CQWR*, 3 Aug. 1996, p. 2192 for a useful overview of these provisions.

18 *Welfare Reform Network News* (*WRNN*), Jan. 1997; *CQWR*, 3 Aug. 1996, p. 2192.

19 *CQWR*, 3 Aug. 1996, p. 2192.

20 *WRNN*, Jan. 1997.

21 *CQWR*, 20 Apr. 1996, p. 1025.

22 *CQWR*, 20 Apr. 1996, p. 1027.

23 See *CQWR*, 20 Apr. 1996, p. 1026 for a nice comparison.

24 See James H. Kuklinski, Paul J. Quirk, Jennifer Jerit, David Schwieder and Robert F. Rich, 'Misinformation and the Currency of Democratic Citizenship', *Journal of Politics*, 62, no. 3 (2000), pp. 790–816. Kuklinski et al. report extraordinarily high levels of public ignorance concerning welfare provision, culminating in a distinct anti-welfare bias. Up to two-thirds of respondents in their Illinois study were misinformed regarding the percentage of black people on welfare and 90 per cent provided incorrect answers when asked about the portion of the federal budget spent on welfare (which

proved to be the most important predictor of their preferences). Most respondents committed errors that were biased against federal welfare provision. Of some importance, the authors contend that 'those who are both highly inaccurate and highly confident [in their misinformed beliefs] tend to be the strongest partisans and thus the very people who most frequently convey their sentiments to politicians' (p. 799).

25 *CQWR*, 25 Feb. 1995, p. 614.

26 *CQWR*, 27 July 1996, p. 2116.

27 *CQWR*, 2 Sept. 1995, p. 2612.

28 *CQWR*, 2 Sept. 1995, p. 2643.

29 The term 'crashing through' derives from Roger Douglas's contentious approach to reform in New Zealand during the second half of the 1980s. The logic of a 'crashing through' approach is that bulldozing a measure through the legislative process overwhelms opponents and lessens opportunities for debate, compromise and failure. The great danger of this approach, especially in a system founded on the principles and practice of power-sharing, is that it marginalizes stakeholders (who have the opportunity to act upon their grievances), and presents the impression of extremism.

30 *CQWR*, 27 July 1996, p. 2116.

31 *CQWR*, 12 Aug. 1995, p. 2444.

32 Ibid.

33 *CQWR*, 24 June 1995, p. 1842.

34 *CQWR*, 24 June 1995, p. 1844.

35 *CQWR*, 12 Aug. 1995, p. 2444.

36 *CQWR*, 2 Sept. 1995, p. 2643.

37 *CQWR*, 29 Apr. 1995, p. 1190.

38 *CQWR*, 2 Sept. 1995, p. 2643.

39 *CQWR*, 27 July 1996, pp. 2118–19.

40 *CQWR*, 12 Aug. 1995, p. 2445.

41 *CQWR*, 23 Dec. 1995, p. 3889.

42 *CQWR*, 23 Dec. 1995, p. 3891.

43 Ibid.

44 *CQWR*, 20 May 1995, pp. 1423–4.

45 *CQWR*, 23 Dec. 1995, p. 3891.

46 *CQWR*, 20 Apr. 1996, p. 1024.

47 *CQWR*, 28 Oct. 1995, p. 3342.

48 *CQWR*, 20 Apr. 1996, p. 1024; 25 May 1996, p. 1461.

49 *CQWR*, 17 Feb. 1996, p. 395.

50 *CQWR*, 31 Aug. 1996, p. 2445.

51 *CQWR*, 25 May 1996, p. 1465.

52 *CQWR*, 25 May 1996, p. 1467.

53 *CQWR*, 17 Feb. 1996, p. 394.

54 *CQWR*, 25 May 1996, p. 1467.

55 *CQWR*, 20 July 1996, p. 2048. Packaging welfare reform into reconciliation ran the risk that the President might not sign the bills needed to fund the

government and that he would call Congress back into session, thus preventing law-makers from returning to their states in preparation for the November elections – a strategy that helped deliver Harry Truman's presidential victory in 1948. See *CQWR*, 17 Feb. 1996, p. 422.

56   *CQWR*, 25 May 1996, pp. 1465–7.
57   Ibid.
58   *CQWR*, 31 Aug. 1996, p. 2445.
59   *CQWR*, 31 Aug. 1996, p. 2418.
60   *CQWR*, 31 Aug. 1996, p. 2446.
61   *CQWR*, 27 July 1996, p. 2115.
62   *CQWR*, 27 July 1996, p. 2116.
63   *CQWR*, 27 July 1996, p. 2117.
64   *CQWR*, 3 Aug. 1996, p. 2191.
65   *CQWR*, 3 Aug. 1996, pp. 2191–5.
66   *CQWR*, 3 Aug. 1996, pp. 2195–6.
67   *CQWR*, 3 Aug. 1996, p. 2216.
68   *CQWR*, 3 Aug. 1996, p. 2195.
69   Ibid.
70   Ibid.
71   *CQWR*, 3 Aug. 1996, p. 2196.
72   *CQWR*, 2 Mar. 1996, p. 558.
73   *CQWR*, 3 Aug. 1996, pp. 2216–18.
74   *CQWR*, 23 Nov. 1996, pp. 3310–11.
75   *CQWR*, 23 Nov. 1996, p. 3311.
76   *CQWR*, 23 Nov. 1996, p. 3310.
77   *CQWR*, 23 Nov. 1996, p. 3311.
78   *CQWR*, 2 Aug. 1997, pp. 1847–8.
79   *CQWR*, 2 Aug. 1997, p. 1848.
80   *CQWR*, 2 Aug. 1997, pp. 1847–8.
81   *CQWR*, 2 Aug. 1997, p. 1848.
82   *CQWR*, 8 Feb. 1997, p. 329.
83   *CQWR*, 2 Aug. 1997, p. 1847.
84   *CQWR*, 25 May 1996, p. 1506.
85   While divided government creates this centrist dynamic with respect to partisan power-sharing, so do American institutions. We noted in the introduction that the critical component of the partisan-institutional relationship found in the American case (that is absent from European-style coalition governments) is that power-sharing occurs within the context of the two-party system, without the need to consult a strong union movement or far left. While veto points are plentiful in the United States, they are not found in a location likely to mobilize political extremes.
86   *CQWR*, 25 Feb. 1995, p. 613.

8

Does Gender Matter? Women in American Politics

Abigail Halcli

Introduction

In the past decade the political profile of American women has been raised by a number of developments, such as the electoral successes of female candidates (especially in 1992, commonly referred to as 'the year of the woman'), the identification of 'soccer Moms' (white suburban women with children) as a key voting constituency, the deepening of the gender gap in voting, and the continuing struggles over abortion rights. These developments have focused attention on the position of women in American politics, and there is some evidence that the past indifference of the media, politicians and those who study politics has given way to an increasing recognition of the salience of gender differences in shaping the ways in which women and men think about politics and act politically. Of central concern is the extent to which gender inequalities have been alleviated and women's access to and influence in political institutions and decision-making has been improved in recent years. In this chapter I explore some of these developments in order to offer an assessment of the current position of women in American politics, and of the ways in which political scientists study gender. I begin by discussing feminist critiques of mainstream political theory and research. I then review the evidence of a 'gender gap' in political attitudes and participation and consider some of the explanations for it. Finally, I discuss the reasons for and consequences of women's underrepresentation in elective office.

Studying Women and Politics

The study of politics, as well as the practice, has been the near exclusive domain of men. Feminists argue that until quite recently politics as a discipline has ignored or simply failed to recognize women's political involvement. This indifference is reflected in the limited amount of research published on the topic. Between 1906 and 1991, for example, the *American Political Science Review* – one of the most prestigious politics journals – published only twenty-four articles about women and politics.[1] When women did appear in political research they were routinely portrayed in a stereotypical and value-laden manner.[2] Women, it was assumed, were not 'politically minded' and were best suited to the 'non-political' private sphere of the family and domestic activities. Differences between men and women were largely viewed as unproblematic and 'natural' expressions of biological differences, and therefore were not accorded the same political significance as those based on what have been widely recognized as the central cleavages in societies, such as class, religion, region and ethnicity.[3]

These conventional and uncritical views of gender relations were challenged by the women's liberation movement which emerged in the 1960s and 1970s. Women worldwide organized to promote their own emancipation, and in doing so they focused attention on pervasive inequalities between women and men in both the public and the private spheres. In the United States a number of new organizations led the campaigns for women rights, including the National Organization for Women (NOW), the Women's Equity Action League (WEAL) and the National Women's Political Caucus (NWPC). The women's movement put pressure on governments to address issues such as sex discrimination in educational institutions and the workplace, violence against women, abortion rights, and the Equal Rights Amendment. At the same time, second-wave feminists proclaimed that 'the personal is political', thus drawing attention to the political nature of the family, interpersonal relations, sexuality, and other areas of life that had previously been deemed personal and private. 'Consciousness raising' was adopted as a strategy by many women's groups to encourage an awareness of shared gender oppression and to identify collective solutions for women as a group.

Feminists also raised challenging questions about the very nature and definition of politics. Conventionally, political science research has been oriented towards the study of formal politics, including political parties and interest groups, electoral behaviour and office-holding, and war and foreign affairs. This focus on distinctly male-dominated arenas of political activity, feminists argued, reinforced the notion that women are less active citizens. Part of the feminist project therefore was simply to make visible women's political involvement throughout history. Feminists pointed out that women have long been politically active in community organizations and social movements, spanning the continuum from progressive to conservative. The suffrage campaign provided a focus for feminist activity in the late nineteenth and early twentieth centuries, but American women also played important roles as leaders and activists in, for example, the abolition, temperance, and settlement house movements. By paying attention to informal and less institutionalized forms of political engagement, such as participation in social movements and local campaigns, feminists unsettled conventional understandings of what constitutes 'politics' and contributed to the broadening of the field of political studies.

In addition to making visible the varieties of women's political involvement, feminists also offer a fundamental critique of the underlying assumptions of political science.[4] They challenge the notion that politics – or for that matter any aspect of the social world – is gender neutral. Feminist theorists are reinterpreting core political concepts, such as citizenship, equality, representation and democracy, and in doing so they highlight the gendered assumptions embedded in these concepts. To say that politics is gendered means that it reflects male experiences and reinforces gender inequality.

To give an example, the liberal democratic model of citizenship, which is central to political theory, assumes a set of rights enjoyed equally by all members of a society. However, feminists argue that this model is based on the false assumption of an abstract, non-gendered citizen, and that this serves to conceal differences and inequalities that exist between men and women in the public and private spheres.[5] These feminist arguments are part of a much wider debate about the relationship between differences based on gender, class, ethnicity and sexuality and general ideas about citizenship and political behaviour.[6]

Feminists have helped to transform the study of politics by making it more inclusive of women's experiences and by developing more nuanced accounts of gender and politics. The extent to which feminist ideas about gender have been integrated into the core of mainstream political science is an important question, and I will return to this in the conclusion. I turn now from feminist critiques of political theory to more empirical political science research in order to review what it reveals about gender differences in formal political behaviour in the United States.

The Gender Gap

The advent of survey methodologies and public opinion polling in the latter half of the twentieth century has helped researchers to document the political orientations and behaviour of large populations. An interesting pattern to emerge out of this type of research is the existence of a 'gender gap' in political participation, engagement, attitudes and voting behaviour. The gender gap is an important focus of political research in that it can help to illuminate the ways in which American men and women think about policy issues and evaluate candidates and political parties. It also raises pertinent questions about the representation and influence of the sexes in American politics.

In 1920, the nineteenth Amendment to the United States Constitution granted women the right to vote. At the time, many wondered whether a distinct 'woman's vote' would emerge, and if women as a group would use the ballot box to pursue feminist goals. To the disappointment of many first-wave feminists, neither of these outcomes occurred in the decades following the granting of female suffrage, and in fact for many years women were less likely to vote than men. This longstanding tendency was reversed in the 1980 presidential election, and since then the female voter turnout rate has exceeded that for males.[7] In the 1996 election, for example, 55.5 per cent of eligible female voters went to the polls compared to 52.8 per cent of males. This gender difference in voter turnout holds across white, black and Hispanic ethnic categories.[8]

However, with the exception of voting, American women are less involved in formal politics than men. Surveys reveal that participation rates – measured in terms of a broad range of activities such as contributing to campaigns, contacting public officials, attending political gatherings and affiliating with a political organization – are slightly higher for men than for women.[9] There is also a gender gap in political engagement, referring to the extent to which individuals are knowledgeable of and interested in politics. Women, on average, are less informed than men about current affairs and the workings of government, are less likely to report being interested in politics and having political conversations with others, and are less likely to feel politically efficacious (or hold the belief that they can have an effect on politics).[10]

A number of explanations have been put forward to account for this small but persistent gender gap in political participation and engagement. Firstly, socialization theories emphasize the role of different patterns of gender socialization in shaping political behaviour. Studies have shown that boys and girls learn different orientations with regard to politics from an early age.[11] Children receive messages from their families, peers, teachers, religious leaders and the media, among other sources, which reinforce the idea that politics is 'a man's game'. If politics is widely viewed as a masculine activity, then perhaps it is not surprising that girls are less interested in politics and have less political knowledge than boys, and that they may carry these orientations on into their adulthood. However, such gender differences in political orientations have diminished somewhat since the 1960s, which may reflect more egalitarian attitudes towards gender roles among younger generations of Americans.

Secondly, the gender gap has been attributed to gender differences in social roles and family responsibilities. It has been argued that women's 'private' role in the family is incongruent with active involvement in the American political system.[12] In this sense, traditional gender roles lead many women to prioritize domestic life and place less value on being informed about and active in the public/political sphere. In addition, some women may find that the demands of family life and childcare are not compatible with the activities required of political activism, such as attending political meetings and volunteering for campaign work.[13]

Thirdly, variations in terms of educational attainment, income and employment have also been used to explain the gender gap in engagement and participation. We know that people with more education tend to have more information about and interest in politics, and they are also more likely to believe that their involvement can bring about political change. This is true of both men and women, and research shows that women with higher levels of education are more likely to vote and be politically active than women with lower levels of education. Work status also has been shown to have an impact on political behaviour, with women who are not in paid employment being less involved in politics than women who work outside the home. It is generally thought that paid employment creates opportunities for people to acquire the political information, civic skills, access to recruitment networks, and personal incomes that are associated with political involvement. However, gender differences in workplace experiences may account for the fact that women are still less politically active than men. Full-time employment and high-level jobs are thought to offer greater opportunities to accumulate the skills, contacts and sense of political efficacy associated with involvement in political activities. As fewer women than men hold these types of jobs, they have fewer chances to acquire these political resources.[14]

It seems evident that some combination of cultural and structural factors shape gender differences in political engagement and involvement.

These factors may also help to explain the well-documented differences between men and women in terms of policy preferences and voting choices. Women have been stereotypically portrayed by some political observers as less interested than men in policies and more interested in candidates' personalities – in other words, women have been thought to 'vote with their hearts instead of their heads'. This conventional view has been challenged by researchers who show that women are just as likely as men to base their voting decisions on issue preferences.[15] What is clear is that American men and women differ in terms of their views on policy issues, and these differences encompass both foreign and domestic issues. American women in general are more likely than men to support government spending on education, health, social security, and services for disadvantaged people. They also show more support for environmental issues and gun control measures. Men are more likely than women to approve of increases in military funding, the use of armed force to resolve conflicts, and the death penalty.

Given these differences in policy preferences it is not surprising that a gender gap in voting choices has emerged, with women more likely to vote for Democrats than Republicans in presidential elections and in some congressional and gubernatorial races. The emergence of the gender gap in voting is commonly dated to the 1980 presidential election when the Republican Party under Ronald Reagan failed to appeal to large numbers of women voters. His administration's tough anti-abortion stance, use of military force, emphasis on traditional family values and lack of support for the Equal Rights Amendment (ERA) are thought to have cemented the view that the Democrats, and not the Republicans, are the party that represents women's interests. The image of the Democrats as 'the party for women' was reinforced in the 1990s by Bill Clinton, whose actions, including appointing a record number of women to his cabinet, signing the Family and Medical Leave Act (which had previously been vetoed by George Bush) and lifting restrictions on abortion rights, were generally viewed as 'woman-friendly'.[16]

The gender gap in voting is generally reported as the percentage difference between men and women in support for Democratic and Republican candidates. Table 8.1 shows that the gender gap in presidential voting has deepened since 1992. In the 2000 election, for example, a 10 per cent gender gap was evident in support for Republican George W. Bush and a 12 per cent gender gap was evident in support for Democrat Al Gore. This is an increase over the gender gap evident in the 1992 election, when there was a 4 per cent gap in support for Democrat Bill Clinton and a 1 per cent gap in support for Republican George Bush.

Table 8.1 Voting by gender in presidential elections (%)

	Women	*Men*
2000		
George W. Bush	43	53
Al Gore	54	42
Ralph Nader	2	4
1996		
Bill Clinton	54	43
Bob Dole	38	44
Ross Perot	7	10
1992		
Bill Clinton	45	41
George Bush	37	38
Ross Perot	17	21

Source: Center for American Women and Politics, 'The Gender Gap', Eagleton Institute of Politics, Rutgers University (www.cawp.rutgers.edu).

Interestingly, these figures also show that men are more willing to vote for third-party candidates than women.

The relationship between voting choices and policy preferences seems clear – the Republican Party is traditionally associated with issues such as law and order, defence spending and patriotism, and these issues appeal more to male voters. The lack of Republican support for affirmative action, abortion rights, and increases in the minimum wage also seems to have limited the party's support among many women. On the other hand, many Americans associate the Democratic Party with social issues such as welfare spending, health care and education, and these issues resonate strongly among many female voters. Differences in workplace experiences also are thought to have an impact on the gender gap in voting choices. Women are more likely than men to be in part-time and low-paid employment, and are more likely to work in the public sector, and traditionally these categories of workers have seen their interests better served by the Democrats than the Republicans.[17]

The level of 'feminist consciousness' among female voters is also thought to contribute to the gender gap in voting. Feminist consciousness is generally measured in terms of attitudes towards the women's

movement, and there is evidence that women with more favourable attitudes towards the movement are significantly more likely to vote for
the Democratic Party, as it is generally viewed as being more inclusive
and sympathetic to feminist causes.[18] The effect is accentuated because
women with higher levels of feminist consciousness also have been found
to be more politically involved in general than women who are less supportive of feminism.[19]

While recognizing the significance of the gender gap in American politics, it is also important to remember that neither men nor women represent a cohesive voting block. As we have seen, gender does influence
political behaviour, but men and women are also split along ethnic, economic, marital, religious, educational and generational lines, and these
divisions also shape people's opinions on policies, parties and candidates.
In terms of ethnicity, for example, we know that African-American
women are stalwart Democratic supporters, giving Gore 91 per cent of
their vote in the 2000 election, while white women were equally divided
between the presidential candidates (48 per cent voted for Gore and 49
per cent voted for Bush). Women of all ethnic backgrounds who are in
paid employment were much more likely to vote for Al Gore (58 per
cent for Gore and 39 per cent for Bush), while homemakers, devout evangelical women and white women with annual personal incomes over
$50,000 were more likely to vote for Bush.

This means that the gender gap in voting is far more complicated than
has often been suggested. There has been a lot of media coverage of
the ways in which the two main parties have tried to capture the all-
important 'women's vote' by adopting electoral strategies that appeal to
women, for example by portraying their candidates as 'compassionate'
and 'caring'. At the same time, politicians recognize that women, like
men, are not a monolithic group, and that the 'women's vote' actually
consists of numerous voter subgroups with a variety of concerns shaped
by their political, cultural and economic circumstances. In particular, the
gender-centred electoral strategies of politicians have targeted key groups
of 'swing voters', notably white suburban women with children, women
senior citizens and women who define themselves as independent voters.
In the 2000 presidential campaign, George W. Bush and his brand of
'compassionate conservatism' attracted more of these swing voters than
Al Gore.

The overall effect of the gender gap in American politics can be interpreted in a number of ways. On one hand, the fact that women outnumber men in the population and are more likely to vote should
increase their political clout. It is also widely recognized that women
have provided the margin of victory for winning candidates in a number

of recent elections, which implies that politicians ignore the gender gap at their own peril. But the fact that women continue to have lower rates of political involvement and engagement undermines the apparent influence that women have as voters in elections, and suggests that they have less influence in important areas such as policy-making and candidate selection. As we will see in the next section, women are also greatly underrepresented in most levels of public office, and this too has consequences for the influence of women in politics and in society more broadly.

The Political Glass Ceiling:
Women's Representation in Politics

In the 1970s the slogan 'A Woman's Place is in the House . . . and the Senate' began to appear on T-shirts and bumper stickers in the United States. The aim of this women's movement slogan was to draw attention to the low levels of female representation in elective office, and particularly to the paucity of women in high-level political jobs. Since the appearance of this slogan over twenty years ago, we can point to a number of developments that have improved the overall position of women in American politics. For one, the number of female candidates and elected officials has slowly increased at all levels of government. In addition, a number of women in recent years have been selected for high-level positions in the governments of both Democratic and Republican administrations, and two women are now serving as Supreme Court Justices. Finally, more egalitarian attitudes towards women in politics are being reflected in public opinion polls. For example, in a 1999 Gallup poll a massive 92 per cent of Americans surveyed reported they were willing to vote for a qualified woman for President, compared to 76 per cent in 1997 and just 33 per cent in 1937.

While recognizing the importance of these developments, women still have a long way to go to reach equality with men in the political arena. Women are far from reaching proportionate representation at all levels of government, and from a comparative perspective American women have lower levels of legislative representation than their counterparts in many other countries.[20] Fewer women than men make the leap from local to national level politics, and there is a striking lack of women in leadership positions in the federal government. All of this suggests that there is a political 'glass ceiling' beyond which few women are advancing. The idea of the glass ceiling was first used to explain why so few women reach senior management positions. It conjures up the image of an invisible yet effective barrier that makes it difficult for women to move up to higher level positions. In this section I look at the evidence of a political glass ceiling in American politics and consider some of the explanations for and consequences of this phenomenon.

When considering women's representation in elective office, the 1992 election – the so-called 'year of the woman' – was widely viewed as a significant breakthrough for women in that a record number stood as candidates and won congressional seats. In addition to these legislative successes, the 1992 election is also notable because of the high level of interest in and awareness of 'women's issues'. Recent Supreme Court rulings on abortion rights and a high profile political debate over the Family and Medical Leave Bill had brought to the forefront issues that were of central importance to women. In addition, this election was held in the wake of the 1991 Senate hearings to approve Clarence Thomas as only the second African-American member of the Supreme Court. Despite allegations that he had sexually harassed Anita Hill, an African-American law professor, his appointment was narrowly approved by the Senate (52–48), which at the time was made up of ninety-eight men and only two women. Though American women were not unified in their opposition to Thomas's appointment (many African-American women, for example, felt divided loyalties), the national debate that ensued from the Thomas–Hill hearings drew a great deal of attention to the under-representation of women in politics, and in the minds of many, to the failure of male politicians to adequately address women's concerns. These events helped to spur more women than ever before to run for political office in 1992. At the congressional level, 117 women stood as candidates (compared to 77 in 1990) and women's representation in Congress increased from 30 (2 senators and 28 representatives) to 53 (6 senators and 47 representatives). The campaigns of many of these female candidates were memorable in that they capitalized on their outsider status as 'women politicians' as a positive attribute, rather than trying to play it down. Some women candidates found it to their advantage to emphasize the gender differences between themselves and their male opponents, thus encouraging people to vote for them because they were women and not in spite of it. Many of them were successful in portraying themselves as agents for change in an atmosphere of 'business as usual' among male politicians. There is evidence that these appeals worked particularly well with women voters, who turned to female candidates in 1992 to represent their concerns on a number of gender-related issues, including abortion and sexual harassment.

Since the 1992 elections there has been a general upward trend in women's political representation in House, Senate and state-wide offices. In the 2000 elections, for example, four new women senators – including Hillary Rodham Clinton – were elected, bringing the total number of women in the Senate to a record high of 13 (10 Democrats and 3 Republicans). Three states – California, Washington and Maine – have two women senators. An all-time high of 59 women (41 Democrats and 18 Republicans) now sit in the House of Representatives. Overall, women now make up 12.7 per cent of the US Congress. The representation of ethnic minority women in Congress has also increased, and currently 19 of the 72 (26.4 per cent) women serving in the House and Senate are women of colour (18 Democrats and 1 Republican).[21]

Some important advances have also been made in state-wide executive offices, with women now occupying 27.6 per cent of the available positions, including a record high of five women governors. The number of women serving in state legislatures has increased more than fivefold since 1969, with women currently holding 22.4 per cent of legislative seats. Women's representation in state legislatures varies considerably across the United States, with the highest levels occurring in western and Great Plains states such as Washington (38.8 per cent), Colorado (35 per cent) and Nevada (34.9 per cent), while southern states such as South Carolina (10 per cent) and Alabama (7 per cent) have the fewest women in the statehouse. Women of colour constitute 3.6 per cent of the total number of state legislators across the United States. Women have also been making political progress at the municipal and county levels. For example, women now account for 17.5 per cent of the elected mayors in US cities with populations over 100,000, including two African-Americans and six Latinas.[22]

As these figures indicate, women are far more visible in politics than they were even a decade ago, but the overall picture is one of limited, if steady, progress. While women have made some impressive gains at the state and local levels, they appear to be far from reaching full integration at the federal level – in other words, a political glass ceiling is evident in American politics. Many explanations have been put forward to account for women's underrepresentation in public office. Firstly, some researchers have tried to explain why women are less likely to come forward as candidates in the first place. The reasons for this are highly complex, and seem to stem from a variety of overlapping factors linked to gendered views and experiences of the public and private spheres. As we have already seen, women exhibit less interest in politics than men, and they may find their roles in the private sphere of domestic life are not conducive to active political involvement. Women as well as men are constantly receiving messages that politics is a male domain, and this is reinforced by the fact that most politicians are male. The pervasive view of the 'typical' politician as a man can also undermine women's ability to picture themselves as 'candidate material' and therefore to pursue political careers.[23] This suggests that the presence of more women in public office should encourage potential female candidates, as well as voters and party leaders, to view women as qualified and electable politicians.

Secondly, from a comparative perspective we know that women's political representation is linked to the opportunity structures afforded by political parties and electoral systems.[24] In reference to electoral systems, it is clear that women do not fare as well in countries like the United States and Britain which operate single-member districts and winner-takes-all systems. Women politicians have been more successful in countries with multimember districts and proportional representation.

Thirdly, researchers have looked at the effects of bias against women by parties, campaign funders and voters. The evidence here is mixed. It is generally believed that since the 1980s both the Democrats and Republicans have been more supportive of women candidates,[25] with the Democrats even breaking new ground by putting forward Geraldine Ferraro as their vice-presidential candidate in 1984. On the other hand, many women continue to report that their sex makes it more difficult to break into the networks that serve as routes to political careers, and this affects their ability to acquire the contacts, financial resources, skills and experience essential to being a serious contender for public office.[26] There is recent evidence, for example, that party chairs, the majority of whom are male, exhibit a preference for male candidates over female candidates, and this obviously can have implications for the amount of encouragement and support offered to women considering or pursuing political careers.[27] Traditionally women have also found it more difficult to raise campaign funds, in part because they are sometimes viewed as weaker candidates by potential campaign contributors. However, as I will discuss below, there is evidence that the emergence of PACs (political action committees) dedicated to promoting women for political office has helped to offset this disadvantage.[28]

The question of whether voters are biased against women candidates also raises complex issues. Some research has found that women do not appear to be discriminated against by voters,[29] and that in fact being a women candidate might have been an advantage in some races, particularly in terms of attracting female voters.[30] Other evidence suggests, however, that many voters hold very gendered views of the relative merits of male and female politicians, and in many cases these views work to the disadvantage of women, particularly as they seek higher level political positions.[31] This type of gender bias is likely to be more evident in particular localities and among certain categories of voters (such as male Republican voters). Overall, these findings indicate that in many cases women still have to overcome negative perceptions of their abilities as politicians.

Women have addressed these barriers to political involvement in a variety of ways. Perhaps one of the most successful strategies to overcome these hurdles has been the formation of an 'old girls network' of political organizations designed to help women advance in politics by acquiring the skills, networks, campaign workers and financial support necessary to launch a political career. PACs and donor networks devoted to funding female candidates play a central role here. Currently there are forty-six PACs that give funds predominately to women candidates,[32] compared to only nine such organizations in 1980. The efforts of these PACs have been greatly assisted by the fact that women as individuals have more money than ever before, and have shown a willingness to use it to support women candidates who reflect their interests.

EMILY's List (which stands for Early Money Is Like Yeast, in that it makes the 'dough' rise) is perhaps the best-known women's PAC, and claims to be the largest PAC in the US. Its members raised over $9.2 million to fund the campaigns of pro-choice Democratic women in the 2000 elections. Since it was founded in 1985 it claims to have helped elect eleven Democratic senators, fifty-two members of the House, and four governors. EMILY's List also operates as a 'full-service political organization' which offers training for women politicians as well as their staff. In addition, its WOMEN VOTE! campaign donated $10.8 million to projects set up to mobilize women voters in important races in 2000. Other important PACs include WISH List (Women in the Senate and House) which supports pro-choice Republican women and the Susan B. Anthony List (named after a leader of the American suffrage movement) which supports pro-life women running for national office.

Women's political organizations such as these continue to play an important role in focusing attention on the underrepresentation of women in elective office and in developing strategies to help increase the numbers and influence of women in politics. It is important to point out that beyond sharing an interest in getting more women into politics, women's political organizations can differ in terms of party affiliations and policy goals. In particular, opinions on abortion rights serve as a dividing point among these organizations. This fact reminds us that American women do not constitute a monolithic group, and that there are significant differences between women in terms of political attitudes and views of what constitutes 'women's interests'.

Conclusion

The study of women and politics has moved on a great deal in recent years. Research has demonstrated that 'gender matters' in terms of political behaviour and attitudes, and therefore it plays a significant role in shaping how men and women operate as citizens. Feminist political theory has made strides in challenging conventional ways of thinking about politics and gender. Their work has helped to blur the distinction between formal and informal politics, and it reminds us that active citizen involvement occurs not only in the voting booth and in political parties, but also in local campaigns and social movements, and that women across the United States are valued participants in these types of political activism. Still, many feminists believe that more needs to be done to integrate women into the study of politics.[33] They argue that feminist theory continues to be marginalized, and that mainstream political science has not yet taken on board important insights about the impact of gender on the practice and study of politics. They also emphasize that feminist interpretations of core concepts such as citizenship, representation and democracy can transform the study of politics in order to make it more inclusive of the social locations and experiences of all members of society.

This review of the position of American women in politics shows that feminist concerns about women in politics have been justified. Slow progress has increased the visibility of women politicians and focused greater attention on a number of 'women's issues'. Yet many women still encounter a variety of barriers to their political involvement, including biased attitudes of party leaders, potential campaign funders and voters. In particular, women have found it difficult to move into leadership positions and high-level national office, which suggests that a political glass ceiling is limiting women's full integration into American politics. As this chapter has shown, the political representation of women is not a straightforward issue: women are divided both socially and economically, and in their views on political issues. Nevertheless, even allowing for such complexities, addressing gender bias in the representation of American citizens is likely to remain high on the agenda of feminists, and others who care about American democracy, for some time to come.

NOTES

1 Rita Mae Kelly and Kimberly Fisher, 'An Assessment of Articles about Women in the "Top 15" Political Science Journals', *PS: Political Science and Politics*, 26 (1993).

2 See, for example, Susan C. Bourque and Jean Grossholtz, 'Politics, An Unnatural Practice: Political Science Looks at Female Participation', *Politics and Society*, 4 (1974), pp. 225–66; Mary L. Shanley and Victoria Schuck, 'In Search of Political Woman', *Social Science Quarterly*, 55 (1974), pp. 632–44.

3 Seymour Martin Lipset and Stein Rokkan, 'Cleavage Structures, Party Systems and Voter Alignments: An Introduction', in Lipset and Rokkan (eds), *Party Systems and Voter Alignments: Cross-National Perspectives* (New York: Free Press, 1967), pp. 1–64.

4 For a useful overview of feminist critiques of political studies, see Anne Phillips (ed.), *Feminism and Politics* (Oxford: Oxford University Press, 1998).

5 See Sylvia Walby, *Gender Transformations* (London: Routledge, 1997); Anne Phillips, *Engendering Democracy* (Cambridge: Polity, 1991).

6 See Anne Phillips, *Democracy and Difference* (Cambridge: Polity, 1993); Iris Marion Young, 'Polity and Group Difference: A Critique of the Ideal of Universal Citizenship', *Ethics*, 9 (1989), pp. 250–74.

7 Female voters have outnumbered male voters since the 1964 election, largely due to the fact that there are more women of voting age than men.

8 Center for American Women and Politics (CAWP), 'Sex Differences in Voter Turnout', fact sheet, Eagleton Institute of Politics, Rutgers University (available at www.cawp.rutgers.edu).

9 Margaret M. Conway, Gertrude A. Stuernagel and David W. Ahern, *Women and Political Participation: Cultural Change in the Political Arena* (Washington DC: Congressional Quarterly, 1997); Kay Lehman Scholzman, Nancy Burns and Sidney Verba, 'Gender and Pathways to Participation: The Role of Resources', *Journal of Politics*, 56 (1994), pp. 963–90.

10 Sidney Verba, Nancy Burns and Kay Lehman Scholzman, 'Knowing and Caring about Politics: Gender and Political Engagement', *Journal of Politics*, 59 (1997), pp. 1051–72; Virginia Sapiro, *The Political Integration of Women: Roles, Socialization and Politics* (Urbana: University of Illinois Press, 1983).

11 Diane Owens and Jack Dennis, 'Gender Differences in the Politicization of American Children', *Women and Politics*, 8 (1988), pp. 23–43.

12 Sapiro, *Political Integration of Women*.

13 Abigail Halcli and Jo Reger, 'Strangers in a Strange Land: The Gendered Experiences of Women Politicians in Britain and the United States', in Laurel Richardson, Verta Taylor and Nancy Whittier (eds), *Feminist Frontiers IV* (New York: McGraw-Hill, 1997), pp. 457–71.

14 Kay Scholzman, Nancy Burns and Sidney Verba, 'What Happened at Work Today? A Multistage Model of Gender, Employment and Political Participation', *Journal of Politics*, 61 (1999), pp. 29–53.

15   Felicia Pratto, Lisa M. Stallworth and Jim Sidanius, 'The Gender Gap: Differences in Political Attitudes and Social Dominance Orientation', *British Journal of Social Psychology*, 36 (1997), pp. 49–68.

16   Not all of Clinton's policies were viewed as being favourable to women, particularly in regard to poor women. For example, his administration's welfare reform legislation, which was supposed to 'empower' impoverished women, was denounced by its critics as having harmful effects on poor women and their children. (See chapter 7 above for a discussion of welfare reform.)

17   Jeff Manza and Clem Brooks, 'The Gender Gap in US Presidential Elections: When? Why? Implications', *American Journal of Sociology*, 103 (1998), pp. 1235–66.

18   Ibid.

19   Conway, Stuernagel and Ahern, *Women and Political Participation*.

20   Inter-Parliamentary Union, 'Women in National Parliaments', 2001 (available at www.ipu.org/wmn-e/world.htm).

21   CAWP, 'Women in Elective Office, 2001' (www.cawp.rutgers.edu).

22   Ibid.

23   Halcli and Reger, 'Strangers in a Strange Hand'.

24   R. Darcy, Susan Welch and Janet Clark, *Women, Elections and Representation*, 2nd edn (Lincoln: University of Nebraska Press, 1994); Joni Lovenduski and Pippa Norris (eds), *Gender and Party Politics* (London: Sage, 1993).

25   Barbara Burrell, 'Party Decline, Party Transformation and Gender Politics: The USA', in Lovenduski and Norris, *Gender and Party Politics*, pp. 291–308.

26   Halcli and Reger, 'Strangers in a Strange Hand'.

27   David Niven, 'Party Elites and Women Candidates: The Shape of Bias', *Women and Politics*, 19 (1998), pp. 57–80.

28   Ibid.

29   Darcy, Welch and Clark, *Women, Elections and Representation*; Susan Carroll, *Women as Candidates in American Politics* (Bloomington: Indiana University Press, 1994).

30   Kathleen Dolan, 'Voting for Women in the "Year of the Woman"', *American Journal of Political Science*, 42 (1998), pp. 272–93.

31   Richard L. Fox and Eric R. A. N. Smith, 'The Role of Candidate Sex in Voter Decision-Making', *Political Psychology*, 19 (1998), pp. 405–19.

32   CAWP, 'Women's PACs and Donor Networks: A Contact List' (www.cawp.rutgers.edu).

33   Virginia Sapiro, 'Feminist Studies and Political Science – and Vice Versa', in Donna Stanton and Abigail Stewart (eds), *Feminisms in the Academy* (Ann Arbor: University of Michigan Press, 1995); Janet A. Flammang, *Women's Political Voice: How Women are Transforming the Practice and Study of Politics* (Philadelphia: Temple University Press, 1997).

9

Multiculturalism and the End of Jazz

Desmond King and Julian Murphet

Introduction

In this chapter we review the origins of multiculturalism in American politics and assess its consequences for the expression of political themes through popular culture. In particular, we consider the ways in which the development of a political multiculturalism has been mediated through popular musical forms.

We examine how black American music has been affected by the rise of multiculturalism and contend that the influence of the latter can be observed in the transition from postwar jazz, a canonically modernist form, to hip-hop/rap, a canonically postmodernist expression. In both processes black musicians and artists appropriated certain pre-existing American musical forms and traditions and assimilated them to progressive political ends, by creating new expressive forms which (with more or less directness) drew attention to the American 'colour-line'. This project can be seen in terms of white American reaction too, which has ranged from bourgeois anxiety through lower-middle-class cool, to bohemian rapture, relative to the market fate of the music in question. Each form is highly urban and has also had mixed receptions (though much more positive) in black American communities.

A preliminary comment about our choice of music forms. We are not claiming that other forms of music particularly associated with African-American communities, such as blues or soul or some aspects of rock and roll, are less relevant as vehicles for the expression of political issues and creative artistic endeavour. But in our view jazz and rap are clearer instances of the political and artistic processes we address.

Multiculturalism

Multiculturalism has become a difficult concept to define precisely since it is employed widely and often very loosely in political discourse in the United States.[1] Most generally, it means the explicit acknowledgement of competing and co-equal sources of cultural and ethnic identity in a political system. Politically, these multiple identities have been integrated into public policy in a way purported to respect the inherent value of each tradition and not to privilege any one tradition over another. As two leading thinkers in the field have insisted, 'the concept of "multiculturalism" . . . is polysemically open to various interpretations and subject to diverse political force-fields; it has become an empty signifier on to which diverse groups project their hopes and fears.'[2] This formulation suggests that the concept of multiculturalism lacks any essence, and designates instead a process of contestation, a politics in action. Left, right and centre in America variously embrace and modify what is at stake in their respective interpretations of it. For us, however, there is nothing to be lost in attempting some more definite critical understanding of the concept's present social meaning.

Multiculturalism emerged as a policy initiative in much of the advanced capitalist world (especially in the US and Australia) during the early 1980s, when widespread immigration from the Third World and increased representation for minority groups in politics and the media at home challenged the bastions of white political privilege. It took shape as an open acknowledgement by 'white' governments that discrete cultural and ethnic group 'identities' had distinctive roles to play in the political system. Henceforth, diverse ethnic groups would be 'respected' and 'protected' rather than absorbed into an abstract model of citizenship. Multiculturalism has had considerable impact on education policy. In this area, it refers to the revision of educational curricula in high schools and universities to include accounts of the historical experience of groups previously accorded a small or no role at all in the standard narratives; a recent example of this pattern is the decision of the University of Maryland, College Park to establish an Asian American Program, after political lobbying and organization by students of Asian background.[3] It was an attack on the allegedly dominant 'Western' conception of the historical formation of the United States. Such cultural and religious diversity is often controversial and opposed but has nonetheless become a political reality.

Here, we want to analyse the shift from a classical American political 'identity' which predicated itself on the image of a 'melting pot' of ethnicities (while privileging the normative status of the 'free white person') to a multicultural model of American political identity which gives the lie to that earlier model and affirms instead a genuine poly-centricity predicated on affirmative ethnocultural identities. Today's emphasis on preserving group distinctiveness and loyalty is the obverse of the assimilationist principle, assumed, until the last twenty-five years, to be the rational aim in all discussions of immigration and the rationale for Americanization.

To approach this macro-shift in policy and culture, we want to consider some of the strategies and tactics used by African Americans, in refusing and/or affirming both versions of an 'American' identity, through the cultural practices of black music. In the first case, that of jazz after the Second World War, it will be seen that the increasing politicization of black musicians led to a radicalization of their musical aesthetics – a radicalization which pulled deliberately away from a consensual 'melting pot' model of American cultural identity, and accordingly alienated the attentions of white jazz 'purists'. The second case of rap music, however, suggests an entirely different cultural and political dynamic, that of 'multiculturalism'. For rap began as a militantly black cultural practice and for that reason became a multicultural national popular phenomenon. Critical to this reorientation of the logic of cultural identification in the American polity is a consideration of the function of the mass media in late capitalist USA.

The blurring of the boundaries between politics and the mass media, a blurring already constitutive of 'white' governmentality itself since the Kennedy era, is central to any consideration of multiculturalism. Minority groups have seized hold of effective media technologies (television, cinema, radio, sound recording) in order to construct effective and affective representations of themselves; both to enhance their own sense of 'identity' and to implement that 'identity' culturally in order to enlarge their role in the processes of national politics. It will be seen that this mediation of identity through the corporate media is precisely the precondition of state-directed 'multicultural' policies.

Politics and Multiculturalism

It is worthwhile considering some of the political contexts of multiculturalism. In the United States a powerful reason for the development of a multicultural agenda lies in the historical injustices suffered by African Americans. Effectively excluded from full rights of citizenship under the system of segregated race relations established from the 1890s until the 1960s, the passage of the Voting Rights Act 1965 and the Civil Rights Act 1964 implied the extent to which black Americans had historically been mistreated. Redress for this past discrimination fuelled the expansion of programmes, including affirmative action ones, to advance the position of those previously denied equal rights, let alone equality of opportunity, within the universal sphere of democratic citizenship.

Multiculturalists would mostly reject the assumption of a uniform American identity, which was held by nineteenth-century nativists and was common among policy-makers when immigration restrictions were enacted in the 1920s; and although there were voices in this latter decade wishing to conceive of a pluralist United States, they were marginalized in policy choices.[4] Multiculturalists challenge the assumption of the United States as stated in its Constitution and inferred from its ideology: in essence, that there is a distinct American identity, formed through an assimilationist melting-pot process in which all ethnic groups and nationalities participate more or less equally, living in a 'Mr Smith Goes to Washington' Capraesque world. As historical record, this version is partial and inaccurate since it overlooks the exclusion of Chinese labourers in the 1880s, southern and eastern Europeans in the 1920s and the retention of a 'free white person' naturalization rule until the 1940s. Multiculturalists reject the notion of a dominant and shared set of values and cultural motifs as the basis of citizenship and politics in the United States;[5] in its place there is a particularist celebration of ethnic diversity and identity. Preserving group distinctiveness and loyalty is the obverse of the assimilationist principle, assumed, until the last twenty-five years, to be the rational aim in all discussions of immigration and the rationale for Americanization. Striving for group identity is also a judgement about the dominant culture, an implicit insistence that culture is a process of interaction rather than a monolith.

Two aspects of the political context of multiculturalism are crucial. First, it can be seen as an extension of the civil rights movement which highlighted the historical mistreatment of African Americans. This historical record created the agenda for affirmative action. Second, partly in response to the civil rights movement and the adoption of affirmative action programmes, white ethnic Americans who felt their traditions and values had been suppressed by the Americanization programme of the interwar years discovered afresh their ethnic traditions.[6] Numerous scholars identified a renewed interest in ethnicity among descendants of European immigrants from the 1970s, which was in part provoked by reaction against multicultural and affirmative action politics, but which was really an extension of them.[7] This revival of interest in ethnicity poses a serious challenge to the core assumptions of the melting-pot assimilationist model as promoted in the 1920s and 1930s. Such Euro-American groups were considered prime candidates for 'melting', their differences eroded in the process of creating a distinct American identity. Yet it was these very groups who now attempted to emphasize or at least to specify the distinctive values, traditions and customs that singled out their ethnic heritage, and whom Alba characterizes collectively as 'European Americans'.[8] There was perhaps a richer tradition of diversity within the groups assumed to be most successfully assimilated in the United States polity than commonly appreciated. However, these intragroup divisions appear to collapse in the face of a challenge to the aggregate's whiteness, thereby suggesting that they are less deeply embedded than this latter factor. Ian Haney Lopez, who argues that the rise of new white ethnic groups should be analysed 'as a means of opposing non-Whites', makes a similar point forcefully: although 'most Whites entertain a subjective belief in their commonality based on descent from European immigrants', this common heritage assumes political significance 'only insofar as it contrasts with that of non-Europeans, that is, non-Whites'.[9] The retention of a European-American ethnic loyalty, however diffuse its constituent elements or voluntary its adoption, assumes significance as a source of identity directly defined in opposition to non-whites. In the 1990s, grievances over affirmative action have accentuated the ethnic identity among some whites. As Haney Lopez notes, the revival of ethnic traditions 'coincided with and came in response to the civil rights movement'.[10] This development points to the importance of the redefinition of race in black–white terms in the decades after 1930: immigration restrictions were enforced but the system of segregated race relations endured, and its dismantlement was the primary purpose of the 1960s civil rights legislation. Electorally and politically, the association of affirmative action with a black constituency has ensured its filtering into racial divisions.[11]

The continuing political salience of multiculturalism is reflected in national political discourse, for instance in debates about bilingual education programmes (Iowa, for instance, with several other states has pursued a state constitutional amendment to make English its primary language) and about affirmative action admissions programmes (with recent changes in California, Texas and Florida all weakening the functioning of quotas). How are these factors reflected in artistic expressions? We argue, in the next section, that the transition from jazz as a primary voice of exclusion to a mainstay of the US's musical canon made space for a politically informed and heterogeneous hip-hop movement.

As we note, the marketing of popular music is a crucial aspect of its development. Often music which begins as radical and dissenting is absorbed and Americanized – a process observable in respect to both bebop jazz and rap. Even free jazz has been Americanized: the initial reception of Ornette Coleman's dissonant free jazz is an example, with extensive coverage in magazines such as *Time*. Radical and dissenting music becomes, in effect, American and thereby its political content and significance is dissipated. The difference, as we shall argue, is where this 'Americanization' springs from: in the first case, jazz, from an extrinsic machine of normative ideology; in the second, hip-hop, from the machine of representation of which it is itself a pivotal element. This is the difference between a centripetal model of assimilationism and a centrifugal model of multiculturalism.

Music as Politics

Jazz

Historians and musicologists of jazz have singled out the 1940s and 1950s as a key era in which a new generation of African-American jazz musicians revolutionized their art. This transformation is associated in particular with bebop, and the music of Charlie Parker among others.[12] Writing over thirty years ago, Amiri Baraka (formerly LeRoi Jones) emphasized both the artistic ambitions of the jazz players working in the 1940s and 1950s, especially their break with earlier jazz, and the centrality of racial identity to jazz's most important compositional works, including those of Charles Mingus.[13] In these decades, modernity in jazz composition meant both musical innovation (and the invention of a new form of jazz which would exclude white jazz players, commonly beneficiaries of the best contracts[14]) and racial equality in politics.

The Second World War exposed domestically and internationally the pernicious reality of racial inequality and segregation within the United States.[15] Wartime and associated labour shortages proved an opportunity for black militancy and protest against racism. These inequalities and contradictions were mobilized in A. Phillips Randolph's March on Washington movement and recognized by President Harry Truman in his establishment of investigative committees on civil rights and on the Armed Forces; in the ten years after 1945 politics were dominated by the injustices of the US's institutionalized racism. Intellectually and artistically, this period was very fruitful for African-American jazz musicians and, as Amiri Baraka comments, despite the initial critical rejection of bebop, 'the young musicians [such as Monk, Parker and Gillespie] began to think of themselves as serious musicians, even artists, and not performers.'[16] Such artistic ambitions translated into not just a distinct musical style but, for male jazz performers, a sartorial one too, conveyed in Dizzy Gillespie's goatee, beret and thick horn-rimmed glasses, and zoot suits.[17]

The bebop jazz revolution was part of a new stance adopted by many African Americans in US society, many politicized by their wartime experiences. Ben Sidran identifies several jazz artists' work as contributing to political activism for civil rights in the 1960s.[18] David Stowe locates this political dynamic in bebop composition itself: 'the sharp contraction of the ensemble in bebop, together with the emphasis on individual maturity and militancy taking root among African-Americans in the 1940s'.[19] Frank Kofsky argues that the combination of entrenched segregation and economic depression in the interwar decades had acted as fetters upon artistic creativity, and the development of African-American autonomy. These fetters were weakened by wartime changes which stimulated an oppositional politics among African Americans:

> this radical shift . . . can be boiled down to the fact that every aspect of Washington's conduct of the war, from employment opportunities in war-production industries to the role of blacks in the armed services, was pervaded by racism, at the same time that blacks were being pushed to support a crusade allegedly directed against the 'master race' doctrines of the Axis powers.[20]

Bebop constituted not simply a new musical form but was 'a musical vehicle for expressing black dissatisfaction with the status quo'.[21] For Kofsky the social context is fundamental to understanding the meaning of jazz music; it gave the music some of its powerful authenticity. The band leader Lionel Hampton also characterized bebop as in part an oppositional black politics.[22]

Against this background, African-American musicians composed artistic work rooted in the experiences of autonomous communities in a segregated society, of which both bebop (a reaction to swing) and hard bop (a successor to cool jazz) were emblematic. (Free jazz artists also fitted this tradition, if more self-consciously.) Artistic struggles were part of the political context of postwar jazz performances, a context defined significantly by segregation. As Ingrid Monson notes, these political features affected the relationship between artistic creativity and politics: 'the conflation of modern musical and artistic traits with the modern struggle against racial discrimination and segregation characterizes the particular meaning of "modern" within the jazz community of the 1940s.'[23] Musical and compositional success became, Monson contends, 'a symbol of racial achievement. The fierce pride in music, one of the few professional areas open to African-Americans, put much more at stake in these musical proving grounds than formal musical innovations.'[24] The initial impact of bebop – as radically different to pre-1940s jazz – was a means for its practitioners to assert themselves as free, creative individuals in a white society.

African-American jazz artists in the 1940s strove to compose music too difficult to be imitated by white musicians. In Steven Elworth's view, bebop permitted 'black musicians to seize their discourse from the white-dominated culture industry and to create something less likely to be appropriated'.[25] For Eric Lott, bebop lay 'brilliantly outside' conventional politics and conveyed the urgency of wartime black militancy and the edifice of segregated race relations: the music 'attempted to resolve at the level of style what the militancy fought out in the streets'.[26] The political (as well as artistic) significance of the bebop-powered jazz revolution was directly traceable to these profound racial injustices and their social effects. Jazz was an expression of both social and political commitment.

The jazz composer and bassist Charles Mingus often gave his pieces titles derived from politics and struggles over civil rights. These include 'Fables of Faubus', a reference to the Governor of Arkansas (Orval Faubus) during the Little Rock crisis, 'Meditations (for a Pair of Wire Cutters)', a reference to the encampment of civil rights protesters, 'Haitian Fight Song', of which Mingus observed that it 'could just as well be called Afro-American Fight Song',[27] and 'Remember Rockefeller at Attica'. Other jazz composers such as Art Blakey, John Coltrane, Eric Dolphy and Max Roach also gave their works appellations referencing the movement to achieve political rights of citizenship for African Americans.

A political agenda more obviously and self-consciously informed aspects of the movement in jazz known as 'free jazz' which emerged in the 1960s and 1970s. Its practitioners were African Americans, many of whom intentionally placed themselves outside the mainstream of existing jazz composition and political structures; it developed in part as a response to the increasing assimilation of bebop into white American society. It is associated with the work of musicians such as Ornette Coleman, Albert Ayler and Cecil Taylor, and several jazz ensembles of which the most important is the Art Ensemble of Chicago.[28] The very term 'free' paid obvious homage to the aims of the civil rights movement which swept across the United States in the 1950s and 1960s. As a jazz form it had two key features: an overt expression of political ambition for a fully democratic society, and a commitment to radical compositional forms, including atonality, liberated from conventional harmonic structures. Ornette Coleman's first recording, *Something Else! The Music of Ornette Coleman*, duly attracted considerable attention as a powerful new jazz voice, rooted in a radical improvisation and style, a promise confirmed with the release of his recording, *The Shape of Jazz to Come*. In 1961, Coleman released his album directly titled *Free Jazz*, recorded with a double quartet, a full statement of the new music. What later became uncontroversial and almost conventional was at the time judged a radical musical intervention which seemed genuinely distinct from existing jazz compositions, although the line-up of musicians, selection of instruments and content were unquestionably products of a jazz tradition. Of this approach, Coleman observed:

> when our group plays, before we start out to play, we do not have any idea what the end result will be. Each player is free to contribute what he feels in the music at any given moment . . . I don't tell the members of my group what to do. I want them to play what they hear in the piece for themselves. I let everyone express himself just as he wants to. The musicians have complete freedom.[29]

This experimental musical modernism functioned as a direct black claiming, within a black musical tradition, of that quintessential 'expressionism' of the Euro-American 'subject' enshrined in artistic movements as diverse as fauvism and German and abstract expressionism. Coleman went on to develop what he called 'harmolodics' culminating in the orchestral composition 'Skies of America' performed with the London Symphony Orchestra in 1972; the result is a remarkable meditation on the US, saturated in political and artistic allusions conveyed in the music and titles of the twenty-one pieces making up the work.

Several jazz groups and ensembles formed in the 1960s and 1970s to further the ideas and philosophy of a free jazz movement.[30] In Chicago, the Association for the Advancement of Creative Musicians was founded in 1965 to provide a forum for progressive jazz playing. Many of its leading lights – such as Roscoe Mitchell, Lester Bowie and Anthony Braxton – went on to major careers. From this background the Art Ensemble of Chicago, rallying under the motto 'Great Black Music – Ancient to Modern', formed and issued important recordings including *Tutankhamun* and *Bap-Tizum*. Ironically – though not without other examples – the Art Ensemble achieved initial critical success outside the United States, notably on European tours, which proved a launch pad for greater domestic attention. Free jazz, however, never attained the popularity of bebop or enjoyed bebop's assimilation into the American modernist canon. To that degree, as a musical line of flight back to Africa and Europe, free jazz learned to challenge white 'Americanization' from without, preparatory to bringing it back home as a corrective cultural force.

Rap

The first thing to say about rap (or hip-hop) music is that, unlike jazz, it defies the pathos of high cultural authenticity. Rap was born out of an essentially amateur musical practice blending electronically generated rhythms and 'two turntables and a microphone': playing other artists' records in inventive new ways, and speaking verbally inventive 'raps' over the synthetic background of programmed beats and poached riffs. Thus the cult of personality and genius with which black jazz had been partially assimilated to the Western concept of art had no initial application here. Rap emerged not from the exquisite development of musical skills in highly professional contexts of 'Big Bands' and experimental quartets, but from the impoverished, musically untrained ghetto youth culture of the South Bronx, just as Reagan's 'war against the cities' was starting to make itself felt.[31] The music belonged to an African-American and Latino urban youth context of graffiti writing, gangs and breakdancing.

'The Message' (1982) and 'Rapper's Delight' (1979), two of the earliest singles to be produced out of rap or hip-hop culture, broached the essential political message of this music at its inception: a bitter but linguistically playful complaint against social conditions in the ghettos, and a barely veiled threat of violence on the part of a black male subject. In part, then, rap was an ideological outgrowth of the black militancy and black arts of the 1960s and 1970s. The decimation of the Black Panthers by the FBI, and the murder and incarceration of many of the black community's political leaders, might have erased the overt street militancy, but it sprang up in raps as a highly adaptive poetic form, linked to the scratched sounds of records also selected from the recent past.

Much of the power of hip-hop stemmed from the unusually confident, convinced and authoritative tones of the rapper's voice as it ran complex and affective black speech idioms over the sounds of drum machines, synthesizers and turntables. It was a tone of voice and a cultural attitude with which young black listeners could identify in a way quite distinct from the melodic structures of soul music, or the abstract experimentalism of contemporary jazz. Rap was aggressively populist, and it addressed a particularly black audience. This specificity of address can be determined through the ethnic idiom of its linguistic structure, the musical referentiality of its sound samples, the fashions and styles worn by its performers (as seen on stage and on video) and the ideological content of its lyrics. And yet, within a few years, the largest demographic market for these singles was not black youth, but white youth, specifically white suburban middle-class boys.[32] This is the singular, and mostly unexamined paradox which defines rap music as having been 'multicultural' from almost its outset.

Moreover, the multiculturalism implicit in that imbalance between a specifically addressed group audience, and a much larger, white-dominated market, has evolved distinctly in the twenty years since rap was first developed as a form. It has profoundly affected the artists, the management structure and recording industry, as well as the global fortunes of the rap form. As Paul Gilroy observes, 'Anyone asserting the continuing marginality of hip-hop should be pressed to say where he or she imagines the center might now be.'[33] Rap music is, in fact, the privileged instance of an aggressively particularist form of cultural 'identity' which became, first, paradigmatically American, and then a pervasive global musical force, a 'dominant' now observable in many youth- and non-youth-targeted advertisements. It is thus peculiarly illustrative of what is at stake in the meaning of the word 'multiculturalism' – a concept with which rap is strictly contemporary.

To underscore the militant 'blackness' of much early rap, it will suffice briefly to consider the important East Coast group Public Enemy. As a group, Public Enemy perfectly combined the articulate black nationalist rapper (Chuck D) with the comic rapper (Flava Flav), the DJ supremo (Terminator X) and the visually menacing black dancers (the S1Ws: Security of the First World). They effectively promoted black nationalist ideology through some of the most creative lyrical structures of all rap music, an ingenious visual style which fused past icons of black power (Malcolm X, Frederick Douglass) with the new consumerism of black youth (Nike), and a musical texture of remarkable complexity – often mixing dozens of sonic layers in one dissonant yet danceable synthetic whole.

One of its songs, 'Fight the Power', was featured as the title track of Spike Lee's breakthrough film, *Do the Right Thing* (1989), and its confrontational style perfectly matched Lee's political concerns in that film. Looking at some of its lyrics, we note the residual tones of 1960s black militancy, fused with a dense rhyme scheme and meticulous rhythmic structure. The key is the denial of the trite, melting-pot Americanism of 'people we are the same', and the transition into a militant ethnic particularism, because it specifically designates the field of 'multicultural-ism' on which rap would be played out. It is a song whose advocacy of black nationalist education, cultural separatism (it yells obscenities at the spectre of Elvis Presley) and the revolutionary seizure of power by a black army would seem in all important respects to have excluded a white American audience; yet it was broadly consumed by suburban whites, at home and abroad. Even the fact that Public Enemy flirted with the Nation of Islam leader Louis Farrakhan, and cited him in their songs, was not enough to dissuade legions of white boys from purchasing their records, wearing their merchandise and attending their performances. And this was explicitly recognized by the group when they re-recorded one of their earlier songs, 'Bring the Noise', with a white heavy metal band, Anthrax, thus confirming the 'cross-over potential' of militant black nationalist ideology with white, or 'multicultural' America.

That is to say, this song marks very clearly a distinctive contradiction: at the level of production a staunch cultural difference and opposition is being asserted, while at the level of consumption a much more power-ful force of equivalence transforms that difference into a source of exchange value. It is this contradiction to which we give the name 'multiculturalism'. If this reversal is particularly 'American', it is so only in so far as America is the epicentre of multinational capitalism itself. (What is at stake in this process is the precise inverse of what happened to black jazz after the war, as it mutated into bebop and free jazz, and became less and less accessible to a white audience. Franz Fanon recalls this process well:

> We remember perfectly ... the reactions of the white jazz specialists when after the Second World War new styles such as the be-bop took definite shape. The fact is that in their eyes jazz should only be the des-pairing, broken-down nostalgia of an old Negro who is trapped between five glasses of whiskey, the curse of his race, and the racial hatred of the white men. As soon as the Negro comes to an understanding of himself ... it is clear that his trumpet sounds more clearly and his voice less hoarsely.[34]

Yet it is that conscious cultural clarity, a Black Aesthetic arrived at after decades of musical struggle and negotiation with white culture, which made white audition so 'difficult' and ultimately alienated this music from any mass popular appeal.)

In rap music, however, the trend began in a clarity of black national-ist understanding, and for that reason became broadly popular within a white-dominated consumer culture. Much of this inversion has to do with a wholesale redirection and expansion of American media society. While mass media culture was in its definitive period of ascension to national hegemony during the 1950s and 1960s, it was only within strictly curtailed ideological parameters. The censorship of Elvis Presley's hip-wiggling on the Ed Sullivan Show remains the quintessential instance of a contradiction between a nascent media society with evident appeal to 'youth culture' and ethnic exoticism, and a puritanical national imag-inary not yet willing to relinquish its Oedipal taboos against pleasure and disobedience. It is in this context that the drift of self-conscious black experimental jazz artists into more and more complex, dissonant forms was strictly inaccessible to media society. It remained at the level almost of artisanal experiment, and no doubt much of its aesthetic achievement rested upon this determinate extrinsicity to the national media culture.

The historic breakthrough came with the counterculture of the late 1960s, a point at which 'youth culture', rock and roll and the spirit of rebellion became cultural emblems which the mass media could trans-mit and stereotype freely. At this point in the evolution of the media, the appearance of 'identities' (hippie, yippie, protester, Black Panther, etc.), whose icons were visual and audible at once, was very much a part of the quantum-shift expansion of the media's hold on the national imagi-nary; Angela Davis is still despairing of the fact that she is 'remembered as a hairdo'.[35] Henceforth, we were not 'all the same', but different, and our differences could be codified, sorted and 'imagineered' by television, radio, the cinema and the popular magazines. In a strictly dialectical process, 'identities' were both the product of and the cause for ex-pansion of the mass media themselves.

The fate of rap music from the very moment of its emergence on the cultural scene of postmodern America was preordained by the media space into which it grew. Consider the strange evolution it underwent in its migration to the West Coast. Here, taking on board a whole slew of other cultural identities wanting to perform in the rap idiom (Latino, Samoan, white, etc.), rap increasingly adopted the trappings of a very coherent media identity: namely, the gangster. 'Gangsta rap', as it was called, continued the aggressively militant anti-white, anti-establishment tone of early rap (NWA's infamous 'F*** the Police' constituting a mem-orable instance), but also assimilated misogynist 'gang warfare' imagery with which the media became inordinately fascinated. To the degree that 'gangsta rap' became codified as a closed system of lyrical, musical and sartorial affronts to Middle America (violent hatred of police, misogyny, anti-Semitism, grating noises, baggy jeans, bandanas), so too it became media friendly.

The critique of rap's violent and petulant style in this phase by figures of national authority (politicians, church leaders, feminist academics, etc.) only confirmed its viability as a virulent cultural 'identity', which had now surmounted all ethnic boundaries, and guaranteed its economic future in the massive youth market. This process underlines the fading importance of traditional political discourses on American identity, and the vital, burgeoning role of the commercial mass media in constructing it, in a dialectical fashion, beyond the walls of politics. This media society depends upon the construction and elaboration of forms of cultural 'identity', which it can then package and promote as commodities. Abstracted into commodity form, the 'identity' loses its moorings in any given ethnic community, and becomes generally available as a style and an idiom to all consumers. This is the new, multicultural America. The remarkable success of white rappers such as Vanilla Ice and Eminem demonstrates the radical separation of form from content inherent in this process.

We have said that this process is dialectical, and that is so. Today, rap music enjoys unparalleled success as a form on a global scale. It can be heard, by local artists, in Paris, Manila, Hong Kong, Sydney and all over the Americas. In each location, it has been harnessed as a tool of protest by young people against stifling ghetto conditions and against the very conformity of life in a global economy. Yet it has also helped to con-solidate that conformity. The profits generated by this form of music, as a critical sector in the recording industry at large, are astronomical, and have produced many millionaires, both black and white – the most famous being Sean 'Puffy' Combs, a major black producer-artist and one of America's most visible 'rich and famous'. Missy 'misdemeanor' Elliott appears in ads for Gap clothing; and Lord Tariq and Peter Gunz make anthemic, karaoke-style hip-hop out of cannibalized and recycled Steely Dan.[36] A form of 'cultural identity' first hatched in the South Bronx ghetto in the late 1970s is now lived as a critical social force by millions upon millions of human beings in all corners of the globe, and is a critical tool in the mass marketing of its own products and many others. It is quite a different experience from that of the bebop jazz artists of the 1940s.

The most fundamental point to make here is this: traditional political critiques of rap music failed to curtail its emergence as a global force, because rap functioned, *avant la lettre*, according to the logic of 'multiculturalism' with which political discourse has been at pains to catch up. That is to say, its very particularism was the guarantee of its universal success. This signals that incontestable rupture in the social definition of Americanness, which policy initiatives have had, by virtue of the salience of this cultural-economic dynamic, to address. By and large, the adjustment to policy along these new, multicultural lines has taken place in the most conservative fashion. What we know as 'multiculturalism' strips the truly radical nature of the dialectic of rap music's success from its formal equalization as a commodity.

The political discourse of 'multiculturalism' is an analogue of the process of commodification itself; and it functions just as Marx once argued 'price' did for the commodity. Different cultural identities, like 'use values', are 'good' because ultimately they are all the same. It is 'good' to enhance and draw attention to these stark cultural differences, because otherwise we might come to realize how identical we have all become as consumers. In this sense, as the Slovenian theorist Slavoj Zizek has argued, multiculturalism is the perfect ruse of contemporary capitalism which 'bears witness to the unprecedented homogenization of the contemporary world' and 'treats each local culture the way the colonizer treats colonized people – as "natives" whose mores are to be carefully studied and "respected" '. He adds:

> it is effectively as if, since the horizon of social imagination no longer allows us to entertain the idea of an eventual demise of capitalism – since, as we might put it, everybody silently accepted that capitalism is here to stay – critical energy has found a substitute outlet in fighting for cultural differences which leave the basic homogeneity of the capitalist world-system intact.[37]

A political concept which was forged in the marketplace, against the 'white' state, as a cultural striving of different groups, now functions at the state level as an ideological justification of the market itself. The irony is that, in rap especially, what Zizek fondly calls the 'horizon of social imagination' has been so open as to include (in Public Enemy) critiques of everything from the World Health Organization, to the history of the slave trade, drug addiction and the extermination of Amerindians. The political crisis of the present inheres in the fact that such radical anti-Americanism can be marketed as an instance of tolerant 'multiculturalism'. When every sign of protest is also a cultural commodity, the possibility of social change is both ceaselessly 'performed' and 'contained' by the market. Ultra-conservative 'multicultural' America reaps the rewards of this paralysis.

Conclusion: The End of Jazz?

We have argued that jazz, broadly conceived to include both music and more general forms of artistic and political expression, was a fundamental moment in twentieth-century US culture which conveyed many aspects of the civil rights movement. We have also suggested that hip-hop, similarly construed as a field of cultural practices denoting 'urban black youth', was a signal development in the articulation of black political grievances in the age of Reagan. Yet what separates these two cultural dynamics is not merely a matter of style or aesthetics; it is rather the determinate shift in the political construction of 'America' which is named by the question-begging concept of multiculturalism.

Jazz, a modernist musical form which valued the development of individual musical expression within an evolving framework of technical and orchestral protocols, attempted to insert the black subject into America's mythic melting pot of free individuals. This effort proved initially very stimulating for white liberals and black progressives alike. Unable to secure this individual emancipation at the political level, black jazz artists harnessed the critical energies of modernist expressivity to articulate a highly codified critique of the limits of subjective freedom in the racist state. True to modernist dicta, these experiments in musical critique rejected market mechanisms of commodification, and so eventually forewent a mass following as their forms became more abstruse.

On the other hand, hip-hop adopted an anti-aesthetic 'postmodern' musical idiom (electronic rhythms and sampled sound-bites) to express a militantly populist defiance of urban conditions for black youth. Rather than appeal to an abstract notion of white 'Americanness' which perforce excluded them, these young African-American rappers aggressively asserted an ethnic 'identity' which was unassimilable into the melting pot. Coinciding with the emergence of a host of new social movements and identities in civil society and the media, such a cultural strategy had the highly ironic and ambiguous effect of becoming a commercial success across the wide ethnic spectrum of the new America. It was the militant proclamation of identity *per se*, rather than the particular identity in question, which appealed to young consumers regardless of race or ethnicity. And this was no doubt a function of the very homogeneity and conformity which a century of 'melting pot' ideology and state practice had wrought; as well as of the standardization of consumer habits on the marketplace. Rap music was avowedly 'different' from white American normativity, and it was a difference which could be bought and consumed as 'authentic'.

Yet its very commercial success and its catalytic enablement of a whole host of competing cultural identities on the marketplace functioned within the construction of a new notion of America not bound to the monolithic discourses and identities of the past. Rap was perversely one of the primary instruments with which America was able to shed its image of white paternalism, and reinvent itself through the consuming power of a number of competing cultural identities. White paternalism is then abstracted from the direct political sphere, into the 'invisible hand' of market forces which dictate the ossification of what Spike Lee has called a new kind of 'black face' in the name of mainly white profits. If 'gangsta rap' continues to sell to white boys, its stereotyped image will remain intact. White America performs and consumes 'blackness' to an unparalleled degree; the perverse logic of multiculturalism is that this exorbitation of blackness in the cultural sphere is not articulated with any transformation at the political level. 'Multiculturalism' is, in this sense, just one more excuse for not redressing the extreme political grievances against urban conditions for African Americans which rap music continues to pronounce.

NOTES

1 S. Benhabib (ed.), *Democracy and Difference* (Princeton: Princeton University Press, 1996); C. Joppke and S. Lukes (eds), *Multicultural Questions* (Oxford: Oxford University Press, 1999); W. Kymlicka, *Multicultural Citizenship* (Oxford: Oxford University Press, 1995).

2 E. Shohat and R. Stam, *Unthinking Eurocentrism: Multiculturalism and the Media* (London: Routledge, 1994), p. 47.

3 'A Multicultural Coup at U-Md: Sisters' Zeal Leads to Area's First Asian American Program', *Washington Post*, 30 Aug. 2000.

4 D. King, *Making Americans: Immigration, Race and the Origins of the Diverse Democracy* (Cambridge: Harvard University Press, 2000).

5 N. Glazer, *We Are All Multiculturalists Now* (Cambridge: Harvard University Press, 1997).

6 King, *Making Americans*.

7 M. Novak, *The Rise of the Unmeltable Ethnics* (New York: Macmillan, 1972); M. C. Waters, *Ethnic Options: Choosing Identities in America* (Berkeley: University of California Press, 1990); R. Alba, *Ethnic Identity: The Transformation of White America* (New Haven: Yale University Press, 1990).

8 Alba, *Ethnic Identity*.

9 I. F. Haney Lopez, *White by Law* (New York: New York University Press, 1996), p. 171.

10   Ibid., p. 170.
11   M. Gilens, *Why Americans Hate Welfare* (Chicago: University of Chicago Press, 1999); E. G. Carmines and J. A. Stimson, *Issue Evolution* (Princeton: Princeton University Press, 1989).
12   See F. Kofsky, *Black Music White Business* (New York: Pathfinder, 1998); S. De Veaux, *The Birth of Bebop* (Berkeley: University of California Press, 1997); F. Kofsky, *John Coltrane and the Jazz Revolution of the 1960s* (New York: Pathfinder, 1970); E. L. Ayers, *Southern Crossing* (New York: Oxford University Press, 1995).
13   D. King, ' "The World's Against Me as a Black Man": Charles Mingus and Segregated America', *Journal of Historical Sociology*, 13, no. 1 (2000), pp. 54–77; G. Santoro, *Myself When I Am Real* (New York: Oxford University Press, 2000).
14   Kofsky, *Black Music*.
15   D. Kryder, *Divided Arsenal* (New York: Cambridge University Press, 2000); A. S. Layton, *International Politics and Civil Rights Policies in the United States, 1941–1960* (New York: Cambridge University Press, 2000).
16   L. Jones, *Blues People* (New York: Morroll Quill, 1963), p. 188.
17   R. D. G. Kelley, *Race Rebels* (New York: Free Press, 1994); I. Monson, 'The Problem with White Hipness: Race, Gender and Cultural Conceptions in Jazz Historical Discourse', *Journal of the American Musicological Society*, 40, no. 8 (1995), pp. 398–422.
18   B. Sidran, *Black Talk* (Edinburgh: Payback Press, 1981).
19   D. W. Stowe, *Swing Changes: Big Band Jazz in New Deal America* (New York: Oxford University Press, 1994), p. 11.
20   Kofsky, *Black Music*, p. 109. See also Kelley, *Race Rebels*; D. King, *Separate and Unequal: Black Americans and the US Federal Government* (New York: Oxford University Press, 1995); Kryder, *Divided Arsenal*.
21   Kofsky, *Black Music*, p. 110.
22   Cited in Kelley, *Race Rebels*, p. 170.
23   Monson, 'Problem with White Hipness', p. 409.
24   Ibid., pp. 410–11.
25   S. Elworth, 'Jazz in Crisis, 1948–1958: Ideology and Representation', in K. Gabbard (ed.), *Jazz among the Discourses* (Durham: Duke University Press, 1995), p. 59.
26   E. Lott, 'Double V, Double-Time: Bebop's Style of Politics', in Gabbard, *Jazz among the Discourse*, p. 246.
27   King, 'The World's Against Me', p. 67.
28   T. Gioia, *A History of Jazz* (New York: Oxford University Press, 1998); P. N. Wilson, *Ornette Coleman* (Berkeley: Berkeley Hills Books, 1999).
29   Quoted in Wilson, *Ornette Coleman*, p. 35.
30   Gioia, *A History of Jazz*, pp. 354–8; G. Giddens, *Visions of Jazz* (New York: Oxford University Press, 1998), pp. 502–4.
31   M. Davis, 'Who Killed Los Angeles? A Political Autopsy', *New Left Review*, 197 (1993).

32 T. Rose, *Black Noise: Rap Music and Black Culture in Contemporary America* (Hanover: University Press of New England, 1994), p. 187n6.
33 P. Gilroy, *Between Camps* (London: Penguin, 2000), p. 180.
34 F. Fanon, *The Wretched of the Earth* (Harmondsworth: Penguin, 1963), pp. 242–3.
35 A. Davis, *The Angela Y. Davis Reader* (Oxford: Blackwell, 1998), p. 273.
36 Gilroy, *Between Camps*, p. 181.
37 S. Zizek, 'Multiculturalism, or, the Cultural Logic of Multinational Capitalism', *New Left Review*, 225 (1997), pp. 44–6.

10

Subverting American Values? *The Simpsons, South Park* and the Cartoon Culture War

Robert Singh

In *Hustler v. Falwell* (1988), Chief Justice Rehnquist wrote for a unanimous US Supreme Court that American political discourse would be 'considerably poorer' without cartoon caricatures. Drawing on a tradition of spirited parody of public figures including George Washington, Abraham Lincoln and Franklin Roosevelt, the Chief Justice noted that: 'The appeal of the political cartoon or caricature is often based on exploration of unfortunate physical traits or politically embarrassing events . . . The art of the cartoonist is often not reasoned or evenhanded, but slashing and one-sided.' The ruling celebrated Americans as 'a good and generous people, but . . . not particularly gentle or genteel; we prefer to speak our minds.'[1]

Notwithstanding the long lineage of cartoon satire, the last decade of the twentieth century saw it assume a new and unprecedented prominence in America. This change was occasioned by two television shows whose main characters have become veritable American icons and whose depictions of American life regularly draw millions of viewers within and outside the United States: *The Simpsons* and *South Park*. Among several cartoons that heralded a new 'golden age' of American animation aimed primarily at adults – *King of the Hill, Beavis and Butthead, Dilbert* – these two have proved easily the most popular, critically acclaimed and politically controversial.

The cartoon depictions of America have been strongly contested by politicians, cultural critics and organized interest groups, generating a politicized controversy about the shows' messages – and effects – on American public and private life. Cartoon culture has thereby come not only to reflect but also to broaden still further the boundaries of America's on-going conflicts about the nature, evolution and future of its culture and national identity. As such, cartoon culture has joined film, music, television and the internet as targets for periodic 'moral panics' about popular culture.[2]

Entertainment with violent, homophobic, misogynist and racist themes has recently been accused of encouraging anti-social behaviour among America's youth, contributing to crises from school under-achievement and drugs to the Columbine High School massacre of 1999. During 2000, the Federal Trade Commission issued a report blaming Hollywood for marketing R-rated movies to children as young as eight and the Senate Commerce Committee under former presidential hopeful John McCain (R-AZ) convened hearings on sex and violence in the media. In the presidential election, the Democratic Party ticket of Al Gore and Joe Lieberman promised to act against the entertainment industry if it failed to self-censor its products (while simultaneously accepting its sizeable campaign contributions). Sexually explicit mater-ial continues to arouse outrage as well as passion, allegedly now consti-tuting 'a major threat to marriages'.[3] Cartoons such as *South Park* have taken their place alongside *Natural Born Killers*, Larry Flynt, Marilyn Manson and Eminem as *bêtes noires* not only of social conservatives but many erstwhile 'liberals', such that Lieberman's top applause line in cam-paign speeches during 2000 was 'Parents shouldn't be forced to compete with popular culture to raise their children.'

In this chapter, however, the argument is advanced that the two car-toons have proved far more supportive than subversive of traditionalist America. Although the satirical commentaries on American life that the shows contain have been at the core of their popularity, the challenge that both offer to established American values is more superficial than serious. Both cartoons comprise remarkably strong affirmations of American traditionalism, lampooning yet simultaneously affirming the centrality and moral strength of the core values and beliefs of traditional life: family, work, community, religion, education, and (since the 1950s) television. Compared to the robust affirmation of Americanism that the shows offer, their subversive content is modest and secondary.

While the chapter is fundamentally in agreement with the arguments of Paul Cantor's influential essays on *The Simpsons*,[4] it seeks to broaden his analysis and introduce some comparisons with television pro-gramming in the UK. This is partly because the UK has proved one of the most important non-American markets for both shows, but also because *South Park* has attracted even more adverse criticism than *The Simpsons*. In addition, Cantor's analysis neglected some important features of both cartoons – concerning issues of race, gender, and their international popularity – that merit scrutiny. The chapter proceeds by outlining the critical commentary on both shows within America, before locating the reasons for their cultural resonance in a highly distinctive representation of the nation and its people, and finally explaining how – despite that portrayal – the cartoons ultimately endorse 'mainstream' America.

Culture Wars and Cartoons

Three developments transformed the place of cultural value conflict – and, indirectly, popular culture – in America after the Second World War. The rise of an 'education class' that embraced progressive rather than traditionalist conceptions of America – for which the civil rights, anti-Vietnam War and feminist movements provided the catalytic momentum – was the first. Compounding this was the judicially driven politicization and nationalization of a range of important social issues previously left largely to the elected branches of government – most importantly, state legislatures and the US Congress – to regulate: contraception, abortion, capital punishment, pornography and gay rights. Third, the rise of a highly profitable and fragmented mass media industry offered new mechanisms by which cultural messages, both subversive and traditionalist, could be disseminated. By the 1980s, the development of cable and satellite television meant that traditional national network programming could be displaced, while the steady increase in access to the internet since the 1990s has ensured that television itself faces many alternative sources of information provision and entertainment.

Even prior to the internet, however, a transformation was wrought in American life by the nationalizing effects of television. With traditional institutions of information provision such as political parties, churches and newspapers now challenged to compete with an avowedly 'neutral' medium, television assumed an unprecedented centrality for millions of Americans. Consumerism, the Cold War and the 'countercultural' protests of the sixties were shaped by television's pervasive influence. Consequently, the content of television messages became a site for contested interpretations by public figures, including politicians. The larger the audience, the more significance was attached to the content of the message – hence the habitual targeting by populist politicians of Hollywood and the music industry for undermining traditional institutions and public order.

The rise to national controversy of cartoons in the 1990s relied on television's ability to reach millions of Americans directly. Matt Groening, the creator of *The Simpsons*, had been recruited by Tracey Ullman in 1987, drawn by his 'Life in Hell' cartoons in a Los Angeles free newspaper. After the family was introduced in a series of shorts on her show, *The Simpsons* were given a regular slot of their own in December 1989. More than 250 episodes on, the show has become the longest-running cartoon (surpassing *The Flintstones*) and the most successful 'situation comedy' in American history. It was dubbed into more than twenty languages, and in 1999 *Time* magazine even declared the cartoon the greatest television show of the twentieth century. In 2001 an edited collection of philosophical essays probed such matters as Homer's Aristotelian qualities and whether Bart could be regarded as a Nietzschean hero or Heideggerian thinker.[5]

South Park, while approaching neither the unprecedented popularity nor longevity of *The Simpsons*, has nonetheless generated a substantial following within and outside the United States since its debut in August 1997. The show attracted approximately 5 million viewers each week in America during 1998, has been translated into several foreign languages (including French and Chinese), and its film-length version, *South Park: Bigger, Longer and Uncut* (released in 1999) won both popular and critical plaudits for its apparent mockery of American public and private life. The cartoon's four 'stars' have been featured on the covers of *Time*, *Newsweek* and *Rolling Stone*. The show has even achieved sufficient exposure in the UK that, by 2000, publications as varied as the tabloid newspaper the *Sun* and the *London Review of Books* employed its signal catch-phrases.[6]

What is most distinctive and important about the two cartoons is not simply the political content that they contain but that both approach the subject of politics explicitly through the institution of the family. As Cantor noted, *The Simpsons* does this directly by focusing on five members of one nuclear family (Homer, Marge, Bart, Lisa and Maggie), with a large cast of relatives, neighbours and other family units in the town of Springfield playing important but subsidiary roles. But *South Park* also achieves this family focus indirectly through the experiences of four boys (Kyle, Stan, Eric and Kenny) from markedly different family backgrounds (respectively, wealthy Jewish married couple, middle-income Protestant married couple, single mother and poor blue-collar married couple). However significant the differences between them, the use of the family as the central motif is a political statement that markedly distinguishes the shows from the bulk of American television output (and has also occasioned imitators in cartoons such as *King of the Hill*).

The shows' most audacious achievement has been to marry animation's 'anything goes' format with day-to-day family life. Yet the satirical purchase of the cartoons rests primarily on the ability to grapple with family mundanity by means of densely written scripts that unflinchingly examine family dynamics in all their aspects, from tenderness to ugliness. Paradoxically, the shows have married a form of communication that is supposedly 'unserious' to a subject-matter – the state of the family – that has become a *de facto* proxy for all manner of what Byron Shafer terms 'degenerative trends' in America:[7] divorce, births out of marriage, single parents, 'alternative' lifestyles, and the place of religion and morality in public life. If there was nothing inevitable about the adverse critical attention that both cartoons ultimately attracted, their shared focus on family matters was deliberately provocative in design.

Consequently, *The Simpsons* and *South Park* have been condemned in clear and colourful ways by American critics. For social conservatives, in particular, their popularity simultaneously reflects and hastens the decline of 'family values'. In 1990, for example, former education secretary William Bennett took Bart Simpson directly to task. Visiting a Pittsburgh drug-treatment centre, Bennett spotted a poster of Bart beside the caption, 'Underachiever and Proud of It'. Bennett commented that 'You guys aren't watching *The Simpsons*, are you? That's not going to help you any.' The ensuing media furore prompted him to admit that in fact he knew nothing about the show (though his wife informed the *New York Times* in 1998 that the Bennett children remained forbidden to watch it).

The most notable public intervention occurred in 1992, when President George Bush Sr declared during the summer of his faltering re-election campaign that: 'We're going to keep on trying to strengthen the American family. To make the American family more like the Waltons and less like the Simpsons' (to which Bart retorted in a subsequent episode that his family were already 'just like the Waltons. We're praying for an end to the Depression, too'). But critical attention extended beyond such soundbites to (in February and March 1997) a discussion among the opinion pages of the *Wall Street Journal*. Therein, Benjamin Steel commented that the show lacked demonstrable political content. In response, John McGrew argued that the show was political and 'consistently' left-wing. Deroy Murdock and H. B. Johnson Jr responded in turn that the show attacked left-wing targets and supported traditional values, concluding that it was 'politically ambiguous' and hence appealed to both conservatives and liberals. Following Cantor's article, and despite his view that on balance the show is 'like most of Hollywood's output, anti-Republican',[8] Jonah Goldberg even sought to commend *The*

Simpsons to the avowedly conservative readership of *National Review* – on the explicit reasoning that it offered more attacks on liberals than the remainder of American media output and the implicit reasoning that American families would be better off being more like the Simpsons than the Clintons.[9]

South Park has generated even stronger traditionalist criticism than *The Simpsons*, despite – or perhaps partially as a result of – its comparative lack of mainstream appeal. For example, the non-profit organization Morality in Media strongly condemned the show's 'unconscionable' use of child characters. *CultureFacts*, a weekly publication of the conservative Family Research Council, noted under the heading 'South Park Perversion' how 'homosexuality visited South Park again.' In response to a comment made by one adult in the show that 'we're all a little gay', Jim Hanes cautioned that: 'Not everyone is just "a little gay" in South Park though. Another character, named "Big Gay Al", is known for his homosexual pet sanctuary.'[10] Describing the show as 'mean and obscene', critic David Hinckley even suggested that American 'indifference to President Clinton's allegedly crass personal conduct' during the Lewinsky scandal of 1998–9 was linked to the cultural decline hastened by *South Park*:

> Mom hasn't noticed the tasteless lesbian jokes. She didn't see the episode in which a teacher decides to kill Kathie Lee Gifford and a helpful cop tells him he can get a good shot from the book depository. She missed the Christmas show in which Santa and Jesus get into a fistfight. So far, *South Park* has been noticed primarily by people who think all this is funny. People who are ready for humor that sometimes hurtles past marginal to become just plain wrong.[11]

Approvingly noting how such sentiments were shared across the Atlantic, the *New York Post* recorded how an English nursery school (in Reigate) had changed its name from 'South Park' to 'The Orchards' to 'shed the image of the foul-mouthed American TV series' (school governor Alan Mayer declared that 'We were aware there was a cartoon called South Park and that it was not a particularly nice cartoon', noting that the school's new name was 'designed to encourage children to love their environment').[12] The cartoon has even been accused of inspiring child suicides by encouraging youngsters to believe that – like the character Kenny – they will come back to life if they die.[13]

Most notable of all was the response of the Christian Family Network, which produced a detailed content analysis of the show that contrasted biblical injunctions with the cartoon's immorality, deviance and blasphemy. Castigating the show for encouraging drug and alcohol abuse, homosexuality, bestiality, and disrespect for authority, the CFN view was especially critical about its irreligious content:

> South Park's content is irreligious and blasphemous . . . Our children need to be rooted in a strong moral foundation, one with a strong sense of faith and values. Parents who have trained their children in these precepts need to have their teaching reinforced to their children. South Park does nothing but undermine traditional, foundational values of our belief systems.[14]

The report went on to note how Jesus ('a recurring character') was negatively portrayed as the host of a failing cable access television show, 'Jesus and Pals': 'On His show, Jesus takes live call-in questions from viewers. He is portrayed as evasive and wimpy. Writers make fun of His humble spirit. South Park dialogue of Jesus has been written to contain four-letter words and to take His own name in vain.'

In a content analysis of one show ('Cartman Gets an Anal Probe'), the CFN noted that an 'offensive use of language' occurred every 18.5 seconds, not including the 'sexual conversations' that took place. (The film version of *South Park* was also noted as containing 399 swear words and 128 crude gestures.)

But however much the history of 'moral panics' over television in America has shown them predominantly to have been the preserve of cultural traditionalists, the two cartoons have also been distinctive in occasioning 'the dog that didn't bark': the silence of American liberals. For progressives, a combination of traditionalist attacks and the obviously satirical intent of the cartoons no doubt deters criticism – but the shows also appear to offer disturbing examples to American youth on an egalitarian reading. For example, *South Park* has featured characters openly espousing sexist, homophobic and racist views. Some of its characters appear as far cruder, one-dimensional stereotypes than exist in *The Simpsons*: Chef epitomizes racist stereotypes about the sexual obsessiveness and promiscuity of African-American men; Kyle's mother Sheila Broflowski of hectoring Jewish women; Cartman's mother of irresponsible and promiscuous single-parent mothers; and the puppeteer teacher, Mr Garrison, of effete, professionally incompetent and self-hating homosexual men in denial about their sexuality. Even the school counsellor, the supremely ineffectual Mr McKay, personifies the well-intentioned but naively indulgent sixties hippie.

Whether for these reasons, or because of the more familiar concerns of traditionalists, critics have condemned the two shows for providing profoundly deficient role models for parents and children. The most common grounds for censure have been those concerning a legitimation of undesirable – even illegal – activities: foul-mouthed kids defying authority, children and adults doing obscene things, children regularly dying in assorted horrible ways, politicians obsessed with their careers and gaining media attention, corporations insensitive to small-town values, racism, sexism, homophobia, violence and bestiality. Even the language that the children use has been seen as setting a disturbing example: Bart's various slogans ('Don't have a cow, man', 'Ay Carumba', 'Eat my shorts') and the *South Park* boys' ready resort to a vernacular of bitches, dildos and, as Eric Cartman puts it, 'It's all a bunch of tree huggin' hippie crap.' Amid such criticisms, the shows are understandably regarded as radically subversive. Such an interpretation, however, is misplaced in the light of the profound support that they offer traditional American values.

Exceptional America: The Politics of Failure

The conventional wisdom about the cartoons is that they are highly unconventional, and it is unquestionably the case that few totems of modern American public life or culture have proved sacrosanct for either show. Presidents, political parties, celebrities, Bill Gates, and television itself have been targets for the type of mockery that is rarely seen on most American television.

But the cultural resonance of the shows is strongly shaped by three complementary elements: their acute sensitivity to the cultural value conflicts that occupy many Americans; the broadly balanced nature of the political commentary that they offer on these conflicts; and the distinctive – even, for American television, revelatory – narrative focus that both provide on the nature of individual failure in the United States.

The on-going battles over cultural values that so distinguish America from other democracies are well represented in *The Simpsons* and *South Park*. In particular, both shows highlight the profound differences and enduring tensions between a traditionalist Americanism (Cartman's regular invocations of the cardinal insult 'Hippy!' are matched by Homer's nativist antipathy to anything smacking of unconventionality or foreignness) and the more progressive, internationalist convictions of Kyle, Stan, Wendy, and Lisa Simpson. The latter especially – vegetarian, feminist, environmentalist, internationalist – personifies modern American liberalism as fully as Homer and Cartman give raw expression to traditionalism. Collectively, the two shows encapsulate broader American conflicts over 'god, guns, gynaecology and gays'.

Yet both cartoons also display strong attacks on intolerance, sometimes explicitly (*The Simpsons* episode 'Much Apu about Nothing', for
example – on Apu Nahasapeemapetilon (the Indian-born illegal resident
operator of the Kwik-E-Mart) and anti-immigration sentiments – and
South Park's satire on homophobia in 'Big Gay Al's Big Gay Boat Ride').
Frequently, the parody on intolerance is pitched through the use of characters who themselves espouse bigoted views – most commonly Homer
and Cartman. Their success in satirizing bigotry, however, seems much
greater than that of comparable shows in both the US (*Archie Bunker*)
and UK (*Till Death Us Do Part, Love Thy Neighbour*) that employed
genuine actors. What is additionally distinctive is that the targets of the
satires on intolerance come from both the left and the right. Uncritical
acceptance of environmentalism, pacifism and multiculturalism receive
as much ridicule as racist bigotry, corrupt politicians and stupid police
officers.

Accordingly, in partisan and ideological terms, neither show is especially doctrinaire or one-sided in its express political leanings. As Matt
Groening has noted, the implicit message of *The Simpsons* is that 'your
leaders may not have your best interest at heart' – be the leaders political, religious, community or otherwise. In itself, such a comment reveals
a characteristic antipathy towards authority in general, and government
in particular, that strongly informs American political discourse.[15] Particularly with regard to politicians, cartoon depictions of untrustworthy
or venal leaders are well suited to a post-Watergate era of cynicism and
distrust, as the following rankings of occupations in terms of 'respect in
American life', published in the *National Journal*, demonstrate.[16]

Scientist	73%	Journalist	28%
Teacher	73%	Federal worker	28%
Clergy	72%	Lawyer	24%
Farmer	70%	Stockbroker	24%
Doctor	69%	Union leader	24%
Engineer	63%	Professional athlete	22%
Judge	63%	Insurance executive	20%
Military officer	59%	Actor	17%
Police officer	52%	Politician	15%
Banker	36%	Prostitute	7%

Thus *The Simpsons* features regular satires on Springfield's mayor,
'Diamond' Joe Quimby, a corrupt, womanizing lush with an unmistak-
able Kennedy accent. When the show's Rush Limbaugh character accuses
Quimby of being an 'illiterate, tax-cheating, wife-swapping, pot-smoking

Spend-o-crat', the mayor responds that he's 'no longer illiterate'. Quimby evidently represents an old-style city boss, head of a corrupt party machine (presumably Democratic in party affiliation). *South Park*'s mayor is a useful counterpoint to Quimby, not only in being female but also in being even more media-obsessed than her Springfield counterpart. Both seem to share little in terms of genuine empathy with their constituents (another reflection of the low esteem accorded most politicians as a class by Americans currently), yet their political ambitions seem to be different. Quimby is committed to sexual promiscuity and material self-enrichment, while *South Park*'s mayor seems to possess wider political ambitions – if only in order to take her away from the uncongenial town and its 'hick' inhabitants.

Since both shows ran during the 1990s – a decade of notable scandals in American politics – the attacks on politicians and politics were perhaps predictable. But the attacks in both shows seem more in the long-established American tradition of anti-authoritarianism and mistrust of politicians than any partisan sniping. In one *Simpsons* episode of notable even-handedness, for example, signs inside the Republican national convention read 'We want what's worst for everyone' and 'We're just plain evil', but signs at the Democratic convention read 'We hate life and ourselves' and 'We can't govern.' In the spring of 1992, after twelve years of Republican dominance of the presidency, an episode featured Sideshow Bob being hauled off to prison for attempted murder, declaring 'I'll be back. You can't keep the Democrats out of the White House forever. And when they get in, I'm back on the street! With all of my criminal buddies!' Perhaps most memorably, when Grandpa Simpson starts receiving royalty cheques for work he didn't actually do, Bart and Lisa enquire about whether he had wondered why he was receiving cheques for doing nothing. Showing the wisdom of his years in post-New Deal America, Grandpa sagely responds, 'I figured, 'cuz the Democrats were in power again.'

What the shows suggest about the nature of American identity is another area in which the ambiguities and ironies of modern life in the United States figure prominently. In particular, the shows offer an unusually clear focus on the politics of failure in America. Rarely can the description offered by Seymour Martin Lipset of American exceptionalism as a 'double-edged sword' have received more vivid and comprehensive expression in American television.[17] The pervasive American culture of material success and rugged individualism is contrasted with – for many Americans – the stark realities of an unrealized 'American Dream'. Authority figures who cannot teach, read or lead, and who resort to short-cuts, subterfuge and illegality to acquire the material benefits that American culture demands, populate the shows in ways largely unfamiliar to non-cartoon programming. Yet in characteristic American fashion, the blame for failure is squarely set on the individual, not collective social structures or the constitution of the general American social order.

Some of this focus on failure finds expression in the very appearance of the show's characters, who provide the cartoon antithesis of the (arguably, more cartoon-like) idylls of *Baywatch*. In an era when over one-fifth of Americans are now officially classified as obese, the cartoons' anti-beautification message is not only resonant but also matched by a broader theme of inadequacy and insufficiency. The shows are populated by characters who are, to a greater or lesser extent, flawed in both physical and ethical terms. Neither an archetype of universal admiration nor a role model of unimpeachable ethical credentials exists in either show (Marge Simpson probably comes closest). By contrast, the express recognition of diverse failings in all the characters suggests a universal vulnerability and a refusal to admit of human perfection that is conspicuously rare in most American television.

In this respect, although much of the power of the shows derives from the mundane nature of their family-centred subject-matter, the cartoons' cheerily satirical content steadfastly rejects timidity in its range of references. As Stuart Jeffries notes:

> The dysfunctional alcoholics of *Cheers* were never depicted as drunk; yet, Homer and the other habitués of Moe's Tavern are virtually always drunk and stupid. The contented smoker is also excluded from sanitised American programming; and yet barely an episode goes by without Marge Simpson's husky-voiced sisters sucking noisily on twin king-sizeds. You will rarely see a parent shaking his boy by the throat; in *The Simpsons* this image of bad parenting is so regularly deployed that it has become a T-shirt illustration. American television culture privileges the beautiful and the healthy, but *The Simpsons* strikes a blow for the ugly and the burger-obsessed. The characters may be two-dimensional and yellow, but they are more rounded, more real than the characters of *Ally McBeal*, *thirtysomething* and *Friends*.[18]

Unusually, the comedy of failure so central to postwar British television comedy is strongly apparent in both shows, populated as they are by a markedly heterogeneous cohort of American 'anti-heroes'. Life is less a constant party than a continuous struggle, relieved occasionally by mostly ephemeral moments of pleasure centred on family, friends and bouts of material consumption. Equally, the cultural milieu of the overwhelming majority of Americans is presented less as a *Frasier*-style mixture of opera, smart bars and avant-garde German book clubs than a vibrantly vulgar blue-collar collage of Kwik-E-Marts, Monster Truck Rallies, Cow Festivals and 'trick-or-treat' excursions. Ironically, given the sophisticated satirical content of the shows, elitism and intellectualism are represented as alien and un-American tendencies (dislike of television as a medium serving as their cardinal expression) in a fashion that Richard Hofstadter would have recognized as part and parcel of American populism.[19] These are Americans possessed less by aesthetic 'hinterlands' than heart trouble.

However, the crucial difference between these American shows and their British counterparts is the former's ability not merely to satirize 'ordinary' life but also to revel in and celebrate mediocrity sincerely and unashamedly, rather than ignore, contest or feel socially inadequate about such human dysfunction. 'OK, brain' says Homer when required to retake his high school exams, 'You don't like me and I don't like you. So let's get through this and I can get back to killing you with beer.' Bart's 'Underachiever and proud of it' slogan sold more than 1 million T-shirts each week at the end of the 1980s and was banned in public schools (schools in Texas and Georgia also banned students from wearing clothing depicting *South Park* characters, citing concerns over the violence depicted in the show). Whereas the British comedic enterprise is one whose most prominent figures are psychologically disturbed and even disgraced by their individual failures in a social and political culture where inegalitarian values concerning class and status predominate – Alan Partridge, Basil Fawlty, Reggie Perrin, Rigsby, Del Boy, John Shuttleworth – America's anti-heroes remain gloriously insouciant about their many deficiencies.

As cartoons – a device almost guaranteed to evade excessively close critical scrutiny – the shows press the boundaries of what is politically acceptable far wider than would otherwise be the case. Yet what is at stake in acceptability is not the conventional criticisms but the refusal in American media to confront the theme of failure. In a culture where material and social success is a cornerstone of life and its elusiveness a product of individual deficiency rather than structural obstacles, the comedy of failure is something far more readily acceptable in cartoon form than through real actors portraying real people. No doubt this also forms part of the explanation for the shows' tremendous popularity outside the States. Notwithstanding their humour, the shows offer a rare example of the nation and people being portrayed – albeit affectionately – in a variety of negative fashions. In an era of American superpower and (at least in the West) cultural dominance, the overt exposure of a relatively dumb, mean and flawed populace reflects and confirms many non-American stereotypes of the United States.

Admittedly, some American cartoons, such as *Doonesbury* and *The Far Side*, had taken satirical looks at American life for several years before *The Simpsons* and *South Park*. Even *Peanuts* featured as its central character a boy constantly doomed to failure in Charlie Brown, a direct precursor of Bart and Kenny. More broadly, as Rehnquist's judgment noted, America has not lacked stinging satire. Historically, Mark Twain and H. L. Mencken proved worthy literary cousins to Swift and Pope on matters political and cultural. But current American television satire is hardly cutting-edge (*Frasier* and *Seinfeld* are justifiably well regarded as sharp, shrewd and sophisticated comedies but are hardly vicious), while much self-consciously 'political' comedy in the US is less satirical than just polemical or declamatory (Bill Hicks, for example). The continued pervasiveness of the 'American creed' as the foundation of national identity means that the type of scathing attacks in the UK made by the likes of TV shows such as *Not the Nine O'Clock News*, *Spitting Image, The Day Today* and *Brass Eye* brook no clear or consistent comparison in the United States. Indeed, it is surely significant that while many nations emulated the *Spitting Image* anti-establishment formula with their own versions (including France and Russia), America proved a conspicuous exception.

Morality Tales: For Family, God and Country

For all their focus on failures of physique, intellect and spirit, *The Simpsons* and *South Park* are remarkably moral series – quintessentially American, even, in this respect. This is an aspect that has been neglected by many commentators yet pervades both shows. Although unconventional and in some respects anti-traditionalist, both are deeply rooted in the American television tradition. For example, in one *South Park* episode, after the adults leave the kids alone to boycott the cable television company in order to get *Terrance and Philip* (the constantly flatulent Canadian cartoon pair) off the screen, the message of the show is stark – if parents spent more time with their children instead of relying on television as a nursemaid, perhaps its baleful effects might be mitigated. Similarly, the message of equal treatment offered by 'Big Gay Al's Big Gay Boat Ride' – in which Stan learns that his dog, Sparky, is gay and thereby embarks on a personal journey towards tolerance – is as surreally poignant as it is progressive on matters of sexual orientation. That it takes children to deliver messages that adults should perhaps already know (a typical implicit message of many episodes) provides much of both cartoons' power and effectiveness.

Where the moralist and traditionalist cast of the shows is most apparent can be best gauged by their shared thematic focuses: the family; children; community; religion; education. The content of the particular messages here is less significant than the choice of motifs. Each individually offers a concise summation about the state of the particular institution, generally of a negative type, but simultaneously contributes to a broader and more positive assessment of social life in America. Collectively, they not only restate the core ideational and structural components of American life but also bask in them, critically aware, ironic, yet simultaneously affectionate for the mainstays of life in the United States as being somehow blessed as special, different from, and better than a world alternately fascinated and repelled by the republic. However much the treatment of American culture is satirical, its introspective cast is more accepted than challenged.

The central irony that confronts moralistic conservative critics of *The Simpsons* and *South Park* is that, rather than challenging or subverting traditionalist celebrations of the family, both shows affirm the importance to American society of the institution, and the nuclear family in particular. If, admittedly, this occurs in odd and circuitous routes that may be easily missed, it occurs nonetheless. As Cantor observed, 'In effect, the shows say, "Take the worst-case scenario – the Simpsons – and even that family is better than no family." '[20] Traditionalists (thanks partly to Cantor's essay) have become increasingly willing to recognize this in relation to *The Simpsons*. But the scope of their affirmation, and the equally robust defence of Americanism offered in *South Park*, remains limited.

The attack on authority that informs both shows is undoubtedly a prominent theme that occasions much of the moralistic conservative disquiet:

> Nearly all authority figures in *South Park* are belittled. The children show little or no respect for teachers, parents, or religious and legal authority. The scripts are written in such a way as to make these authority figures appear inept. The one adult figure the children seem to confide in and respect is that of the school cafeteria chef.[21]

But in spite of the concern that some young boys might imitate Bart's open and consistent disrespect for authority, Bart undeniably represents a modern American icon. As Cantor notes, he is essentially an updated version of Tom Sawyer and Huck Finn. *South Park*'s Kyle, Stan, Eric and Kenny seem less iconic in comparison, partly because they occupy equally prominent roles in the show and partly because of a relative lack of both individual and collective self-confidence compared to the slightly older Bart (who manages to glean advice from a wider array of sources than the *South Park* boys' near-total reliance on Chef). Yet the political legitimacy of disrespect for authority and rebellion was the very foundation of the American republic. Moreover, the enjoyment that attends breaching conventional rules and norms is one that extends to the figures of authority as well. American antipathy to power has been the *leitfmotif* of its political culture from the revolutionary era to today.

As Cantor has argued, the really problematic character for critics of *The Simpsons* – and its authentic stroke of brilliance – is Homer Simpson: dumb, uneducated, weak in character, unprincipled and selfish. The critic Gilbert Adair, in celebrating *The Simpsons* as 'a *chef d'oeuvre* to which the work of no currently practising English-language novelist is comparable in importance or greatness', claims that Homer is:

> One of the most credible portraits in any art form of an ordinary man, your average Joe Sixpack, not undeserving of comparison with Joyce's Leopold Bloom and Hasek's Good Soldier Schweik . . . He is the Platonic ideal of the slob, the pure repository of base human appetites, an obnoxious Everyman emancipated from all the fetters of psychological 'spirituality' which mawkishly cling to practically every depiction of ordinariness in our culture.[22]

Yet for his obviously chronic and seemingly inherent dysfunctionality, as Cantor argues, 'He fulfills the bare minimum of a father: he is present for his wife and above all his children . . . He continually fails at being a good father, but he never gives up trying, and in some basic and important sense that makes him a good father.'[23] He loves his family, and they return that love. The obvious counterpoints – the Simpsons' pious neighbours, the Flanders – seem to offer no better a world, for all their devotion to faith and virtue.

South Park too, while casting a far more caustic eye upon the distinct family units inhabiting the town, nonetheless maintains a consistent affirmation of their centrality. Families are represented as fundamentally positive sources of nurture and guidance against a hostile world. In spite of their marked differences in terms of education, employment and empathy, the boys can rely to a greater or lesser extent upon their respective parents for emotional support (even if Chef provides a more reliable source of practical guidance). Indeed, the scenes of genuine crisis in *South*

Park frequently occur when the parents argue or seem to be on the verge of separation or divorce. Moreover, for all their frustrations and acts of rebellion against parental authority, the shows invariably resolve these squabbles within the family unit, directly and strongly reaffirming its worth. For the children, the mistakes and misunderstandings that accompany growing up are matched by an equal bemusement at the ways of the adult world, but they are also willing – Kyle and Stan in particular – to state their love for their parents, affirm their loyalty, and declare their need for love and guidance.

Ironically, the movie version of *South Park* was especially moralistic in this respect; consistently and explicitly so. The plot – a vulgar Canadian cartoon film prompts the children to mouth obscenities, which in turn leads to citizen action by 'Mothers Against Canada' to censor the movie and get the US government to declare war on Canada (which in turn allows Satan and his boyfriend Saddam Hussein to take over the Earth) – yielded ample opportunities to make commentaries on the evils of war and the absurdities of much in contemporary culture (the Devil reading the self-help guide, 'Saddam is from Mars, Satan is from Venus', was one of the more inspired). The insertion of a V-chip into a child's head in order to deter swearing by the emission of a small electrical charge was an absurdly surreal, yet absurdly logical extension of moral censoring of the content of American television. The film's climactic coda – in which Eric Cartman's verbal dexterity with swear-words foils Saddam, and Kenny enters heaven – offers yet another explicit message, both figuratively and literally.

Indeed, nowhere is this juxtaposition between the centrality of family and its problems more apparent than in the character of Eric Cartman, only a slightly less bold and imaginative cartoon creation than Homer Simpson. Cartman's combination of selfishness, indolence, stupidity and intolerance seems to be a direct commentary upon being raised by a promiscuous and irresponsible single mother.[24] Ironically, for their shared obnoxiousness, Eric's (ultimately fruitless) quest to discover the identity of his absent father seems to serve only to reinforce Cantor's view of Homer's beneficial role: that merely by being present, a dutiful and attached father can provide a meaningful influence despite his dysfunctional behaviour and errant educational ways. The reaffirmation of the family is all the more notable for its relative infrequency. Most American sit-coms since at least the 1980s have instead sought to reflect and legitimize 'alternative lifestyles': the normality of one-parent and even no-parent families, the significance of being single and/or gay in shows such as *Ellen*, *Alice*, *My Two Dads* and *Love, Sidney*. Without belittling these at all, the message of the two cartoons is a highly distinctive endorsement of traditional family structures as the definition of American 'normality'.

Simultaneously, though, an important aspect of the shows is the direct challenge they pose to the pervasive cult of childhood in America. Antonin Scalia has argued persuasively that the marked elevation of childhood has attained a position such that even longstanding constitutional rights can face erosion when issues pertaining to children are involved.[25] Certainly, the children in *The Simpsons* mostly represent fundamentally innocent individuals whose lives are more or less wholesome. Bart, in particular, is essentially a lovable but fundamentally harmless – if persistent – rogue. However, *South Park* offers much less endearing or conventional images of children. The show provides a pointed rejection of the Rousseauist notion that children are innocent angels corrupted by a mean world, and not foul-mouthed, competitive brats obsessed by the senses whom society is charged with the difficult task of educating into semi-decent human beings. That this view has still not been embraced when gun murders by children have become disconcertingly familiar in America reveals much about American sensibilities. For Christian evangelicals to excoriate the 'unconscionable' images of children presented in *South Park* suggests either an uncertain or a highly distinctive grasp of the doctrine of 'original sin'.

The other key feature of American life that the shows treat with an irreverence that nonetheless affirms its centrality is religion. Both shows are too cynical and iconoclastic to be explicitly pro-religion, and both can be considered to be anti-religious in ways rarely seen on American television. Pious Ned Flanders is a regular target for derision in *The Simpsons*; in *South Park* 'Jesus and Pals' is not only relegated to public access television but also regularly fails to attract viewers (when asked about the morality of assisted suicide, Jesus replies: 'I'm not going to touch that one with a six-foot pole'). Yet in satirizing religion, both shows acknowledge its importance in American life in ways that few others concede. The punchline of the boxing bout between Satan and Jesus in *South Park* is that only Satan was willing to place a bet on Jesus, the message being more about the frailty of American religious belief than its futility. Similarly, in demonstrating the ecumenical appeal of *The Simpsons*, the Most Reverend Dr Rowan Williams, Archbishop of Wales, describing himself as a 'great enthusiast', recently noted that: 'The good people always win in the end. A lot of people attack the show but there are good strong Christian morals there, too.'[26]

Education also merits consideration. In both shows, school is seen as a necessary but largely unfulfilling environment, inhabited by professionals who are either demoralized and/or woefully inadequate at their jobs (the teacher Mr Garrison, the school counsellor Mr Macky) or largely preoccupied by petty but pervasive bureaucratic politics (Principal Skinner). The state school system is seen to breed teachers and students with a shared combination of lack of interest and cynicism. At the same time, however, the children are portrayed as at least willing to learn, if not necessarily eager. In regulating their lives, the school authorities also regularize them and offer a stability and predictability otherwise rare in their towns. Again, some of the most familiar aspects of schooling – peer competition, status, bullying, crushes (on fellow pupils and teachers alike) – are represented in ways that few other shows tackle so directly, regularly and in a fashion bereft of sentimentality. The message that children are neither uniformly nor consistently angelic creatures of universal goodwill is, again, loud and unequivocally clear.

Paradoxically, the farcical nature of the shows allows them to deal with serious issues in ways that many other American television programmes either cannot or will not. Over recent years, both have dealt with issues that have real importance and arouse deeply divisive, polarizing reactions in America: firearms, immigration, gay rights, nuclear power, criminal justice, genetic engineering, environmentalism, immigration, and even women in the armed forces. Law enforcement authorities also receive regular exposure as a combination of poorly educated, ignorant and venal forces who – despite, or perhaps because of the everyday vulnerabilities they share in common with ordinary folks – nonetheless provide a measure of stability and public order to community life.

The absence of criticism from progressives, mentioned earlier, is especially notable given the place of race and gender in the shows. Neither Springfield nor South Park are populated by many 'people of color'. Other than the doctor and one of Homer's co-workers in the Springfield nuclear plant, black Americans are mostly absent in *The Simpsons* – although Apu, as an Indian immigrant, provides an interesting contrast. Latinos and Asian Americans are almost entirely absent in *The Simpsons* as in *South Park*.

The key exception here is *South Park*'s Chef. Both shows have employed celebrities to substantial effect, both as characters in the shows proper and as voiceovers. That Chef should be voiced by the musical icon of 1970s 'blaxploitation' movies, Isaac Hayes, accounts in part for the relative lack of adverse criticism. For an artist whose career rested in large part on the cultivation of a 'love-God' persona, with lengthy monologues about love on much of his recorded work, the path from Hayes to Chef was hardly a creative gulf. Some crude racial stereotypes are afforded ample sustenance here ('Now I know how all those white girls must have felt' was one of the more subtle efforts in the episode 'An Elephant Makes Love to a Pig').

To some degree, a potentially repellent message is tempered in two respects. First, Chef is effectively the only reliable authority figure to whom the boys can turn for advice and who is consistently solicitous of their welfare. In America, the symbolism of four white boys having as their most respected adult and friend a black male canteen worker is as striking as it is innovative. Second, several episodes contain scenes in which the history of American racism, prejudice and discrimination is confronted directly – nowhere more so than in the film version where the all-black US army regiment is given the task of leading the first (suicidal) assault in the war against Canada. Such scenes not only reflect and remind viewers of the history of segregation but also help to challenge complacency about contemporary practice in America's most successfully integrated institution.

Nonetheless, the shows conform to the more general approach of American comedies that refuse to acknowledge the centrality of race to American development. For example, *Friends* and *Seinfeld* – set in cosmopolitan and ethnically diverse New York City – rarely feature any non-white characters. *Ally McBeal* and *Frasier*, though set in less diverse cities, equally present a view of America as essentially white (in marked contrast, for example, to the genre of American detective programmes where issues of race and ethnicity loom large). How much this relative lack of diversity is a function of sensitivity on race rather than neglect is unclear. But the few non-white characters in both cartoons reinforce a representation of America that does not comport with the demographic reality.

To the extent that the shows lack a genuinely subversive message, however, this is perhaps clearest in regard to women. On gender, there are relatively few 'strong' female characters in either show. The women represented in the cartoons are hardly subversive figures; most appear in the home. In *The Simpsons*, Marge Simpson attempts to combine the traditional roles of a mother and wife with a mild feminist streak, while Lisa conforms to what most would see as an ideal child (loyal, diligent intelligent and empathetic). In *South Park*, the women are portrayed as primarily homemakers whose lives are effectively incomplete or unhappy if they have no male partners and children. The special maternal role is also accorded particular emphasis.

However, the variety of female characters is salutary, and the direct confrontation with the complexities of post-sixties identity politics is sometimes acute. Marge, for instance, is often seen as eager to 'snuggle', but is mostly frustrated in her amorous attempts by Homer's excessive eating and drinking binges. In *South Park*, Mrs Cartman represents a marked departure from traditional portrayals of women. Indeed, one analysis of cartoon sexual politics even sees her as the 'first TV mom to completely subvert all traditional maternal roles': 'She recognizes motherhood as a role, even a façade (and she is not very good at it), as she drinks, smokes crack, and is sexually promiscuous.'[27] Wendy Testaberger, also, is not only precociously intelligent but also a wily seductress able to manipulate her erstwhile partner, Stan, with the greatest ease. Sexuality is an issue that is generally broached with a degree of moderation that is both judicious and supremely effective in *The Simpsons*, especially in comparison to the plethora of mainstream television programming that has sex at its core. There exists a degree of innocence in this regard that recalls the fifties despite its ironic and satirical acuity – many commentators have referred to watching the show with their families (an act that admittedly is less feasible with *South Park*'s more anarchic assaults on conventionality and ready references to sex).

That ability literally to bring families together owes much to the quality of the plots and the content of the dialogue of the shows. *The Simpsons* and *South Park* are superb – albeit markedly variable – comedies. For all the flatness and unsophisticated imagery, the characterizations are well developed, the dialogue is typically rich in its barbed familiarity with American idioms, and the surrealism provides a sublime reminder that these are cartoons. Any show in which a little boy (Cartman) hopes to seduce his lesbian substitute teacher by noting that 'my grandmother was Dutch-Irish and my grandfather was lesbian, so that makes me a quarter lesbian' deserves praise not only for the preposterous premise but also for the evocation of American preoccupation with immigration. Moreover, the shows are sufficiently ambitious and self-confident to be replete with references that many adults (much less children) will fail to identify. As James Watson noted of *The Simpsons*:

> Children are unlikely to be provoked to tears of mirth by the sideswipes at J. D. Salinger, Gore Vidal or Saul Bellow, let alone to chuckle knowledgeably at the pastiches of *A Clockwork Orange*. The show's creator, Matt Groening, has pointed out that younger fans will get a shock when they first see *Citizen Kane* – almost every scene has been parodied in *The Simpsons*. Nor can adult viewers ever feel too smug. Plenty of the gags will fly over the most polymathic head.[28]

Equally, the willingness of the shows to rubbish and even demonize celebrities (Barbara Streisand, Celine Dion, Patrick Duffy, Alanis

Morrisette, Bryan Adams) and foreigners (the British, Australia, Canada) provides a rare departure in an American public life whose professed individualism frequently yields a powerful conformism. Homer's laughter at the names of other countries (pronouncing Uruguay as 'You are gay') at once reflects and confirms small-town parochialism. The rest of the world is a source of curiosity and trepidation for a citizenry firmly located in a particular community, for whom travel narrows rather than broadens an American mind not so much steadily closing in Bloomian fashion as only ever having (for non-college graduates) been very slightly ajar.[29] Intra-American prejudices – the sign informing one trip out of South Park, Colorado: 'You are now entering Nebraska. Sorry' – also form prominent themes that remind us of the marked heterogeneity, relative insularity and strong territoriality of American states.

The final element that distinguishes the shows is their ability to deal directly with the central role of television in American life, not least by regular self-parody – the reliance upon television that characterizes the lives of millions of Americans being represented explicitly in the cartoons themselves. At the beginning of each show, for example, the Simpsons return home after their respective days to sit together on the couch to watch television (just as many of their viewers are doing in reality). Homer and Eric Cartman in *South Park* combine watching TV with excessive consumption (of 'Duff beer' and 'Cheesy Poofs' or 'Snacky Smores', respectively).

But in the most brilliant representational coups, the types of 'moral panics' that are generated by television shows like *The Simpsons* and *South Park* are themselves parodied. The children in both shows are seen zealously watching cartoons whose content seems designed to offend adult sensibilities by a preoccupation with flatulence and vio-lence: respectively, *Terrance and Philip* and *The Itchy and Scratchy Show* (the latter itself a satire on the violence of *Tom and Jerry*). The movie version of *South Park* was a ninety-minute lampoon (that America should embrace the violence of war in order to clean up smutty language). And in one episode of *The Simpsons* Grandpa Simpson writes to TV advisers specifically to complain about issues of minority representation:

Dear Sir

I am disgusted with the way old people are depicted on television. We are not all vibrant, fun-loving sex maniacs. Many of us are bitter, resentful individuals, who remember the good old days, when entertainment was bland and inoffensive.[30]

Conclusion

As Peter Cook's remark about modelling his Establishment Club on 'those satirical Berlin clubs of the 1930s that had done so much to prevent the rise of Adolf Hitler' suggested,[31] the political influence of satire is strictly limited. Nonetheless, it is a mark of the complex conflicts over American cultural values that *The Simpsons* and *South Park* have generated such strong critical attention from traditionalists who have more reason to celebrate than censure the shows. Despite continuing popular references to the shows as 'critiques' of the United States,[32] the examples and role models that the cartoons offer are more reassuring to traditionalist conceptions of America and Americanism than they are subversive critiques or indictments. However much they zealously avoid moralizing, notions of right and wrong are prominent – inextricable – themes in both shows. Part of the reason for critical concern may be knowledge of the cultural dominance of American television and the mixed assessment of America revealed in the cartoons. Yet for all the ironic commentary that the shows offer on the United States, it is salutary to note the less sardonic and avowedly positive, even patriotic features of their representations.

  The Simpsons and *South Park* have achieved a remarkable, if hardly unique, political double: occasioning condemnation for subverting traditional values when they instead affirm them, and being seen as attacking America when their lampoons instead celebrate its many successes as much as castigate its relative failings. Yet millions have recognized and acknowledged the imperfect but powerful mirrors that the shows hold up to the United States. Springfield and South Park have now entered the American topographic lexicon alongside Dallas, Washington and New Orleans and, while the latest occupant of the Oval Office remains a temporary custodian of the ultimate prize in American politics, the United States has acquired in the Simpsons a permanent 'first family' worthy of that title. As the Court opinion in *Hustler* suggested, America is considerably richer as a result.

NOTES

A version of this paper was presented at the Philosophy, Politics and History Wye Weekend at Wye College, Wye, Kent on 26 February 2000. The author would like to thank Samantha Ashenden, Paul Hirst, Desmond King, Judy Oliver and Bill Tompson for their comments on earlier versions of the paper.

1   Rodney Smolla, *Jerry Falwell v. Larry Flynt: The First Amendment on Trial* (Chicago: University of Illinois Press, 1988), p. 303.
2   John Street, *Politics and Popular Culture* (Cambridge: Polity, 1997).
3   One critic claims that pornography is now cited with 'alarming frequency' in American divorce and custody proceedings; see Holman W. Jenkins Jr, 'Pornography, Main Street to Wall Street', *Policy Review*, no. 105 (Feb.– Mar. 2001), p. 6.
4   Paul Cantor, 'The Simpsons: Atomistic Politics and the Nuclear Family', *Political Theory*, 27, no. 6 (1999), pp. 734–49; and 'At Home with The Simpsons', *Prospect* (June 2000), pp. 58–61.
5   William Irwin, Mark T. Conrad and Aeon J. Skoble (eds), *The Simpsons and Philosophy: The D'Oh! of Homer* (Chicago: Open Court, 2001). A comprehensive guide to individual episodes is Warren Martyn and Adrian Wood, *I Can't Believe It's a Bigger and Better Updated Unofficial Simpsons Guide* (London: Virgin, 2000).
6   After the first London mayoral election, the *Sun*'s front page (5 May 2000) featured a picture of the head of successful Independent candidate Ken Livingstone superimposed on the orange-coated body of Kenny accompanied by the headline, 'Oh No, They've Elected Kenny!'; the *London Review of Books* headed a review of a book by Paul Feyerabend with one of Eric Cartman's signature exclamations, 'Screw you, I'm going home' (22 June 2000, p. 28).
7   Byron E. Shafer (ed.), *Partisan Approaches to Postwar American Politics* (New York: Chatham House, 1998), p. 122.
8   Cantor, 'At Home with The Simpsons', p. 58.
9   Jonah Goldberg, 'Homer Never Nods: The Importance of *The Simpsons*', *National Review*, 11, no. 8 (2000), pp. 36–7.
10 Jim Hanes, 'South Park Perversion', *CultureFacts*, 28 July 1999.
11 David Hinckley, 'Crude Awakening: It's Taking Us Too Long to Realize that "South Park" is Mean and Obscene', *New York Daily News*, 19 April 1998.
12 'Toon Tossed for Tots', *New York Post*, 31 Aug. 1999, p. 89.
13 'In his Suicide Note, Boy, 12, Points Parents to TV Show', *Washington Times*, 23 May 1998; 'Mother Says Son Died Emulating South Park Character', *National Liberty Journal*, Nov. 1999.
14 *The Problems with South Park* (Christian Family Network), p. 5.
15 See the essay by Anthony King, 'Distrust of Government: Explaining American Exceptionalism', in Susan J. Pharr and Robert D. Putnam, *Disaffected Democracies: What's Troubling the Trilateral Countries?* (Princeton: Princeton University Press, 2000), pp. 74–98.
16 The survey question was: 'How would you rate the ethical standards of people in the following field?' Percentages record those answering 'very high' and 'high' combined. See *National Journal*, 3 June 2000, p. 1775.
17 Seymour Martin Lipset, *American Exceptionalism: A Double-Edged Sword* (New York: W.W. Norton, 1996).
18 Stuart Jeffries, *Mrs Slocombe's Pussy: Growing Up in Front of the Telly* (London: Flamingo, 2000), pp. 237–8.

19 In this regard, see the essay by Aeon J. Skoble, 'Lisa and American Anti-intellectualism', in Irwin, Conard and Skoble, *The Simpsons and Philosophy*, pp. 24–34.

20 Cantor, 'The Simpsons', p. 738.

21 *The Problems with South Park*, p. 9.

22 Gilbert Adair, 'Ecce Homer', *Independent* (*Review section*), 21 June 2000, p. 1.

23 Cantor, 'The Simpsons', pp. 738–9.

24 The most obvious representation of this occurs in his constant change of identity to reach his 'roots' when he learns of each new probable father – from Native American to African-American 'homeboy', for example – in the episode 'Cartman's Mom is a Dirty Slut'. See Trey Parker and Matt Stone, *South Park, The Scripts: Book One* (Basingstoke: Macmillan, 1999).

25 Scalia refers to *Maryland v. Craig* (1990), a case where the US Supreme Court upheld a Maryland law – by a 6–3 vote in which he dissented – that allowed a child to give testimony about an alleged abuser on video. As he notes, the case reflected more about American sensibilities over child abuse than it did a concern for the Sixth Amendment rights of the accused 'in all criminal cases' to be able to confront directly the accuser. See Antonin Scalia, *A Matter of Interpretation: Federal Courts and the Law* (Princeton: Princeton University Press, 1997), pp. 43–4.

26 Quoted in the Diary, *The Times* (London), 27 Apr. 2000, p. 22.

27 Dale E. Snow and James J. Snow, 'Simpsonian Sexual Politics', in Irwin, Conard and Skoble, *The Simpsons and Philosophy*, p. 132.

28 James Watson, 'D'Oh! Bart's Unbeatable', *Daily Telegraph*, 20 June 2000, p. 15.

29 It seems unlikely that Allan Bloom would have found either cartoon admirable, given his views on popular culture more broadly; see *The Closing of the American Mind: How Higher Education has Failed Democracy and Impoverished the Souls of Today's Students* (New York: Simon and Schuster, 1987).

30 Quoted in Watson, 'D'Oh! Bart's Unbeatable'.

31 Quoted in Harry Thompson, *Peter Cook: A Biography* (London: Hodder and Stoughton, 1997), p. 42.

32 In commending the UK's BBC2 television channel for commemorating ten years of *The Simpsons* with a 'Simpsons Night' of programming on 23 June 2000, John Davies argued that the show was not only the funniest but 'also the most acute critique of United States culture and politics'; see *The Times Higher Education Supplement*, 23 June 2000, pp. 30–1.

Index